What people are saying about

Amazing Grace

Serge's journey from titled entitlement to spiritual seeker, told with panache and humour, shows us how staying true to our deepest vision brings profound, lasting changes in our outer world, and the worlds of those we meet. This transformation inspires us to rebalance our lives, valuing Self over ego, having the courage to face mistakes and discover the ordinary; and with it find the extraordinary, the miracle of being human. To step free from 'material blessings', he explains, is not a sacrifice, but a gift—personal freedom. If you feel trapped by this too, here is a guidebook towards an ever-opening inner door.
Dale Mathers, Jungian Analyst & Author of *Alchemy and Psychotherapy*

In *Amazing Grace* my dear friend Serge has described not only his own transformational journey, but he also speaks for many of his generation who grew up in the ferment of 1960s hippiedom, looking for new ways of being and living. This is a passionate and engaging narrative by a man of unique style who has lived fully while also often suffering deeply as he struggles to break through to a whole new way of living. Born into a hugely privileged background entailed its own dysfunctions and wounds, and these very much shaped the agenda of Serge's life journey as he felt that many of the values which he had been raised to subscribe to were the very ones which needed to be surrendered if one was to have a world that worked. A deeply humane and wise book.
David Lorimer, Programme Director of the Scientific and Medical Network and Author of many books including *Resonant Mind* and *Science, Consciousness and Ultimate Reality*

A marvellously entertaining account of Serge's adventures through the material and spiritual worlds, filled with equal measures of humour and spiritual insight. Serge writes as if speaking to a close friend, and offers the distilled wisdom of a lifetime of spiritual exploration.
Steve Taylor, PhD, Poet, University Lecturer and Author of *The Leap* and *The Clear Light*

Serge Beddington-Behrens is a unique person and friend, whom I met in England in the mid-1970s. We shared much in the area of spiritual search. In *Amazing Grace* he opens his soul, mind, and heart with honesty in looking-back at his personal development from his British aristocratic upbringing in his childhood to the present mature phase of his life journey. He conveys beautifully the challenges and conflicts of growing-up in this context and his struggles to become his own person with a deep vision, concern, and sense of identification with the perils and opportunities we are all facing on Planet Earth in this crucial phase of our collective evolution.
Abelardo Brenes, PhD, Co-author of *Earthly Dimensions of Peace: The Earth Charter* and Author of multiple academic publications in Psychology, Peace Education, and Sustainable Development Education

In our present times of obsessive consumerism, billionaires who spend fortunes going into space, media moguls and false information to say nothing of hogging the limelight film stars, it is refreshing to read the memoirs of someone who was born with a silver spoon in his mouth, the son of a Russian princess and a very successful businessman, educated at Harrow and Oxford, but who decided to put all that behind him and seek another way to live.

Serge Beddington-Behrens has travelled the path to self-enlightenment through experiences via Carlos Castaneda, Findhorn, fasting, Shamanism, Zen Buddhism and much more. He readily admits that without his financial inheritance it would have been a much more difficult journey, but the importance of this memoir lies in the fact he chose a difficult path to follow in life rather than the one, given his upbringing, which would have been much easier to follow.

As he says, we need a new vision of life––one with heart, compassion, and wisdom. Read this book and hopefully you too will start to search for a new vision in your life.

John Bell, MA (Oxon.), Educational Consultant

Reading Serge's book will take you on a fascinating journey. You will look forward to the next chapter and regret having finished it, but you will be left with a true taste, a thrill in your soul, a desire to shine and honour your own nature as the author has so skilfully done.

Pier Luigi Lattuada, MD, PsyD, PhD, Transpersonal Psychotherapist, Author and Spiritual Teacher

Amazing Grace

Memoirs of a Transformational Journey

Amazing Grace

Memoirs of a Transformational Journey

Serge Beddington-Behrens

Winchester, UK
Washington, USA

JOHN HUNT PUBLISHING

First published by O-Books, 2023
O-Books is an imprint of John Hunt Publishing Ltd., 3 East St., Alresford,
Hampshire SO24 9EE, UK
office@jhpbooks.com
www.johnhuntpublishing.com
www.o-books.com

For distributor details and how to order please visit the 'Ordering' section on our website.

ISBN: 978 1 80341 214 6
978 1 80341 215 3 (ebook)
Library of Congress Control Number: 2022908274

A CIP catalogue record for this book is available from the British Library.

Design: Lapiz Digital Serivices

UK: Printed and bound by CPI Group (UK) Ltd, Croydon, CR0 4YY
Printed in North America by CPI GPS partners

Contents

Nothing is more dangerous than to be the offspring of a millionaire.
Theodore Zeldin

I live my life in growing orbits
Which move out over the things of the world.
Perhaps I can never achieve the last,
But that will be my attempt.
Rainer Maria Rilke

For my family and all my dear friends, teachers and students who have played such important roles in helping me become a little more human.

Acknowledgements

My dearest friends, I want to say, first of all, that I feel terribly grateful towards Amazing Grace for having connected me with you and for the huge difference you have all made to my life in your different ways. I feel very blessed. A huge thank you to my darling wife Martina, for your loving support at all times––three books have emerged over the ten years we've been together. Lovely Kathi Bota, I don't know what I would have done without you tirelessly helping me prepare all aspects of this manuscript for publication. I also want to express my gratitude to all the many teachers I have had, including the many people whom I have been privileged to work with over the years as all of you have helped give my life so much meaning.

Introduction

My dear reader, I am choosing to write about my life because I believe I have a not uninteresting and, in places, quite an amusing story to tell, especially for people who are familiar with the kind of background I came from, or who would like to know more about the journey of personal transformation and its many challenges. Also, as my profession requires that I'm always listening to and working with other people's stories, and as I've already written two books about transformation, I feel it is now time to say a few words about my own personal odyssey.

Joseph Campbell, the great mythologist, with whom I once had the honour to study, always stressed the importance of this. 'We all need,' he said, 'to tell our story and really understand it...' He went on to say that

> *We're so used to only being engaged in doing things to achieve outer purposes... that we forget the inner value, the rapture that is associated with being alive... People say we're all seeking a meaning for life... I think what we're also seeking is an experience of being alive... We're looking for a way of experiencing the world that will open us to the transcendence that informs and that also forms ourselves within it.*

I fully agree, and I don't think we can experience that rapture or sense of aliveness unless we are able to begin living the life that our soul or our deeper truth tells us is right for us, and this book is essentially the story of my adventures in trying to do just that. In fact, my journey of gradually discovering who I really am—that is, finding the 'real me' behind the mask or 'false me'—has been, and still is, very important for me. As such, this is not like most memoirs which ordinarily explore all aspects of a person's life. Here the prime focus is on my evolutionary or my transformational journey and so I say very little about those areas of my life and those people in my life who are not directly part of that particular adventure. And most of my greatest teachers are completely unknown.

So don't expect to be overly titillated. I haven't done a lot of externally daring things, This is about inner journeying. I've been more of an inner explorer. I've not travelled much in the East; I've not gone over the Niagara Falls in a barrel or gone to live with a tribe in Brazil or ventured bravely out into the rainforests to personally challenge those guys who are cutting them down. I've never had an affair with Madonna or started a revolution, or hang-glided off the top of Mount Kilimanjaro (as some of my old Oxford mates who were members of the Dangerous Sports Club) have.

I'm a gnarled old toad now, but, as you'll be seeing, I think I've been a fortunate one. I've had one or two narrow escapes, but I've always managed to land on a secure water lily. Apart from the odd debilitating disease that has knocked me from time to time, I've been blessed in that I've never had any truly grave tragedy to face. In fact, from very early on, I've always felt that a graced or a 'helping' presence has been with me, protecting and guiding and often challenging me, often in very amazing ways.

I also have another agenda in telling you the story of my transformational adventures, and that is that I'd like to inspire you, dear reader, to perhaps consider embarking on a similar enterprise (if, that is, you are not already doing so), and if so, hopefully pick up a few tips about what you might expect to confront along the way.

I believe that given the dire state of our planet at the moment, the coming into the realisation of our deeper humanity—which I believe exists inside all of us—can serve as a key antidote to the chaos and confusion all around us, to say nothing about the great personal benefits that it can confer upon us. Yes, my friend, our world is a much more dangerous one than it was half a century ago, and I believe that the more flexible, clear, strong, centred and open-hearted we become, the better our ability to navigate ourselves through its many quagmires. Indeed, the more evolved we become, the less we are part of the problems around us, and the more capable we are of becoming part of their solution.

However, to arrive at that place, we will need to work at it which among other things requires that we confront where we are wounded or dysfunctional and what it is about ourselves that blocks our deeper humanity from emerging. As you will be seeing, I have not shied away from presenting the many darker sides to my nature as I feel that I have carried many of the more unpleasant wounds afflicting Western man. In fact, I regard making the effort to heal myself and deepen my inner life as one of the most important things that I can do, not only for my own personal well-being, but—much more important—also for the health and well-being of our planet. As the great Indian sage Sri Aurobindo put it:

> *To hope for a change in human life without a change in human nature is an irrational proposition... an impossible miracle.*

So *that* is precisely why I have a second agenda. I also ask you please to make sure you read my epilogue as it explores what I see happening in the world from now to the end of the century. While I feel that humanity will continue facing tough challenges over the next eighty years—in fact, we've already begun doing so—I believe that as a species, we will break through to a whole new global way of operating, and that a new and better world will gradually arise, phoenix-like out of the ashes, and so in the long run I am very optimistic.

The question to ask is this: how in hell did the only son of a multimillionaire, titled industrialist and a Russian princess—and who was educated at snooty old Harrow and Christ Church,

Oxford (where he was a member of the infamous Bullingdon Club) and well trained in the dark arts of snobbery and elitism—gradually move away from the world that he was born into, to become (in a small way) a spiritual educator, a soul-centred psychotherapist, a teacher of transformation and an activist for a transformed planet? Here is the story of how it all happened...

Chapter 1

Vignettes of Childhood

I was born with a silver or a gold spoon (depending how you see it) in my mouth on 29 June 1945 in a hospital in London situated within the sound of Bow Bells, which technically, someone told me, makes me a cockney. A cockney, however, looked after by a big staff. To cater for the requirements of my father, mother, and me, we had sixteen servants. Two cooks, two chauffeurs, a butler, three gardeners (we had a large country house that my father had inherited from his aunt), a groom (my father loved riding), two cleaning ladies, two maids, a nanny, who lived to be 109, and later two governesses.

If I look back at photos of myself in old albums, I always looked rather a forlorn and lonely little fellow, with sticking-out ears and a kirby grip to hold my hair back. I have never seen pictures of myself as a child smiling. I was an only child and the only people who'd ever play with me were the servants. While at a physical level I wanted for nothing, at other levels I wanted for everything as there was little sense of joy or love in our household. No spirit. Everything was big but there was a deadness to it. Yes, I was glad of this big staff because it meant I was not alone; my father was always away on business trips and always got my mother to come along with him, as he felt that having a pretty, young princess on his arm gave him a bit of panache, a bit like how Donald Trump always dragged Melania along with him to make him appear more virile.

As I grew up, it was therefore left to the butler and the chauffeurs to play football and cricket with me, as my father never once played with me. Bless him, he didn't know the meaning of that word; his obsession was with his work—with doing, with achieving, with filling every moment with something considered purposeful, and which happened to be an agenda that excluded me. Here are one or two snippets of memory from those early days:

Going to see my father's 'Aunt Violet', who would be lying stretched out on a sofa—poor thing had a bad back as her house got bombed in the war—and always feeling extremely uncomfortable in her presence.

Being in a post office and my mother holding a 'ration book' in her hand. I was born just after the Second World War had ended and there was strict rationing. I think my mother went without some essentials to give them to me.

Going many times with my mother to Hampton Court to see her great friend, the old Grand Duchess Xenia Alexandrovna of Russia, the elder daughter of Tsar Alexander III, who was looked after by a very loving nun, Mother Martha, always dolled up in full nun regalia. The grand duchess was a sweet, gentle person and gave off very loving vibes. After seeing her, I would go and get lost in the Hampton Court maze and the chauffeur would be sent in to find me.

Going in the car with my father to appointments in London. The chauffeur would deposit us and my father would always say, 'I don't know how long we'll be, so best you circle the block, Vickers.' Real echoes of *Downton Abbey*!

Often having lunch with American friends of my parents who had their own private zoo. In the house was a macaw that for some bizarre reason would repeat over and over, 'Don't you get fresh with me, or I'll slap your face, you poor sap. I'm not that kindava girl.'!

Borrowing my father's trilby hat and overcoat, buying a packet of Will's Whiffs cigarettes and, puffing away to look grown up, going with my friend Edward Hulton—also a six-foot twelve-year-old—to see what then used to be called X-rated movies. The first one we went to see was *The Fly*. Pretty scary for us little fellahs, though Edward was more scared that we'd be recognised as underage and turfed out!

Playing hide-and-seek in the hay at our farm with my best—indeed my only—childhood buddy, Michael McInnes, and watching the cows get milked by hand.

My father had bought the farm adjoining the country house that his Aunt Violet had left him, and one day my mother was out walking in the field and happened to see a piece of flint on the ground. She picked it up and took it to an expert, who told her it was a perfect Stone Age arrowhead. One thing led to another, and the great archaeologist Louis Leakey came down with his family and excavated the field and discovered the oldest Stone Age site in Britain. It was very exciting. Hundreds of important flints were found and my father had a museum built in the field.

His son, now the famous Richard Leakey, who was my age, was allowed to run wild with no shoes on. I wasn't in case I caught a cold. Nanny and Mummy were very protective of their little Half-Princeling. What I found was that as I began to copy him, and also started running wild with no shoes on, I stopped getting colds.

My father, who identified himself as something of a tough guy, felt that my mother mollycoddled me too much and that I needed introducing to the 'tough life', that I needed manning up. 'I'm going to introduce you to camping—to things that real men do,' he told me when I was about seven. 'We're going to go into the wilderness and live in a tent for a few days!' I was quite excited at the idea.

Well, my tough experience of camping was this. The wilderness was in the field under a big tree near our house. The chauffeur drove us there. The farm manager erected the tent. The maid came and made the camp beds. The cook came and cooked us dinner over the campfire, and the butler served us. In the morning, the chauffeur came with my father's daily papers, after which the cook came again to cook a fry-up, a 'real man's' breakfast. Afterwards, the groom showed up, bringing my father's horse and my pony, so we could go for a ride together! Yup. Real tough-guy stuff. That's why I'm such an outdoors 'manly, self-sufficient fellow' today… Ha!

I remember playing with Lizzy, alias Princess Elizabeth of Yugoslavia, who was the daughter of my father's good friend Prince Paul of Yugoslavia. Goodness, she must be well over eighty today. She was then a teenager and she'd gang up with my half-sister Evelyn (whom we called Chuchie) and I'd climb through their bedroom window, and they'd throw me out and then I'd climb in again. Lots of fun.

Being continually surrounded by lots of people who were Prince or Princess this or that, I never quite knew who was who. Royals, I found, like to hang out with other Royals. I remember Prince Michael of Kent's mama was one of my mama's best friends—they liked to play canasta together—and so when they would meet, us two boys would often spend time together and play with our electric trains. I was very friendly with him when we were little boys, but then lost touch completely as we grew older. In my forties, I discovered he lived close to me in Gloucestershire, and wrote him a friendly postcard: 'Hey Michael, gather you live near me. Still playing with trains? It'd be nice to say hi again.'

I was invited to dinner at his country house. And boy, what a palaver. I had to bow and scrape and call him 'Sir' and I forget what I had to call his wife. Was it Your Highness? He politely and formally asked me what I did, and I politely and formally replied. No human connection. Not a fun evening. I felt a bit sorry for Michael. I think he is a lovely man cocooned in all that ghastly formality. Thank goodness, the world of British royalty has toned down today and has become more human. I think William and Harry have done a great job there.

When I was a little boy, we'd have huge meals. A normal breakfast would be cereal and toast and a full fry-up of eggs, bacon, sausages, tomatoes, fried bread. Then sandwiches and biscuits for 'elevenses', and a five-course lunch consisting, say, of soup, hors d'oeuvres, a fish dish, meat, potatoes and vegetables, a dessert and then cheese and biscuits. Tea at five would be chocolate, fruit and sponge cake, chocolate biscuits and hot buttered toast, and dinner the same as lunch. God only knows how we all survived these onslaughts as in those days, gyms didn't exist and everyone smoked like a trouper; and my father, not surprisingly, was always overweight and on some extreme diet.

I remember we'd have guests for dinner and he would be served his diet plate first—a favourite one was steak and pineapple—and he'd have gobbled his down before the last guests had been served, so what he'd do was to have little nibbles off their plates. 'I say,' he'd say, 'that foie gras looks awfully good, mind if I have a taste?' This led to me thinking it was normal to do the same thing and eat off my neighbours' plates. Thus, my table manners were not the best.

I remember a powerful experience I had—I must have been about seven—when, after a particularly large lunch, I went to my bedroom and became consumed with sadness for all the poor, starving people in the world. I remember crying uncontrollably and when Nanny or whoever came to see what the matter was, me telling them that 'I am such a bad person. I have so much food and luxury and I feel I ought to starve like the poor people in the world. I want to leave my family and go out and live with them.' In retrospect, I see this as a little 'awakening' experience. It lasted all day and perhaps was a sign of things to come. My rage at the injustices and corruption in the world, which lies behind much of the work I do today, must have existed in embryo even then.

Let me now tell you a bit about my father as he played an important role in my life; mainly, I'm afraid to say, as a model of what I didn't want to be like.

Chapter 2

Chappy Happy World

My father was called Edward, though we had nicknames for each other—I was Chappy Happy mi, and he was Chappy Happy ma—and when I was eleven, he was knighted and became Sir Edward. He was born in 1898 and was a contemporary of Robert Graves at Charterhouse. In his autobiography my father wrote that he always beat Graves in the school boxing competition, but I heard from other sources that the poet, who was a bit older, used to win! What they also had in common was that both survived the Battle of the Somme.

But there the comparisons stop. Edward was no poet, but he was a brave and resourceful and, in many ways, a brilliant man, and he embraced many different worlds. He got an MC and bar in the First World War before he was twenty and was the youngest major in the British army. He was also a banker, an entrepreneur, he sang, he drew; he was involved in politics; he collected art and patronised several very famous artists and was chairman of many big companies. Interestingly, his vision for a better world was not wholly dissimilar to mine, although he realised it in a very different way. Basically, he was a mixer-in with world leaders. Macmillan, Churchill, and de Gaulle were frequent visitors at our house. He also played a key role in having England enter the European market and essentially was a great mover and shaker, and I suffered for this as I wasn't. When I got a bit older, I sometimes wondered what I'd done wrong and why 'the great and the good' weren't also coming flocking to my door!

I don't think my father ever quite recovered from the death of his nineteen-year-old twin brother at the Battle of the Somme—he felt guilty for having survived—or that of his mother when he was thirteen, which left him with a real curmudgeon of a father who didn't know what to do with him and so parked him with his Aunt Violet (who was married to the writer Sydney Schiff), and they virtually brought him up. He also suffered severe shell shock in that battle (as post-traumatic stress disorder used to be called in those days), but his condition was never treated and when he emerged from the First World War, I believe that something had been broken in him that I don't think ever healed.

Materially, pretty much everything my father engaged in turned to gold, but at an inner level the story was very different. As I said earlier, many people cultivated his acquaintance, not necessarily because they liked him—my father lacked charm and was not personable—but because they felt they could get something out of him financially. And many did. He told me once that he handled the portfolios of Macmillan's entire cabinet and would guarantee to repay anyone if they ever lost any money. I don't think he was interested in money per se but more in the power he felt when handling large sums.

My father was very generous, and he helped many people, including everyone in my mother's Russian family who had escaped from Russia during the revolution and who were very impecunious. He saw that my grandparents had a lovely flat in a good part of London to live in, and he also financed my Uncle Misha's training as an accountant. He was also a patron of both Oskar Kokoschka and Stanley Spencer. As a little boy, I especially remember the sweetness of Oskar when he and his wife Olda lived with us at 99 Park Lane for about a year, which gave him a space to paint. Oskar and my mother were especially close, and I have framed some letters that Oskar wrote to her calling her 'darling Irena' with little drawings in them. It hurt my father a lot when Oskar wrote an autobiography and barely mentioned him.

My memory of Stanley Spencer is more vague, although I remember once saying to him something rather cheeky along the lines of, 'Why do you look like a little boy?' He always had a schoolboy's haircut. I can't remember what he replied. Chappie also helped his friend Charlie Chaplin in many ways, including assisting him to get his money out of America into Switzerland. In fact, he let Charlie dump his family on us for a year and it was good to have the company of his son Michael and daughter Geraldine—the beautiful actress of *Doctor Zhivago* fame. Michael also suffered from having a highly successful and egotistical father and later wrote a book called *I Couldn't Smoke the Grass on My Father's Lawn*.

I read some of the love letters my father wrote to my mother—which, interestingly, were very similar to the language I would later use in my letters to girlfriends—and I do believe that there was love between them at the start of their marriage, despite a twenty-year age difference and them having completely different interests. My father was essentially an intellectual—he had a law degree and a doctorate in economics—and my dear mama, a refugee from the Russian Revolution, had been working at Elizabeth Arden as a beautician and when my father met her, at Norman Hartnell's.

Over the years I believe this love waned as they realised how very different they were from one another and that really the only thing they had in common and which they could talk about was me. The first French words I ever learned were 'Pas devant le petit'!

Nonetheless, they would join forces at weekends when the rich and famous from all walks of life would congregate to stay at our big country house. If our guests did not necessarily 'go for' my father, they all adored my mother, who had a wonderful social manner and, I am sure, enjoyed being hostess, just as I am sure our guests particularly appreciated being in the presence of a young and pretty Russian princess. I feel my daughter Irena, named after my mother, has inherited something of my father's 'get-up-and-go' as well as my mama's charm.

But no one was really interested in me except when Nanny would dress me up in a little sailor suit to meet the important guests so they could pat me on the head and say 'What a sweet little chap' before I was wheeled away to bed. I therefore always needed to do things to get people's attention.

Once when I was about three or four, my parents were having one of their smart weekend parties and I felt particularly unnoticed, so I jumped off a sundial in the garden in front of all the guests and broke my leg. It certainly did the trick. Suddenly, I got everyone clucking around me as the main centre of attention. And here I will namedrop just to make the point that the guests who my parents had invited that weekend were the kind of people they surrounded themselves with all the time. I got this information many years later from looking at the photo album from that day. The guests who attended that weekend of my leg breaking were Coco Chanel, Lord Jellicoe, Harold Macmillan, T.S. Eliot, Emilio Pucci, Oskar Kokoschka, Chips Channon, and Prince Paul of Yugoslavia. No wonder my parents had a big staff. They were needed!

Here's an example of the way my father used to operate. I must have been about ten when he decided to take me to a boxing match in the East End of London (he'd boxed for the army) and the chauffeur in our Rolls-Royce dropped us off at the head of a long queue.

'Hey guv,' people started to shout. 'Yer toffs can't come 'ere. There's a bloody line.' A uniformed doorman came to confront him. My father's response was to brush him out of the way, showering him with a wad of notes, and addressed the angry crowd with the words: 'I used to own this building.' He probably did. Well, we got in and I saw the boxing match, but this was one of many incidents involving my father where I wished the ground had opened under me and swallowed me up and perhaps why I've never ever wanted flashy cars or ever to draw attention to myself as being someone with a bit of dosh!

I have to say, though, that I am grateful to Chappy for many things. At a physical level, nothing was wanting. I had the best of everything. I went to the best schools and university and as soon as I was old enough, my father whisked me off to his tailor to have a couple of elegant suits made for me. In fact, I have inherited his taste for being snappily dressed and today, seven years older than he was when he died, I am still happiest in a well-cut blazer and with a brightly coloured silk handkerchief peeking out of my top pocket, although beneath that I generally sport a denim cowboy shirt, blue jeans, and cowboy boots. I guess it reflects my stance: part English gent and part cowboy. I've basically dressed like this my whole life.

I had a pony called Tiddles and I was taught to ride at an early age, and when I was still a little boy my father would take me hunting with him, though I must confess I found it bizarre, when I arrived on the scene of the kill my first time, to have the blood of the fox smeared on my cheek. I was told that as this was my first hunt, this was my initiation, and that I wasn't to rub it off all day. I felt sad for the terrorised fox and later in my life when I went to live in Gloucestershire, right in the middle of huntin', shootin' and fishin' terrain, I felt completely disinclined to partake in any of these country sports. For me, there was nothing sporting about them.

For a lot of my early life, then, I felt very much like a fish out of water. It took me many years to realise that people existed at different levels and inhabited different worlds or realities and that the worlds that I felt most comfortable with were not those that I had been brought up with. Nonetheless, I enjoyed my riding, which I continued for many years, but not as much as I did my tennis, which I was also taught at an early age and which has been a sport that has given me huge pleasure all my life.

My father also introduced me to skiing when I was very young. We had a chalet in Zermatt and all my memories from there are delightfully happy ones. As I write this, I am once more hearing the sound of the old church bells and I am opening my bedroom curtains to a beautiful sunny day and there, spread out in front of me, is the majestic Matterhorn. I haven't been back to Zermatt since my father died and I have a dream that I would like to do so before I am eighty and take my daughter back there with me.

My skiing career began with my being carried down, aged two, in a rucksack by our ski guide, the wonderful Willie Perren, and by the age of five I was joining the grown-ups. Indeed, as I will be explaining later, skiing has been a huge source of joy in my life and some of my happiest moments have been on the ski slopes out in the sun where all the various demons that used to dog me so much would leave me alone. I have a memory of going on a skiing expedition with my parents where I fell and broke my leg, but Willie always carried a grain or two of morphine for emergencies like that, and I am told that he carried me down on his back with me singing cowboy songs.

I loved everything about Zermatt, and so many happy memories still come wafting back of walking down the main street of this beautiful resort, which only had sledges (cars were banned). We'd always go to the same place, the Alpina, for an *après-ski* tea, and we'd have ice cream and delicious cakes. In the evenings, I would often play canasta with my mother, the only card game I ever learned. I have another memory of my father, my half-sister Chuchie and me all having hurt ourselves skiing and all three of us walking down the main street together on crutches!

I think what I am most grateful to my father for, as well as his introducing me to these sports, was his impressing upon me the need to keep physically fit. He had never drunk or smoked, and he encouraged the same inclinations in me. While I admit I puffed away a bit at Oxford and for a couple of years after, on the whole it has never been part of my life. Nor has alcohol. Or drugs. Later I used to see myself as a non-druggie hippy!

While I know that my father did his best for me, given his wounds and limitations, I also suffered because of him. As I grew older, he was continually on my case, never accepting me as I was and continually telling me I should have more backbone and willpower! What he did not know then and what I did not also realise myself until much, much later, at fifty-four, when my first wife gave me a textbook on Attention Deficit Disorder (ADD), was that many of my numerous deficiencies, which include vagueness and a difficulty in being organised and handling money, could be put down to this disorder.

Like many people of his generation, Chappy had little or no psychological insights, and at no point did he ever realise the price I paid as a result of his continually projecting his fears and weaknesses onto me, thus enabling him to bask in the illusion of his potency! The result was that I felt continually weighed down, depressed, disempowered, weak and lacking in confidence, and this all tied in with my ADD. I think what probably 'saved' me was the fact that I was good at sports and that people generally liked me—I was told I had a certain 'sweetness' about me—and so I received a fair share of positive projections from people.

It pains me to say this, but the truth is that after the doctor rang me to say, 'I am afraid your father has passed away,' I felt a huge sigh of relief. It was so strong that even before I had put the phone down from talking with the doctor, I thought, 'Thank God. At last.' It was either him or me and I mean it seriously when I say that if he had gone on living, I would probably have died very soon, as I could not go on shouldering the weight of all his misery and inadequacy. It wasn't that I hated him. I just found his presence monstrously oppressive.

Yes, my friend, my life can be divided into different stages and new beginnings, but this new beginning was the most important one. I felt that my real life started on the day of his death, 28 November 1968, just a few months after I had finished doing my final exams at Oxford. Many of the anxieties, fears and depressions that had so plagued me at university and caused me to fail to appreciate how special that time was, utterly vanished and never returned.

I feel sad when I tell this story, as my father was in no way a bad man or a crooked or sleazy one. He was just a very wounded person and very self-centred, and wounded people inevitably project misery around them. My father had collected art most of his life. He told me that he bought his first Picasso when he was twenty-five—his good eye, I think, was all about what paintings would go up in value—and although I received some of them when he died, I had no appreciation of them whatsoever.

In fact, I was embarrassed by his art and kept de Chiricos and Kokoschkas and Gaudier-Brzeskas and Utrillos etc all hidden away in a warehouse, then later either gave them away or sold them for very little. I really didn't want to have anything to do with his world, as for me it was one woven around materiality, status, and power, and so all the symbols of his world carried a bad odour for me. In fact, this Jewish money side of him absolutely gave me the creeps.

There was no doubt that my father was proud of his only son, but I also felt he was jealous of me, as he felt unloved—his father had never loved him and his mama had died when he was so young—and I was always quite popular, and I think he felt this somehow showed him up. He was also an old dad; he was forty-eight when he had me. I think he felt that for all he had achieved and done—and he'd achieved a lot—nobody really appreciated him, and I know it saddened him when I showed no inclination whatsoever to follow in his footsteps into the corporate world.

His daughter from an earlier marriage was my beloved half-sister Evelyn, whom I adored. My mother gave Evelyn her nickname, Chuchie, which was Russian for 'scarecrow', because she always looked a total mess. Chuchie was kind and compassionate. She was much older than me and so we were never brought up together, but she would always play with me when I was a little boy, and she worked teaching children with disabilities to play musical instruments. When I was older, I went with her to some of her classes and I think I fell under the spell of her goodness, which first sparked in me the idea that one day I too might work helping people. Sadly, Chuchie in her massive untidiness and scatter-brainedness—far more so than me—was made into the black sheep of the family, which meant that everyone dumped their negativity onto her so they could feel self-righteous in her presence. I felt terribly sorry for her as I adored her.

Also, she infuriated him because she had money on her mother's side, so he could not control her, and she always answered back. She had a lot of chutzpah. When my father wrote his autobiography, he did not mention his first marriage or that he had a daughter, and this naturally riled her. She gave interviews to the newspapers in which she would ask why he had never mentioned this.

Sadly, his admonitions of the dangers of smoking went unheard by her, and (I am sure to handle her stress) she would often go through eighty cigarettes in a day; in her late forties, not unsurprisingly, she died of a very virulent form of lung cancer. I mourned her terribly.

If Chuchie had the courage to rebel outwardly and stick up for herself around my father, I was much more timid. I did resist but it was more covert.

I was about fourteen, I remember, when my father announced proudly that Charles de Gaulle, then president of France, and other heads of state were meeting at his posh London flat, so I went to the joke shop Ellisdons and bought some stink bombs in tiny bottles, and I planted them all over the room where he was to have his meeting, where he would also be showing off his collection of Degas, Utrillos, Kokoschkas, Chagalls and Picassos.

Well, the servants smelled the room but couldn't find the source and the meeting had to be moved and take place in a small room instead, which I think greatly embarrassed him. Afterwards, I removed my little bottles and threw them away and no one ever solved the mystery of how it was that that room had suddenly been assailed by such horrible smells.

My father often used to have guests for dinner and would sing to them. Somehow, his singing always annoyed me; all show, why don't you ever sing and play with me. Once, when we were in our chalet in Zermatt—I think I was about ten—just as he was in the middle of his entertainment, I burst into the room firing my toy machine gun. He exploded in rage and smacked me hard. Crying uncontrollably, I ran out barefoot into the snow and of course all the guests had to go out and look for me.

Another incident. It was a very important day in 1952; it was the coronation of the queen, and my parents had invited about twenty guests to watch it as the carriage would pass right in front of our house in London and the servants had therefore hired some wooden chairs that needed assembling. And guess what? At the very moment when the queen's carriage passed in front of our house, I got my finger caught in my chair and howled and howled. Of course, everyone had to stop watching and pay attention to me.

What do all these incidents say? You don't have to be a psychoanalyst to realise that this little boy felt neglected. Everything was always being done 'for the guests', to create a particular image, and this little fellah always felt left out. It's not enough to be 'seen but not heard'. He wanted to be heard; he wanted to feel he counted for something more than being just a decoration in a sailor suit with his hair held back in a kirby grip, who, at the end of the evening, would be presented to the guests in order to get those head pats!

If the world of my childhood was lonely, it nonetheless reeked of extravagance. A vast London mansion in Park Lane, the chalet in Zermatt, and our manor in Surrey, and as I said, oodles of servants to bow and scrape. Expensive pictures adorning the walls. But I repeat once more: no soul. No heart. That's why these two things became so important to me and why I later wrote books about each of them. Yes, my friend, the world of my childhood was financially full, but it was emotionally barren. As I said, my father felt unappreciated by my mother, and she felt he had no time to devote to her. Neither had the faintest idea how to accommodate each other's worlds.

I had a profound insight into how truly unhappy my childhood had been when, in my mid-forties, I was driving to a wedding in Surrey and my path happened to take me near our old country house, Abinger Manor. Turning into a familiar wooded lane, I suddenly found myself engulfed by tears. They sprang up very suddenly and seemingly from nowhere. I sobbed and sobbed, and it went on and on. I had to stop the car. I couldn't drive. I arrived at the wedding an absolute wreck. How adept we all are at burying painful memories. Maybe suppression isn't all bad and in order to allow ourselves to survive, we need to do it. However, given the appropriate trigger—in this instance, driving up memory lane—all my suppressed grief just exploded out.

Yes, despite all those servants and nannies and governesses and gold spoons; despite all that material plenty, I felt I lived in a desolate world. I hated all those big snazzy expensive hotels that I was constantly being parked in when we'd go away on holiday, and I'd get dumped there with the nannies and governesses. I remember my father selling the big house we had in Park Lane and us spending six months living in the Dorchester Hotel before we moved to a new address. I hated it. All those staff and all that fancy food. Everyone bowing and scraping and trying to please you all the time. That's why I've avoided such establishments ever since.

But the split I felt outwardly entered me inwardly. On the one hand, the world of expensive things and engaging in extravagance made me feel increasingly uncomfortable, and so a part of me rejected this world. It became imprinted in my psyche that materiality and happiness lived in different zones and so later I felt that in order to feel happy, I needed to divest myself of all that materiality. For example, after my father died, I inherited an apartment in a chalet near our old chalet in Zermatt, and I gave it away to an impoverished friend. I also later gave away a Picasso painting to an old girlfriend to whom I was not especially close. At this time, the world of 'things' had little meaning for me.

Yet, at the same time, this 'soulless' materialistic world was also my ally as it gave me comfort and security. After all, it was the only world I knew growing up. And in this world, I never needed to lift a finger. Everything was always done for me. I could throw my clothes on the floor and they'd be picked up by the maid, and so it was strongly imprinted in me that everyone had a duty to look after me—to be my servant and pick up for me (leading many girlfriends over the years to tear out their hair in despair over this spoilt, demanding and precious little prince). My wonderful friend, Alan Gordon Walker, whom I met at Oxford, would become increasingly infuriated by my unconscious desire to somehow turn him into my batman. 'I am not your damn servant, I am your friend,' he'd angrily tell me.

Thus, there has always been an ongoing battle between these two parts of me, as the very world that I despised also gave me comfort and security. As I grew up I would find myself veering from one extreme to the other. Later, as I said, I developed an identity of what I'll call the loose, free-wheelin' cowboy-booted, cool dude 'Californian Serge', and when this role took me over, I'd always be at war with the somewhat pompous, smoking-jacketed 'precious toff' side of me—and of course also with that dimension of the world outside of me. This 'me' thought all rich, classy people were a bunch of wankers!

Conversely, when I was with my snootier, 'wankier' friends and nestled back into that identity, I found myself slightly looking down my nose at my more 'lefty-inclined' mates, who were more interested in climate change than in the cut of their blazers. In earlier years, although I had gone to live in California, I still owned a lovely old barn in the Cotswolds, very much in 'toff land' (Prince Charles was a close neighbour), and I liked the contrast between these two worlds. I would act out each identity, hanging out with my spiritual friends in California, wearing my cowboy boots and talking about consciousness, and then returning for a couple of months to live in my barn in Gloucestershire and hosting dinner parties dressed in my green velvet, tailor-made smoking jacket and wearing my Gucci shoes!

Often these worlds would clash. I remember once bringing one of my California girlfriends, a disciple of the spiritual teacher Osho, back to Gloucestershire with me for a month, and being horrified at her inability to dress properly when I gave one of my dinner parties. To say that I didn't have—indeed still don't have buried inside me somewhere—a very superficial 'sub-personality' that a friend once appropriately named 'Lord Snooty' after the character in the *Beano* comic, and to pretend that it hasn't taken many years of hard inner grind for him finally to relinquish his top hat and striped trousers, would be to tell a big lie. But before I go on, let me say something about my mother, or 'Moonie' as I used to call her.

Chapter 3

Moonie World

My dear mama, Irena, whom I always called Moonie (I can't remember where the name originated) was also the source of many obstacles in my life, playing a central role in the often-convoluted relationships I would have with women!

Moonie was from an aristocratic Russian family and was born two years before the Russian Revolution. Her father, Prince Serge Obolensky, had been aide de camp to a series of Moscow governor-generals, and had owned very large estates near Moscow. According to my grandmother, who was a wonderful, strong woman and whom I loved very much, they were told that the Bolsheviks were on their way to murder them. Thus, with their five young children and knowing that they just had a few hours to flee, they stuffed a few pieces of jewellery into their clothes and took off, leaving everything behind.

Further trauma occurred when the battleship that they boarded to take them to France was torpedoed. However, the Obolenskys all managed to arrive in Paris unharmed and, once there, they received help. In those days the lot of refugees was not steeped in the dire tragedies that we see today.

Nonetheless, being born within the violent birth of a revolution is a traumatic experience, and as small children always pick up the anxiety of their parents, my sense is that Moonie, together with all her brothers and sisters, was in some way damaged. I say this as all of my uncles and aunts, who were delightful human beings—and I was very fond of all of them—seemed to have problems and to find it difficult to live happy lives. I was especially close to my lovely Uncle Misha, and on several occasions in his life I needed to step in and, in a small way, help him out. I think that my mother who was naturally a strong character, came out the best of the lot.

How this 'revolution trauma' affected Moonie was that it inclined her to a certain rigidity that remained all her life and which certainly had a damaging effect on me. I never felt that she could let me in—that is, allow me to come close to her and love her, which I did very much—or be fully real with me, and it was not until the very end, when I bade goodbye to her in the hospital as she was dying of cancer, that she opened up her thin little arms to me and hugged me and gave me a despairing look that said, 'I am very sad I am dying and I love you, doucie moy (meaning "little darling" in Russian), and I have always loved you.'

It was true. Moonie always did her best for me; she loved me to the extent that she was able and I deeply acknowledge her for that. But because of the difficulties in her early life, she had a great reluctance to face dark or unpleasant things. In Jungian terms, you could say she never wanted to confront her Shadow! This can be summed up by the fact that despite having a bad cough for a long time, she refused to go to the doctor. When her lung cancer was at last discovered, it was of course much too late to do anything about it.

Moonie married my father in a beautiful little Russian church in London. The father of my good friend and cousin Prince George Galitzine (who had been at Harrow and Oxford with me), who was also called George, was her best man, and afterwards there was a cocktail party to which, glancing at the guest list, I see that pretty much all of London society, including most of the royals, seemed to have been invited. My father was so proud of my mother and got the great fashion photographer Cecil Beaton to take many pictures of her. I have two of them hanging in my office today.

I don't know how long my parents were happy together. Perhaps for the first few years, but certainly by the time I was old enough to observe things, I could see that they were not at ease. My father just worked and was not personable, whereas Moonie was wonderfully charming with people and everyone said she should have been an ambassador's wife. Certainly, on paper it was a good fit. He gave her financial security and she gave him beauty, youth, and aristocracy. They stayed together for ten years and then my father, who was always complaining to me how lonely he felt with her, decided to leave her. I am happy to say that soon after she divorced him, she married a lovely man, George Morton, who was her age and who knew us all well as he'd worked for my father in the past.

I was very fond of George. We also had nicknames. I was 'Soidge' and he was 'Goidge' and Goidge was always very kind to me—he went to great efforts to teach me the ukulele—despite finding me abominably spoilt, which of course I was. He'd often remind me of the following story. Long before he married my mother, he had come to stay the weekend with my parents in Abinger and was playing football with me in the garden. I kicked the ball over the hedge behind him, which meant one had to go a long way around to retrieve it. I waited for him to do so. He was quite rightly outraged and made me go and get it. This surprised me as I was not used to people telling me off. I was used to the servants always being at my beck and call! I may have been a sweet, shy little boy when presented to guests, but I also think I was brought up to be a very spoilt one. My father always accused my mother of spoiling me, and I am sure he was right.

I am delighted to say, however, that, unlike my father, George made my mother very happy. His mother had died just before they got married and he did well from her inheritance. The result was that they spent their winters in a beautiful chalet in Gstaad and the summers in a lovely, huge, fresco-adorned palazzo in Venice. Moonie went on to have two more children with him.

George was also interested in spiritual things and when I was older and living in California, we had a very active correspondence as we found that we both spoke the same language. I have just reread some of his letters to me and I was impressed with all the trouble he took. George was a very good man and his coming into my life was a great blessing. It is not easy being a stepfather and inheriting other people's children, but he took great care of me.

I loved my old Moonie and when I was a little baby, she did her damndest for me. In looking back, I feel that she was as present with me as her 'clenchedness' allowed, except for all those occasions when my father would whisk her away to accompany him on his business trips just when I was feeling happy and comfortable with her.

This, however, set in place a pattern for me with women whereby, just when I was starting to feel settled and secure with them, they would suddenly, without warning, take off and leave, and the abandonment I would always feel echoed the abandonment I had experienced with Moonie. The result was that I grew up with a big rejecting pattern inside me, and as a result it would often be me who would run away from the girl I was dating *first,* in order to anticipate the pain of my unconsciously feeling that they would do the same thing to me.

My problem with darling Moonie was not that she didn't love me and do her very best for me; I know she did. For example, I clearly remember once forcing her to walk for hours to find a particular shop that I thought sold a particular toy soldier that I wanted, and her traipsing along with me despite the fact that she was weak and had just got out of bed after having pleurisy. Yes, I was quite a taskmaster!

The problem was that her love was limited in scope. It was OK when I was a little baby and a young child, as then I needed comforting and soothing. Problems emerged when I started growing up and needed other kinds of love that were simply outside of her repertoire.

I needed the kind of love that comes from being intelligently listened to and understood, the love that comes from being seen for who I was, but this kind of love required that Moonie inhabit a domain of being that she had no experience of. When she sensed me moving away from her as I grew up, because she needed very much to hang on to me as a substitute for the loveless relationship she had with my father, her strategy was to try to infantilise me, try to hold me back from developing—keep me as her sweet little 'doucie moy' (Russian for darling), because only then could she properly relate to me.

Moonie also wanted to keep her little boy 'special', so he wouldn't get sullied by connecting with the not-so-special, grimy outer world. One of the external forms this took was making me wear little white gloves when I went outside in London so as not to catch nasty germs! One particular episode is etched strongly in my mind.

I had just walked up to the local church a few hundred yards away from our country house, and I'd seen a group of young boys who also lived in our village. I asked Moonie, 'Please can I go up and play with the village boys?' Her reply was—and it made my heart freeze—'No you can't. They are common!' I was not to mix with the world of the lower classes, the hoi polloi. It was imprinted in me early on that I was part of a superior species and should only mix with my kind. How painful it was to be told you are special and then when you grow up and start mixing with the big bad world, you find that for some inexplicable reason, not everyone agrees with you and bows down to you!

I was special, then, for no other reason than that I was the son of my parents and so I had to be 'special' to reflect well on them. The price I paid for this, especially for much of my early life, was that the false face I chose to put on for the world was one of superiority. In my Christ Church freshmen's photo, for example, I have my hands in my waistcoat pocket as I look arrogantly at the camera, but underneath lay hidden another me that, if the truth be known, was a singularly unconfident little boy!

At the same time as I felt Moonie desperately trying to keep me as her little boy so she could feel close (this all vanished when she had her new family with George and could coo over her new 'babylings', as she called them), I always felt there was a barrier between us in terms of real intimacy. I remember if I hadn't seen her for a bit, I'd run to hug her and want to put my arms around her, and I'd always feel her tighten and emotionally pull back as if this degree of closeness was uncomfortable. Which of course, for her, it was.

This set another pattern in motion in my love life, whereby if women opened to me lovingly and offered genuine intimacy, I simply wasn't interested. Conversely, if they were beautiful-looking and had a kind of ice-queeniness about them that echoed my mama, I would be instantly hooked and, generally, would fall in love! Indeed, 'fall' was the right word as my emotional tumbles and dramas around women during my twenties, thirties and yes, even my forties, constituted, as you'll be seeing, a significant part of my life challenges.

The biggest wound though, which I received and which so many of us unwittingly receive and at huge cost—and here my father and mother and nannies were all unknowingly complicit—was what I call the *great soul wound*. This particular wound occurs when we are born and are still connected to the world of soul, where, to quote Wordsworth in his great poem 'Intimations of Immortality', we are still 'trailing clouds of glory... from God, who is our home'.

What happens when those who welcome our birth into this world are people whose own soul life has closed down—or, in most cases, has never properly opened up—is that we, the child, also learn to close down to this most important part of who we are. Put another way, for our own soul life or soul light, which is present as we are born, to remain open, and to grow and continue to shine and thus for us to start connecting into the deeper or more essential part of ourselves, it is necessary that, as a newborn, we experience soulfulness being mirrored in the consciousness of those who welcome us into the world and care for us.

If we are 'un-soulfully welcomed'—that is, received by parents who are basically not very conscious human beings and have a minimum of genuine inner life and who see their baby primarily as being an adjunct to them—what happens is that we, the children, take on these conditional projections. We grow up feeling that to be accepted or loved, we have to be what our parents secretly want us to be. The price we can pay for this is that we grow increasingly away from who we truly are, and our false face or 'societal mask' begins increasingly to dominate.

This certainly had been the case with me, and basically the story of my life has been about all the many different activities I have embarked on to try to discover the 'me' that had not properly had a chance to emerge. And this retrieval of my soul self didn't occur overnight. It took me a long time to understand that all my ideas about who I *thought* I was actually had very little relevance to who I *truly* was. I also think my real problem was that I didn't ever really feel at home in the world that I had been born into. It was not that it was in any way a 'bad' world, and there was certainly a bit of love in it, it was just that as a pea, I felt that I didn't quite belong in that particular pod.

Chapter 4

Funny Money

Most people have complex patterns evolving around money, and I was no exception. A spiritual master called George Gurdjieff once said that if you want to know about a person, just observe how they relate to money and sex. Well, in my own case the answer in both areas was 'extremely messily'. We'll get to sex later, but at this stage I will look at money.

As I explained earlier, there was a lot of confusion for me in this area. At one level, I realised I needed it for my survival; and later on, it saved me from having to sit in an office from nine to five doing some boring job that I despised. However, at another level, I saw it as being tainted and so didn't want it. I saw that my father's obsession with business and with making money was what stood in the way of his having time for me. I disliked his 'world', which seemed so materialistic. In fact, when Chappie was sixty, he wrote his autobiography and devoted entire chapters just to describing in great detail his many important business deals and all the famous people he hobnobbed with and how successful he was. And he only gave two lines to mentioning me, his only son! That really hurt me, but it seemed to say it all: what he considered important and what he saw as unimportant.

While I have no doubt whatsoever that all his money was earned honestly—as I said, Chappy was brilliant in this area and was no sleazeball or cheat and there was nothing 'Trumpian' about him—for me it was all tainted. When he died, everything that got left to me in his will smelled of a world that I had little respect for.

As a result, for many years I had a curious kind of love/hate relationship with money and especially the idea of engaging in 'business' or being a 'businessman', as for me it had unhealthy connotations. So instead of initially being grateful that I had a support, as it were, to start my life off from, I saw it more as a noose around my neck making me different from others and in some way holding me down. The result was that I would go to great lengths to conceal the fact that I had money. All the valuable paintings I inherited from my father at his death, I had no respect for. I never had them on my walls and would hide them away in storage places, sell them cheaply or give them away. I never had flashy cars and always drove Minis, though I have to admit that they were pretty cool Mini Cooper S's with black windows!

If we don't respect something—or someone, for that matter—we tend to treat it, or them, shabbily, and that's how I treated money during the earlier part of my life. It confused me and I had no interest in looking after it properly and would spend it indulgently on useless things like, for example, going everywhere in taxis. In my early twenties I never ever went on the tube or took a bus. Now, in my seventies, I never take a taxi!

However, the problem is never money. Money is neutral and will take on whatever identity we choose to project onto it. It can be a source of great evil if used unwisely and great good if used wisely. If I am honest, I didn't do much good with my money—except when I gave large chunks away, generally to undeserving individuals or causes—but I didn't do anything bad with it either. While in my early twenties I was certainly a bit of a dandy and spent quite a bit on poncy clothes and nightclubs, I was never one of those 'decadent youths' who used his money to give himself baths in champagne, stay in hideously expensive hotels, travel first class, engage in high-stakes gambling (I've never gambled in my life) or satisfy some monstrously depraved habit. Actually, I think there was always a certain innocence and naivete to me and I think one or two people took advantage of this in the early days.

In retrospect, I just wish that my father had thought it relevant to have taken me out for lunch—just us two—and explain money to me, tell me how important it was, how lucky I was that I was going to receive some when he passed away, and that I should do my best to invest it wisely. I also wish he'd educated me as to the aesthetic as well as the financial importance of the paintings I inherited. If I had just bothered to hold on to them, they would probably be worth many millions of pounds today. But I never thought along those lines. My father never took the trouble to show me anything, just to criticise me for lacking in 'get up and go'!

In those days, I disliked everything about his world, together with all the things it embraced, which very much included Renee, a distant cousin of his, whom he married after divorcing my mother, and this is why over the course of my life, I gradually rid myself of everything that reminded me of it.

But he did test me out. Just before I went up to Oxford, he insisted that I have the experience of working in a stockbrokers firm and as he knew the director of Greenwell's, he arranged for me to be taken on as an apprentice. I remember every morning travelling to the City on the tube, dressed in a 'gent's uniform', namely, a pinstripe suit, a white shirt and blue tie with little white dots, a rolled-up umbrella and my father's bowler hat that he used for hunting. I refused to get my hair cut and so instead I would tuck it down inside my collar. I felt right out of a Monty Python skit!

While a couple of chaps (poor devils) were put in charge of me to show me the ropes, I have to confess that, aged nineteen, I had not the slightest idea what was going on, nor the remotest interest in being enlightened. Two incidents stand out for me. Being caught reading a comic hidden inside the *Economist* magazine by the boss, who, walking by, also saw me playing with my long hair that had fallen out of my collar. 'Ah, Serge,

I am so glad you don't bother with haircuts and like reading Marvel comics,' he said.

The other incident was pretty symbolic. I was in a room alone. Everyone else had buggered off somewhere, and suddenly the phone rang. Help. What do I do? After letting it ring for a bit, I felt I should answer it. Probably someone wanting to know a share price. I remember on the wall was a chart with the names of shares on it. I wasn't quite sure if the number written after them in blue meant they had gone up and if the red number meant they had gone down, or if it was the other way around. Oh well. Tremblingly, I picked up the phone and a voice barked out: 'What are bats?'

What are bats! What a curious question. My stammered reply was something along the lines that I thought they were mouse-like creatures with wings who flew at night, had a good radar system and—I was interrupted. 'Who the hell are you?'

I stammered out my name. It was my father. I can't remember what he said to me, but I later learned that bats stood for B.A.T.S. or British American Tobacco shares. I imagined that this experience prepared him for the further disappointment when, a year or so later, he asked me to come to a meeting at a new business he had bought a year or so ago and which he told me he had turned around and was now making a huge profit. I think it was called BedCo and it employed several hundred people and made office equipment. He wanted to make me a director and also promised the same thing to my great school friend Johnny Reed, whom he also asked along, thinking this might arouse some interest on my part. Sadly, it didn't. (Today, I think that I would jump at the opportunity if I were offered a successful business. Today, I also read the *Economist* very carefully and, over the years, have worked for several small businesses, helping them bring more heart and soul onto the shop floor.)

I sometimes ask myself this question. If, when I left university, I had focussed my energies on honouring money and taking responsibility for it, would I have been the person I turned out to be? Would I have championed the causes I stood for? In other words, if I had focussed on remaining wealthy, would the need to lead a simple life, which became so important to me later on, have been possible? Certainly, I had friends with backgrounds similar to mine and who never needed to lift a finger and consequently never did, spending all their time just amusing themselves, and their money actually turned out to be a veritable noose around their necks.

Put simply, if I'd have stayed the rich kid I started out as, would my spiritual life, which I will discuss later as being so important to me, have been less important? I don't know. Maybe. Maybe not. At that stage, spirituality, and materiality, which today I see very much as integral parts of one another, existed in very separate worlds. All I know is that having wealthy parents embarrassed the hell out of me. Just as I never wanted my fellow pupils at Harrow school to see me arrive at the beginning of term in a chauffeur-driven car—I'd always ask Vic, our chauffeur, to park the Rolls half a mile down the road—I would also have been mortified to have had friends see paintings by Kokoschka or Utrillo or Chagall adorning my walls, and so I hid away all the paintings, preferring gaily coloured Japanese prints. One thing I did like, however, was a sculpture of the Beatles by David Wynne and this had pride of place in my sitting room, together with *The Dancer* by Gaudier-Brzeska. I gave the Beatles away to a friend and later sold *The Dancer* very cheaply. Many years later, I heard the Beatles sculpture had been resold for a huge sum!

In retrospect, the biggest regret I had with my father is that I wished that instead of constantly lecturing me about how I could be more like him, he'd taken some time alone with me, bothered to find out about me and talked to me about life and how to handle it and, so very important, told me more about the art adorning his walls. He never did. He was too self-centred to bother to try to enter into his son's little world!

What I found for quite a long time was that I couldn't do anything that my father did or was any good at, as this reminded me of his world. Even today, I ask my wife to talk to my accountant about tax or our landlady about rent because I am so bad at it, and I once ended up paying more for a carpet I bought from a carpet dealer in Marrakech than he had asked for. He looked rather a sad, skinny little fellow and I felt sorry for him. Yes, I realise that I inherited shame about my money and background because in some sense I was ashamed of my father, and the idea of wheeling and dealing just horrified me.

I also found that the kind of 'important people' that my parents mixed with, i.e., royalty (because of my mama), business tycoons and well-known society people, made me feel uncomfortable. It was not that many of them were not decent people or without substance, but because I saw them just as characters peopling my parents' world. As a young man, when encountering these people on my parents' turf I'd always feel that I had to put on some kind of performance, and that just being my own rather laid-back self was not good enough. And I was probably right!

That said, it is interesting how often we may have the same traits as our parents even if we see ourselves as being very different. I mentioned earlier how the language in the love letters my father wrote my mother was very similar to the words that I later used in my letters to girlfriends. And I also confess that while I thought nothing of divesting myself of my father's entire art collection, I had nevertheless inherited the 'collector gene', and have taken pleasure over the years in gradually building up a small collection of my own, only in a very different area.

My great love has been African tribal art, which I was first turned on to by my dear friend Peter Adler, who at that time was a dealer in this genre. African civilisation is very complex, hierarchical, ritualistic, and deeply beautiful. I began collecting in my mid-twenties and it became a great love. It is interesting how much artists like Modigliani, Paul Klee, Giacometti and Picasso owe to this art, which in the past used to be called primitive, but in reality is extremely sophisticated. The point is that tribal art is made for a purpose. For example, in one tribe in Nigeria it was felt that if a twin were to die, his spirit needed to be kept for the twin still living and so he would go to the village sculptor and ask him to craft a figure to represent his dead sibling. Similarly, a figure may be created to appease an ancestor or appeal for favour with the gods, or to ensure a good harvest. Certain figures are power figures that protect the tribe from its enemies. African shamans also like to use masks to perform their rituals. Today, I have a lovely little collection containing one or two really fine pieces and I don't mind at all that a lot of people find them weird, although my wife has gradually come around to having a certain fondness for them.

I always see my sculptures as holding the consciousness of their creator, and I sometimes think of what an extraordinary journey they have had to make, from their existence in a tribal village where they were originally created to perform a particular function, to being scooped up and taken to an auction house, and maybe then to journey into other people's western drawing rooms! I also feel that because my little pieces have been loved and appreciated by me over the years, that they have also undergone other subtle changes. We think that only people benefit from our affection towards them, but it is not the case. My African pieces resonate with the affection I have put into them. In a way, I feel I've given them a new kind of life and I know they feel happy being with me!

Beauty has always been very important to me and I have always appreciated Keats's remark about 'beauty being truth, truth beauty. That is all we know and all we need to know.'

A good friend of mine felt that she healed herself from cancer by meditating daily on beauty, surrounding herself with beautiful things and beautiful friends, reading beautiful literature and listening only to beautiful music by the great composers. Beauty so filled her heart that there was no space for anything else. I have been much inspired by her.

Over the years, I have also collected other artworks that I have found beautiful, such as Tibetan thangkas, Indonesian mandalas, Japanese prints, Aboriginal paintings and Russian icons, and the little office where I now work is absolutely chock-a-block. For me, Russian icons and tribal art figures each represent different aspects of what I see as constituting sacred art, one looking more 'up to Heaven', the other reminding one of the preciousness of things earthy and grounded.

I think that what was important was that my little collection reflected my taste and not Chappy's. I am happy that when I pass away, my daughter will inherit a few beautiful pieces. I hope that she will have felt sufficiently loved by me, and that the meaning of these pieces will have been sufficiently explained to her, as to induce her to want to keep them and perhaps obtain the same joy from them that I have experienced.

Looking back on Chappy some fifty years later, having done a lot of inner work on my relationship with him, I now feel very warm towards him, and I see that everything that happened or failed to happen between us had a certain OK-ness about it. I have fully forgiven him. I am grateful that he was my father and I understand that no one can give to another what they have not yet uncovered inside themselves. I also understand that the pain he gave me led me to ferret out some wonderful teachers and healers and to be moved to explore myself and so indirectly led me to do the work that I have been doing for the last forty-five years, which has always given me so much pleasure. As I sit at my desk today, a big bronze sculpture of Chappy by the artist David Wynne gazes down at me from my bookshelf. His expression is sweet and a bit quizzical and my heart goes out to him, as it also does to dearest Moonie. My parents were both basically good human beings. Given their various wounds and deficiencies, they both did their best for me and for this I am grateful. It is challenging being a parent, as I am always finding out with my own daughter, and I am sure she will one day tell me about areas where I might have been better. If so, I will try to be open to discussing everything with her as truthfully as possible.

Over the years I have learned about reincarnation and past lives, and so have come to see that before ever I incarnated in this life, I probably 'chose' both Moonie and Chappy as my parents, to set up certain challenges for me. I have also come to see that many of my difficulties in life were the working through of old karmas and even of human collective karma. We'll get into all this later, as right now it's time to say a little bit about my schooldays.

Chapter 5

School Days

I always enjoyed going to school and in London, the pre-prep school I first went to was called Wagners. I remember us little boys dressed in our school uniforms, ties, blazers, shorts and caps, walking the streets in a crocodile fashion, and me collecting cigarette cards very seriously. I was also a good yo-yo player and I liked to play the game of trying to smash my opponent's conker with my conker. I very much liked a master called Mr Harold and despite his dragon breath. I wrote a poem to him that went: 'Mr Harold so kind so good, you should go to Heaven, you should, you should.'

From pre-prep school I went on to Summerfields prep school, and at thirteen I passed my Common Entrance exam to Harrow. I think the reason I always enjoyed school was because I enjoyed my friends and I was quite popular. I was never bullied and I never bullied anyone. I seemed to have the knack of being able to get on with the other boys. And this is important. Also, if you are tall and good at sports, that helps! At thirteen, I was the same height I am now—6 feet 2 inches—although then I was as thin as a rake. I remember I once got out of bed and broke a leg as I stood up, as my little ankles were so wisp-thin! Interestingly, they have stayed that way throughout my life despite my doing huge amounts of sport.

My prep school, Summerfields, was in Hastings. The headmaster was a raving paedophile and got away with it for a long time, as in those days, I don't think awareness around these issues really existed. Years later, I heard, he went to prison. I was very lucky; I was not a 'pretty boy' and so was left well alone by him.

Basically, I enjoyed prep school and didn't have all that homesickness that so many boys seemed to have. I was always top of the class in English and generally bottom in maths, but I was in the first team for all the sports and remember well the football match where I got my colours. I was playing centre half and the opposing goalie kicked the ball and it rolled to my feet on the halfway line. I booted it right back and it went over the goalie's head and into the net. This goal from the halfway line won us the match. Perhaps my main claim to fame, though, was that I won the school essay-writing competition on the bizarre subject of being a *Fly on the Wall,* and I also won the throwing the cricket ball competition, chucking it further than anyone else in the school had done. I wonder if my record still holds!

One of my best friends there was called Dennie Dixon Boardman. He subsequently became a great whizz-kid in the States; I heard that he only deigned to handle the investment portfolios of people if they had over £500 million. I bumped into him many years later, only to realise that we had little in common anymore. I have no doubt he felt exactly the same about me. I have found that there are certain friends whom it is lovely to see again; you discover that you still have a lot in common and would like the relationship to continue. With others, while it is pleasant to see them once more and find out what they're doing with their lives, you realise that after half an hour there is nothing much more to talk about.

Another of my contemporaries was Prince Hassan Talal of Jordan, the younger brother of the former King Hussein. Hassan was not only at Summerfields with me, but he also accompanied me to Harrow and later to Christ Church, Oxford. I was sad that he never became king after the death of his brother, as I think he would have done very well as he was a man of great integrity and had a profound understanding of Middle Eastern politics. The title went instead to King Hussein's oldest son. Hassan and I kept in touch for many years, sending each other Christmas cards, and I would occasionally go to parties he held when he was in London.

From Summerfields, I went on to Harrow aged thirteen and was there for five years and, again, public school worked for me in that I was not unhappy, enjoyed my sports and had plenty of friends. The indoctrination of me being a higher-class kind of person and not 'one of the plebs', however, continued. Our school was up on a hill and it was impressed upon us that we should not mix with those 'yobs' or 'oiks' who lived in Harrow town ('Arrow taon') down below. Perhaps my mother not allowing me to play with those 'common village boys' was good preparation!

Snob that I was, even in my early teens, something of my future or my soul was beginning to beckon to me. I was fascinated by the whole beatnik movement and absorbed all the novels of Jack Kerouac and William Burroughs and, though I never actually wrote poetry then, I sometimes would imagine myself being a beat poet 'on the road' with a woman who didn't 'care shit for all that dumb white machinery in the kitchen' (Jack Kerouac). I also bought books by Alan Watts on Zen Buddhism (I saw him speak, many years later in California, shortly before he died) and read everything that Allen Ginsberg ever wrote.

It made me feel cool and rebellious and I was always furious that I was never allowed to grow my hair long, and whenever it might threaten to reach down to my ear tops, I'd be sent to the barber shop. I'd be depressed for weeks afterwards as no matter what you'd ask for, they'd give you a short back and sides (which, interestingly, today is very much the fashion for the young).

I always felt rather self-conscious about my big sticking-out ears. I sensed they gave me the same slightly gormless look as the then-young Prince Charles, and I kicked up such a fuss that when I was sixteen, my mother sent me to a plastic surgeon, who pinned them back for me. Of course, no one noticed any difference, but I felt so much better.

If I am really to speak the truth, in my pre-ear-pinning period, I was a most uncool teenager. I was tall, gangly, and supremely unconfident, especially with the opposite sex. When I'd go on holiday with either of my parents—say to Zermatt, Gstaad or Venice—I'd often find myself at some *thé dansant* where a band would be playing and there would be lots of girls with their parents and there was a possibility of meeting someone. Summoning up my courage, I would walk stiffly and self-consciously up to a table where a girl was sitting and would say in my then very English-accented French (most girls were French), *'Voulez vous danser avec moi?'*

What would invariably happen was that they would pick up my trembling and say, *'Merci,'* but not get up, so I would stand there and repeat my question and still get the same answer. It confused me. If they said, *'Merci,'* surely that meant they were thanking me and wanted to dance!

I never got it until it was explained to me by my cool Italian friend Paolo (who, tiny and ferret-thin, nonetheless had the capacity to charm every girl he met) that if a girl said *'Merci'* to me, it did not necessarily mean 'Yes'. 'You've got to be more sensitive, Serge,' he'd tell me. '"*Merci*" can mean "thank you, yes," as well as "thank you, no," and you've got to tell by their body language and their eyes what they mean. If they smile and turn towards you and start to get up (something that very seldom happened to me), it means they are accepting your invitation. If they say "*Merci*" and then turn their heads away, it means thank you, but no thank you. How they react is all about what energy you project out to them. *Capice*?'

At last, the message sank in and observing how Paolo operated and trying to copy him—and feeling I no longer looked so much like Prince Charles—made me feel a bit more confident, which of course the girls picked up and I began to get one or two positive thank yous and yeses!

The Teddy boy movement was also in full swing. I was too young to be a Ted, so I just let myself dream about decking myself out with a Chuck Berry ducktail haircut and wearing those black crepe suede shoes with enormous sponge soles and green luminous socks and long padded-at-the-shoulders, Victorian-style jackets, and drainpipe pants that the Teds wore. The best I could actually do was get myself an electric guitar and learn all the old skiffle and rockabilly songs. You could play most of them on three chords and I never advanced much beyond that. In those days Duane Eddy was my hero, and I loved Cliff Richard—*Move It*, Cliff's first ever record, was one of the great rock 'n' roll numbers—and I learned to play all the songs of Ricky Nelson, Buddy Holly and the Everly Brothers and still play them today, as they are the only songs whose words I remember. I didn't get on to Bob Dylan, my great hero, until I was about nineteen as he hadn't yet arrived on the scene.

But I did come across Lightnin' Hopkins, the great blues guitarist, and thus began a lifelong romance with the blues; I am as in love today with B.B. King, Leadbelly, John Lee Hooker, Robert Johnson (what a maestro) as I ever was then. Blues music is not just about our ladies leavin' us and our wakin' up in the mornin' and feelin' blue. They are also very positive songs. I have just written a blues song called *Corona Virus Blues* to the tune of *Sweet Home Chicago* and put it on my Facebook page and YouTube channel and got one or two laughs!

Today, my great blues heroes are the great guitarists Eric Clapton and Steve Winwood, the latter of whom became my next-door neighbour when I went to live in Gloucestershire and with whom I got to play on my fiftieth birthday party. But that's another story and I'll save it for later. In those days I also loved Ray Charles, the high priest of soul, and I never tired of hearing *What'd I Say* together with all his other great songs like *Hit the Road Jack* and *I Can't Stop Loving You*. So many teenage memories get hooked into songs. I remember listening to *Hello Mary Lou* by Ricky Nelson when I was fifteen or sixteen at a party and met Carolyn Holmes, who gave me my first 'proper kiss'; I will never forget that moment. It is interesting how many old memories get interwoven with songs you heard at the time. Hear the song again and the memories come flooding back. How obsessed with girls I was in my teenage years; and, if I am being honest, that obsession has remained with me for much of my life. While some might have described me as a naturally 'hot-blooded young man', in retrospect I would now say that I exhibited many of the features of patriarchal man at his most wounded!

When I was much younger, my father had got a music teacher to teach me the piano and, trying to help me be light-fingered, she told me to imagine my hands were like a cat on hot bricks. This had the opposite effect and made me feel my fingers were being burned, so I never played again. But I wish I'd been taught the guitar as I secretly had a desire to be a blues musician. Years later, when I began teaching my spiritual retreats, I would always start the day with the whole group singing and would play lots of shamanic songs that I had picked up from some of my teachers. I still sometimes toy with the idea of getting guitar lessons in the blues and reinventing myself as a blues singer. Perhaps call myself something like 'Sergie Boy Behrens' or 'Lightnin' Beddington'…

But back to school. One of the worst things about Harrow was having to dress up every Sunday in Lord Snooty gear—striped trousers, tailcoat, and stiff collar (I hope this absurd pantomime has now been discontinued). We'd also have to wear a straw hat or boater, and, when we passed a schoolmaster (called, for some reason, a 'beak'), we had to bow our heads and lightly tap our boaters—and woe betide you if you didn't!

At chapel every morning, one had to listen to sermons by pious—although well-meaning—clergymen who would continuously exhort us never to forget that Jesus died on the cross for our sins and that woe betide us if we were not as 'perfect as our Father in heaven was perfect'. Having these guilt trips foisted on me for five years is why all my life since, I've been interested in finding my spirituality outside of religion.

What I also discovered later was that unless those who chose to teach about religion worked on themselves to be connected in some way to that source which they purported to represent, their words would be hollow. I always felt that the true Jesus was no guilt-tripper. On the contrary. I felt that the true Jesus talked about higher states of consciousness and was a genuine mystic and healer, a lover of nature and women. A totally cool guy. Just read the gospel according to Thomas, one of the gospels discovered at Nag Hammadi, in Egypt, which included secret gospels, poems and myths very different from the New Testament, and you'll also find out that he was a teacher of transformation. I had to venture far away from religious institutions to experience that Jesus, as I'll be sharing later.

My housemaster, Charles Lillingston, an archetypal bachelor with a dreadful stutter, was a terrible snob and was delighted to have a prince in his house, even if it was only a half one. Though he continually told me that I was 'vague and woolly minded' and caned me a few times for various miscellaneous offences (once, for not having enough 'house spirit', whatever that meant), he was basically a good egg. Here's an example of his decency: I had acquired a tendency occasionally to break out of the house at night if there was some good party going on in London, and I always got away with it. Then a bombshell dropped. I'd gone to a rather smart 'do' that had been given a centre spread in the society magazine the *Tatler* and there was a picture of me. I trembled when I saw that issue under Lillingston's arm as he beckoned me to come to his office. 'O Gawd, I've got it coming now,' I thought.

'I like boys in my house to look smart,' Lillingston told me, and, opening the *Tatler* with the picture of me, said, 'Ob (the name he called me), you either ought to learn to tie your bow tie properly, or even better, desist going to occasions during termtime where this requirement is needed.' Bless his heart. I could easily have been expelled.

On the whole, though, I enjoyed my time at Harrow. I was an average student. One sadness was that although I loved rugby, I never made the first fifteen, probably because I had the weight of my late uncle, Prince Alex Obolensky, my mother's wonderful brother, sitting on my shoulders.

Alex had escaped out of Russia as a small baby with my mother in the Revolution. Enormously handsome, Alex was known as the 'Flying Prince', because when he was at Brasenose College, Oxford in the 1930s, he was asked to play in the England rugby team against the hitherto unbeatable All Blacks. In doing so, he utterly pulverised their defences with two legendary tries that rugby aficionados still talk about to this day. A book has recently come out about him entitled *The Flying Prince*.

I played on the wing, like he did, and was also a fast runner—I did the 110-metre hurdles and represented Harrow and later Oxford in this sport—but each time I was given a trial for the first fifteen in rugby, fear would creep into me. Memories of Alex would always be there even though I of course never met him. I would be passed the ball and would invariably drop it!

I feel very proud of Alex and was so sad that he was killed at the age of twenty-four, just at the start of the war, when the Spitfire he was flying failed to land properly and he broke his neck. He played for Rosslyn Park and there is a statue of him outside the clubhouse. I read all his correspondence with my mother, with whom he was very close, and learned that it was very tough for him being a prince up at Oxford, with all the expectations projected onto him and yet having very little money. I also found him to be a very spiritual young man with high ideals. I feel that the world is very much the less for his only having inhabited it for a short time and I wish I had met him. Like James Dean, who died young when he crashed his sports car, so my dear Uncle Alex who crashed his plane, will also always remain youthful and beautiful.

It's not just Alex, but the truth is that I have always identified much more fully with the Russian side of my family. On my father's side, I haven't a clue who I'm descended from, and I am not especially interested; those members of his family whom I've met, I've never particularly felt in harmony with. Truth is also that I am more interested in what will happen in the future than in knowing about my past.

One last Harrow story. Perhaps twenty or so years after I left, I was at a school reunion, and bumped into the guy who used to be my 'fag' when I was a prefect. (Fagging was a custom where a younger boy acted as a kind of servant for the older boys, cleaning their shoes, running errands for them, that kind of thing.) Well, in the intervening years, my 'fag' had become a big noise in the property development world and had become a millionaire and been handed a knighthood.

I greeted Sir Whatsisname (I won't divulge his name) in a very friendly manner: 'Good to see you again after all these years'— and then, turning towards his rather toffee-nosed wife, I said, 'Sir Whatsisname used to be such a sweet little fella; he cleaned my shoes so well, pressed my shirts,' and then, turning back to him and pointing at my shoes, I said, 'Look, I wonder if you might just give them a little spit and polish...'

Sir Whatsisname, my ex-fag, responded with a lot of harumphing. He was now a very important person and was not the least bit amused.

Chapter 6

A Dandy at Oxford

Going up to Oxford represented a huge shift in my life. My father wanted me to go to Christ Church as that was where he had gone, and also to read history as he had done. (Actually, I passed into Selwyn College, Cambridge off my own bat and wanted to read theology, but my father would have none of it.)

There has been a long-standing joke among my friends that my father bought my entrance to Oxford, and I believe it (though whether or not I would have still got in without his actions, one will never know!). But you can't refuse the son of a man who raised vast sums of money to create the Christ Church Museum of Modern Art, giving Christ Church extra prestige. Yup, that's what my father did. He subscribed to the dictum that money talks and he got Charles Clore, the multimillionaire, to put up the money to build the museum.

I had a measly two A levels, in which I achieved very low grades, and I still got accepted.

Also, later on, I failed my history prelims twice, and for this you were supposed to be sent down. I was called into the dean's office and he said to me, 'Well, Serge, really I should expel you but you are a good fellow and a good athlete—you represent Oxford for skiing, water skiing and hurdling, and Christ Church doesn't want to lose you, so I'll give you another chance.' I do believe my sporting prowess helped keep me there, but I'm betting that the Russian half-prince bit and the Christ Church art museum probably also played a part.

I went up to Oxford in 1964, when the romantic echoes of *Brideshead Revisited*, though certainly fainter, could still be heard resonating across the Christ Church Meadow. In those days, students still took their lady friends punting on the River Cherwell with a bottle of champagne!

In my first year, I had a room in college, in what was called Peck Quad, and had a lovely chap called Cyril as my scout, or a college servant, to look after me. Michael McIntyre, who has remained a loving and loyal friend all my life, was in the room below me also studying history. Christ Church was full of rich kids like me and had generous dollops of Honourables, Lords, Viscounts, and Earls and about to become (on their dad's death) Dukes—and of course there was dear Prince Hassan.

So, I entered a socially elite world, for which Harrow had prepared me well. While the me that loved Zen Buddhism and Jack Kerouac sometimes felt rebellious, if I am honest, due to my insecurity, I found this new, rather conventional world quite comforting, as a) it was familiar, and b) I got on well socially with all my Etonian and Harrovian contemporaries. I knew how to play the game! We were all united by our sense of superiority and entitlement. We all spoke the same language and had the same obnoxious and prejudicial sense of humour. Just by looking at the freshmen's photo, you can tell by the expression on our faces who'd been to public school rather than a grammar or secondary modern; we looked directly at the camera with an arrogant 'we are born to rule' pout. My pals were all those public-school boys, and I quickly found myself invited to be a member of two elite clubs: the Gridiron, a luncheon club where I would go every day, and the Bullingdon Club.

I don't quite know how that happened, as I am not and never have been a drinker; and when I was invited to join, I didn't even know what the Bullingdon Club was. But I went along and, I have to say, joined in the rabble-rousing, where the definition of a good evening was one where you can't remember what the hell went on. To give you a sense of it, I'll tell you the story of my first Bullingdon Club outing, or rather the little I can remember of it!

About twenty of us were taken in a bus to a very smart hotel, drinking vodka solidly en route. A special room had been arranged for our carousing. It was on the first floor and, in staggering up the steps, some of us grabbed the pieces of wood that held the banisters together and pulled them out of their sockets.

When we got to the beautifully furnished room—all French antiques—at the top, we proceeded like vandals to smash it up. I particularly remember that two people, who will remain nameless—one subsequently became a prominent member of the House of Lords and the other a Minister in the Conservative government—grabbed some beautiful eighteenth-century tables, broke off their legs, smashed a window and hurled the tables out of the window like frisbees, watching them bounce off the roofs of the cars parked below, a bit like the game of throwing pebbles into a pond and getting them to skim. When we'd finished a glass of wine, we'd lob the glass over our shoulder for the 'flunkies' to pick up, leaving an utterly devastated room.

Our bus driver had been left with two bottles of vodka while we were dining, so he was totally pie-eyed as well and on the way back, he crashed off the road and we found ourselves stuck in a muddy field in the pouring rain in the middle of the night. I have no memory regarding what happened next, but the fact that I am here to tell this tale obviously means that some rescue operation or other was launched.

But that evening was mild in the context of some Bullingdon outings. The story goes that one night, all 550 windows in Christ Church got smashed; and at another, the club invited a string band to play, then proceeded to destroy all the instruments, including a Stradivarius. I am told that the Bullingdon Club had a fund of about £10,000 a year to account for vandalism. In those days, that was an enormous sum of money—you could buy a very decent house in a smart area of London for five grand!

I had a friend at that time called David Potter (he later changed his name to Kirke to spare his family the disgrace his exploits would have heaped upon them) and he started an organisation called the Dangerous Sports Club. Here, all sorts of insane sports were invented, including going down the Cresta Run in St Moritz on top of an inflatable woman instead of a bobsled, traversing a ski slope attached to a grand piano on skis, hang-gliding off Mount Kilimanjaro—this nearly led to several deaths—and bungee jumping off several high bridges. David assured me he invented this sport but I'm not so sure.

Many years later, the Dangerous Sports Club came to visit me when I was living in California, because they wanted to jump off the Golden Gate Bridge. I and another friend were positioned at either end of the bridge with walkie-talkies to warn the jumpers if the police were coming. Next day, there was a front-page photo in the *San Francisco Chronicle* of David leaping off the bridge wearing a top hat and tails and striped trousers, with a pipe in his mouth. I'll give it to old Davey; he certainly had a lot of chutzpah. I confess I stayed away from engaging in any of these escapades as I didn't have his strong death wish. Perhaps David also wished he hadn't been so immersed, after one trick went badly wrong: he had himself shot out of a cannon but they miscalculated the distance and he shot a full fifty yards further than expected. His back has never been quite the same ever since.

I am told I was quite a 'colourful character' around Oxford, sadly not for my razor-sharp wit or vast academic prowess! I think it was probably more for my general style and taste in clothes. Indeed, I resonated much more with the archetype of fop or dandy than I did with that of the scholar. But, hell, this was the era of dandy fashions, Carnaby Street, large kipper ties and long-waisted velvet jackets. I have various photos of me with very long hair and huge sideburns, otherwise known as mutton chops or bugger's grips. The Kinks' hit song *Dedicated Follower of Fashion* well encapsulated those flower power days.

I would flounce around wearing green and purple silk shirts with very high collars and black velvet trimmings, made for me at the famous shirt shop Turnbull and Asser near Fortnum and Mason. I had roll-neck silk shirts made for me by my delightful friend with the exotic name of Mr Fish, who started a shop also with that name that only catered to dandies such as myself. I frequently visited two other shops that were well known at the time, Granny Takes a Trip and Hung on You. I liked my jackets to have four buttons, to be very long and waisted, with waistcoats that came up very high and to have about fifty buttons. I always had cuffs on my sleeves. Quite a few of my friends fell under my foppish spell and also began poncing around in equally bizarre get-ups. I would have these Victorian-style suits made up for me by a Mr Green of Billings & Edmonds and one of my prime role models at the time was the seasoned dandy and extremely delightful and eminent interior decorator David Mlinaric (over eighty now and still going strong). You could not imagine a sweeter human being. He tried later on to help me find a house in the country.

These were the outfits I wore when I used to go to debutante parties during the 'season', a term that referred to those months when wealthy, socially well-connected parents decided that it was time for their teenage daughters to be launched into 'society'. To this end, they would host expensive cocktail parties and grand balls and invite other debs, as well as young men especially vetted by someone called Peter Townend, as sweet as he was snobbish, who worked for the magazine the *Tatler* and whose job was to vouch for their 'eligibility'. Basically, this meant that however degenerate they might be, they were deemed 'respectable' if they'd been to the 'right schools' and their parents had 'class' and money, though often the latter counted for more than the former.

Well, apparently I qualified, and thus I joined that gang of young reprobates (who included many of my Bullingdon muckers) who satisfied Peter's snob chart to become what was known as a 'deb's delight'! Whether 'delight' is the right word I am not quite sure, as most of my fellow invitees saw these parties as an opportunity for free hospitality and to meet and hopefully be intimate with as many girls as possible. This was the sixties, I remind you, the era of free love and Germaine Greer and Female Eunuchs and women's liberation, all of which meant that for those thus inclined, it was basically much easier to get girls into bed than in yesteryear. In those days, these high society connections were very important to my image, and I rather liked to be seen escorting pretty debutantes even if nothing was necessarily going on between us.

Yes, my dear friend, I enjoyed these parties and I went to a hell of a lot of them. My mantelpiece groaned under the weight of all the 'embossed' invitations from affluent people, most of whom I'd never heard of. Basically, you'd be invited for dinner near to where the party was being held, and friends of the host would put you up for the night. Then you'd drive to the party after dinner and, in the early hours of the morning, you'd return to your hosts and sleep it off.

One thing I particularly loved about these deb do's were the breakfasts served the morning after. You would go downstairs and find a side table well stocked with fried bread, poached and scrambled eggs, tomatoes, black pudding, chips, chops, bacon, sausages, kedgeree, and kidneys. Absolutely scrumptious. No wonder I had high cholesterol and heart trouble later on in life!

At this phase in my life, I loved going to a club called Sybilla's which was a very fashionable disco and always played the most up-to-date soul music and a lot of blues. These were the days of masters like Smokey Robinson and Otis Redding; the Beatles and the Stones were just creaking into gear. I had a particular friend, a little younger than me, who would often come to Sybilla's with me and who would regularly pass out dead drunk, and many times I would have to help him into a taxi and take him home. He also became one of the more prominent members of the House of Lords!

At about this time I was introduced to a very beautiful girl—she was a top model in Toronto—called Pamela Andras, and the moment we met, we became, as one would say, 'an item'. I was away from Oxford a lot with Pamela and we'd spend our time in a flat in Cadogan Place that my father had bought for me, just round the corner from where he lived. Come the summer holidays, I told my mother I was bringing a friend to Venice with me, and she almost had a fit when my friend turned out to be a girl. 'So, you think you can bring your mistress into my house?' she said to me and promptly put Pamela in a room right at the top of the house and me on the ground floor and slept with her door open so she might hear whether or not there was any tiptoeing going on in the middle of the night. As things turned out, Moonie was very sweet to her and the holiday was a great success.

My gossip columnist friend Nigel Dempster, who worked for the *Daily Express*, wrote an article saying that 'Serge, Pamela and her cat are holed up in his London flat and they are engaged to be married very soon.' My father saw this article, summoned Pamela to his door, told her never to darken it anymore and that she was bad for me and was stopping me working, and put her at once on a plane back to Canada. If Chappy set his mind on something, there was no turning back!

While at the time I found this very upsetting, in the long term I think it served my greater good, for it was not as if the academic me was particularly flourishing and our relationship certainly did not help. But Pamela and I have remained good friends all our lives.

I was not only the dandy, or 'exquisite' as they also used to be referred to in Beau Brummel's day. There was another side of me that I have already briefly touched on and that had been encouraged by my father and which, in retrospect, I think 'saved' me from going too far down the foppish route.

I also put a lot of time and energy into my sports and there was a side to me that was very much a jock. Like my father, the idea of keeping physically fit was very important to me and I took my athletics seriously and as I said, represented Oxford for the 110-metre hurdles, even if not particularly gloriously. None of my running-track mates from the athletics track on Iffley Road in Oxford had the faintest idea of my other, Bullingdonesque, deb's delight, socialite side, any more than those who were familiar with that part of me knew anything about my jock-hood. I kept these two worlds far apart.

My captain of athletics was Jeffrey Archer, who, after Oxford, became the youngest person ever to become an MP and then became a writer of bestselling books and became hugely wealthy. He was also made a Lord. After Oxford, we saw little of each other for many years but have recently reconnected as we have both found ourselves with homes in Mallorca, his being about 200 yards longer than mine! Though I have little in common with dear Jeffrey except for our love of sports and chatting about the 'old days', I like him very much and admire his chutzpah. It is so important, I think, to have friends who are vastly different from ourselves, as in this way one finds out about how other tribes operate! Interestingly, the lifestyle that dear Jeffrey so desperately aspired to and has devoted his whole life to achieving, was pretty much that lifestyle that I subsequently worked equally hard to divest myself of!

Chapter 7

The Joys of Skiing

I enjoyed my hurdling and also my water-skiing, and, in the years I represented Oxford, we always beat Cambridge, but my favourite sport was snow skiing, and as this has been one of the great loves of my life—and bless old Chappy, he did so much to encourage it—I'm going to say a bit more about it.

I had been skiing ever since I learned to walk—actually, since before I learned to walk—and for many years, all my Christmas and Easter holidays were spent in Switzerland, first in Zermatt and later in Gstaad, where my mother, by now married to George Morton, had a beautiful chalet. When I was about fifteen, I began serious competitive training with a club based in Wengen called the DHO (Downhill Only Club), so by the time I began skiing for Oxford, I was already a seasoned ski racer, having competed in lots of races for juniors. I had a strong competitive spirit in me when it came to sports.

I was rather amazed when, at nineteen and representing England, I managed to come fourth in the Lowlander's Championship Downhill in Courchevel, which consisted of the best skiers from all the non-Alpine countries. There, I managed to beat a lot of people who were professional racers and who did nothing but ski. Although I did not realise it at the time, this race gave me my first spiritual awakening experience.

If you watch downhill ski racing, you will observe a few things: one, skiers travel at huge speeds; two, there are big jumps built into the race, where the racer takes off and launches him or herself into the air for 80 metres or so; and three, protections are built alongside the whole course, so if you crash badly, you have something soft to shunt into. Well in those days, the early sixties, courses were not built with the extreme care that they are today, and the protective barriers were not of the same quality. In this particular race, I had taken the wrong line. I was much too high, was approaching a particular jump diagonally instead of straight on, and was headed for a very serious landing on some rocks at about 80mph!

But then something extraordinary occurred; although I was actually travelling very fast, everything began to happen in slow motion. As I approached the jump, I became conscious of what I can best describe as a soft, loving presence around me enfolding me. It seemed to lift me up and very slowly turn me around. I heard soft music and everything felt jellylike and peaceful and I observed myself land perfectly on the snow with my skis pointing in the right direction; and this mysterious 'rescuing presence'—I can't think of a better way to describe it—continued to guide me for the rest of the race.

I could not put a foot wrong; everything I did from then on was perfect, and when I went through the finishing gate less than a second slower than the winner, I learned that I had somehow beaten some of the most experienced skiers around.

The story did not end there. After the race, this mysterious helping presence remained with me. I felt full of vigour and confidence. This lasted about two weeks and then it gradually petered out and life went back to normal. I thought no more of it until several years later, studying the teachings of George Gurdjieff, I came across two important ideas: one, that the universe is basically 'on our side' and in times of crisis, we can evoke or invite in what he called the presence of a 'cosmic energy' that can assist us; and secondly, that if we take ourselves to the edge—as I had done in this particular race as it was of a far higher standard than any I had raced in before—we can sometimes activate whole new dimensions of strength and expertise inside ourselves. This idea of 'help forces' existing in the cosmos to assist and guide us has continued to resonate with me and as I began later to consciously 'work on myself' to try to 'evolve' my humanity, I began to experience this presence increasingly seeming to manifest itself in my life.

From very early on, then, skiing has had a powerful and mystical pull for me and has given me enormous joy. All my winter and Easter holidays were spent on the ski slopes. Sometimes, going off the piste on a beautiful sunny day and feeling pure powder snow under me, I would have the sense that it was not me that was skiing but that a presence was skiing through me—that I was 'being skied', and that there was no separation between myself, the process of skiing and the snow, and that we were all flowing together. Indeed, before I knew anything about mysticism, skiing became a trigger that would very often propel me into very joyful and very expanded states of consciousness.

Chapter 8

Amphetamined Up

It is time now to return once more to Oxford as certain storm clouds were starting to gather. I feel sad when I say this, but the truth is that despite my sports, my Bullingdon experiences, my making good friends, I didn't feel I was getting the best out of university, as I continually felt anxious, depressed and lacking in confidence and gradually all these symptoms were beginning to worsen. In retrospect, I put this down to the fact that my father's unhappiness, expectations, and insecurities that were projected onto me had increased and had conspired to increase the severity of my ADD. One way that this manifested was that I found it increasingly impossible to concentrate; I would sit in libraries with my books for hours on end, unable to take in a single fact, and this made me feel rather scared. I also didn't much like my subject, history, and with ADD, if things don't interest you, you can easily fall asleep.

At Oxford in those days, all the work you did and all the essays you wrote over the years didn't count towards your degree. You may have got A plusses every week, but it was all about how you did in your final exams. In other words, everything boiled down to the marathon six straight days of a three-hour exam in the morning and another three-hour exam in the afternoon. (Actually, as you'll be seeing, this happened to serve me rather well.)

Anyway, things were getting worse and worse and eventually my symptoms, amplified by continual sinus infections, got so bad that I just couldn't continue. It was suggested I take six months' leave and it was thought that it would benefit me to spend some time in mountain air. My stepfather, George, managed to get me a job as—of all crazy things—a cricket teacher in a school modelled on English public schools, situated at Zuoz near St Moritz, called Lyceum Alpinum. I felt rather like one of the characters suffering from TB in Thomas Mann's novel *The Magic Mountain*. It was rather amusing me teaching cricket, as at Harrow I had hardly played it at all, focussing all my afternoons on the running track. But I was a good bullshitter and managed to reinvent myself accordingly! I enjoyed being away from the pressure. I had a lot of time on my hands and I used this to read *War and Peace*, *Anna Karenina*, and Dostoevsky and sometimes rather identified with the main character in *The Idiot*!

During my months away from Oxford, I began to feel a little better; but, on my return, I made the firm decision that I did not want to go on studying history and insisted on changing to what I'd always wanted to read: English literature. I moved into a little cottage on Plantation Road with my close friend Dan Topolski and two others. Dan and I had been buddies since we were fifteen. Many years after we'd left Oxford, we were both diagnosed with chronic lymphocytic leukaemia, which we both felt sure was due to the fact that the cottage was situated close to a large electric pylon. I got my diagnosis randomly in a medical check-up many years later. I was lucky; I never had any symptoms and never required treatment. I still don't.

Not so with old Danny boy. This lusty, bonny, beautiful, full-of-life guy (even if he did pinch a girlfriend or two off me) who rowed for Oxford and England and wrote travel books, as he grew older, he gradually grew thinner and thinner and, reduced to skin and bone, died five years ago. And when a great buddy dies, it feels as if something of oneself has also died. I mourned Danny greatly. In latter years, we'd always meet at the Royal Marsden Hospital in London to have our blood tested and then we'd go out and have lunch together.

But to go on, I was allowed to change subjects but was told that because of the time I already had had off, I could not have any extra time. So, I had four instead of nine terms—just over a year instead of three years—to complete the whole of the English literature course, a pretty daunting task.

By this time my father had cottoned on that there was something badly amiss with his son, and he got a psychiatrist, Michael Davys, on my case. Michael, who subsequently became a close friend, literally saved my life. Though he never told me what was wrong with me—the word ADD was never mentioned—I am sure that he diagnosed it at once and I was put on the amphetamine drug Ritalin. It doesn't go to the cause of ADD—no one really knows what causes it—but it sure takes away its symptoms. I remember the first time I swallowed that little yellow pill, all my bleakness evaporated; for the four hours that the effects lasted, I would feel rosy, focussed, and my confidence would return.

It was decided that I needed ongoing psychiatric help, which could best take place in London, so I decamped from Plantation Road to my Cadogan Place flat and set up base camp there, with dear Michael looking after me. He realised that it was very important for my self-confidence to get my degree—I had all my father's expectations sitting on my shoulder—and that on top of my emotional disabilities, I also had a mammoth intellectual task ahead of me in getting my degree.

So, in addition to Ritalin, Michael would arrive at my flat early every morning to give me an injection of vitamins and amphetamines, and I have to say that this speed concoction saved my life. Ritalin, Dexedrine and Drinamyl were my good mates over the next months until after my finals were over. Yes, for the next eight months I was permanently Dexedrinned, Ritalinned and Drinamylled up.

I ordered all the textbooks I needed, got old exam papers, and embarked on my mammoth task. *And I never wrote one essay*! The first essay I wrote on English literature was in the examination hall. Isn't that crazy!

But I have to say that these were blessed months. The drugs allowed me to focus and concentrate as never before. I would sit in my armchair in my drawing room, with about fifty books encircling me. I not only needed to read the literature but also the books on literary criticism, and as I have always found that the best way to take in information was to make notes—I am still a fanatical note-taker today—I had piles of notebooks.

Here was my routine. Up at eight, start work at nine after my injection from Mike the Psych. Work all morning. Half-hour break for lunch. Work all afternoon until 6 p.m. Outside my front door was a garden and every day I would go for a two-mile run, eight times around it, doing my best to keep physically fit. Then more work, a break for dinner and carry on until midnight and then bed. I ordered Dial a Meal for lunch and dinner, and that is how I lived for all those months, amphetamined up to the eyeballs and with all my ADD and my anxiety tendencies around my father being suppressed. I didn't see anyone but worked with an intensity I have never done before or after. I took in everything I studied, and I enjoyed my studies.

In fact, I loved them. This was a truly joyful time. My heart was being fed by my stimulated intellect as I entered the creative and imaginary worlds of the great literary geniuses; this so expanded me that I am absolutely certain that it wholly offset the effects of the drugs. Yes, I was continually high, but, interestingly, at no stage did I ever feel drugged out or overstimulated.

I didn't miss the parties or the sports or the Bullingdon do's one iota. No girls or skiing or hurdling. Just working. Very monk-like. I surprised myself by how capable I was—we never really know our capacities unless we are put to the test—and I can say that over those months I taught myself how to study and it has stood me in good stead all my life. For many hours each day I filled myself with the beautiful thoughts of all those great literary figures who collectively embodied the British literary soul and when later, in my seventies, I began writing about soul, I realised that that time at 58 Cadogan Place, alone with the thoughts of Keats, Pope and Wordsworth and Jane Austen and Shakespeare and all those other literary giants, was truly a joyful time.

When my ordeal was over and I'd done the exams, I was able to stop taking these pills, and I never once missed them. No addictions set in.

As final exams beckoned, I moved back to my old digs at Oxford. A taxi would collect me every morning at 7 a.m. and I'd be driven to the doctor's surgery and given my amphetamine concoctions, then driven back and for six days in a row, at nine every morning, and again at three every afternoon, I was present in the examination hall wearing my gown and mortarboard, and ready to sit for my exams. Pretty crazy, eh?

I made it. Just! Like my dear friend Danny, we both got a fourth-class honours degree. But I got a degree. That was the key thing.

So, thank you, dear Mike the Psych. I couldn't have done it without you. We remained close friends until his death about twenty years ago.

Chapter 9

Death and Rebirth

Hardly were my exams over when a new drama emerged on my doorstep. My stepmother, who belonged to my father's 'Jewish world', and whom I had never liked and who had never liked me, would not let me see my father. 'He's not well. He doesn't want to be disturbed,' she kept telling me, and I accepted it. I didn't realise that my father had been very ill and was dying and that the reason why she wouldn't let me see him was because she was in the process of getting him to change his will to cut me out and leave everything to her and her two children; she didn't want me around as she was afraid that perhaps if he saw me, he might change his mind. What she needed was his signature on the codicil to his old will, which I presume she had had written up.

She had always been jealous of me and seen me as a useless, self-indulgent, and spoilt boy. Indeed, she was continually reminding my father what a good son she had—there she was right, her son Steve was—and still is—a lovely, honourable man, a good friend of mine, a surgeon who passed his finals with a first—and what a ne'er-do-well I was by comparison. Actually, a lot of truth there. We were both at Christ Church together although he was a couple of years older. After Oxford, Steve and I lost touch for many years. He married while at Oxford to a delightful lady, Judy, also a doctor and they both only came back into my life about twelve years ago. But our relationship has been precious to me, and over these years, Steve could not have been more supportive of me. Not quite on my wavelength—he always felt rather mystified by my books—but a good, good human being who meant well to everyone. Whenever I'd go to London, I'd always arrange that we have a meal together. Steve, thank you for being in my life and for your generosity at so many levels.

But Steve's mama's little wheeze backfired. My father died a few hours before the lawyers came for him to sign the codicil to have me cut out, so it was never activated. I found this out because the law firm whom my father had used for many years, who knew me well, told me later how shocked they were at being asked to change his will and how glad they were my father died when he did. So old Dad's last deed was a great gift to me. Chappy died in time. What a blessing. Was this amazing grace at work again?

While, as I said, I had little respect for my father's inheritance, I nonetheless very much needed it, and it kept me going for nearly twenty years, as God knows what would have happened if I'd been left out in the cold. I felt unprepared for life in so many ways, and while his death eliminated the direct source of my unhappiness, in truth I was a bit of a lost boy. In Jungian psychology, I discovered later that I was what was called a 'puer aeternus', which refers to a person who is fixated on his boyishness and who is resistant to the responsibility of growing up.

I had recently been introduced by my friend Moyra Swan to a spiritual healer called Gwennie, who helped me a great deal over the next six years. She had powerful psychic abilities that enabled her to connect with people who have passed over, and she channelled, among other things, a Chinese discarnate spirit whom she called Wongie, who would speak through her and give me good advice. The evening of the day my father died, Gwennie rang me in a terrible state.

'Duckie,' (old Gwen was a cockney) 'has your father just died?'

'Yes, Gwen, just this early afternoon, how did you know? I was going to ring and tell you.'

'Well, duckie, a few hours ago, I was sitting in my armchair having a fag and a cuppa tea when suddenly I felt a thunderbolt slam into me. I thought I was having a heart attack. It was your father crying and crying and coming through me (Sounds typical of my father. He never did anything gently.) wanting me to give you a message.'

'Your father was distraught,' she went on. 'He kept saying to me over and over again, "Please tell Serge I am sorry for having caused him such pain in his life. I had no idea. Please tell Serge I love him and am so sorry for everything." He kept repeating it. The jolt was so strong, it nearly laid me out…'

This sounded very plausible. I have no doubt that when my father passed over to the 'other side', he encountered his spirit guides and helpers, who pointed out the damage he had unwittingly done me. He must have been guided to Gwennie and thundered his spirit into her, desperate to use her as a mouthpiece to tell me how sorry he was! Or at least, that's my take.

Well, I felt touched. I knew, from having read cases of people who had had near-death experiences, that the first thing that happens when a person passes over is that they are given a full reckoning of their lives. Of course, while he was alive, Chappy never knew the negative effect he had on me; he never knew anything about Shadow projection. But as I have myself over the years developed some toeholds in other realities, Chappy and I have become close and I feel that from the 'other side', he has kept a watch over me and given me the support that he didn't know how to when he was alive. So, Chappy, I say this again: 'Thanks for apologising. I love you a lot. You were never a bad person. In many areas you were a genius; but you were very wounded and without a lot of awareness. You meant well. Thanks for getting Michael Davys to rescue me and thanks too, for dying when you did and not two hours later!'

The other consequence of his death was an immediate breakthrough in a very welcome direction. My friend Johnny Reed had recently come back from university in Canada with a girlfriend called Connie, a model, and Connie had with her, her flaming-haired friend, Carol, also a model. And Carol and I had taken a shine to one another and she happened to be visiting me in my flat when the doctor's phone call came through about my father's death.

I have to say that one of the effects of my father's pressure on me was that it often affected my sexuality. At times with women, I would feel very nervous; a significant dimension of the sorrow I went through over the years was that often I couldn't come up with the goods! About an hour after my father's death, I found myself making passionate love with Carol. And I have to say that from that moment, I never looked back. With the death of my father, my manhood that he'd unwittingly stolen from me was now fully returned, his death having opened up a space for my new life. My real life, I often tell people, began on the day my father died. I no longer had the weight of his misery and expectations pressing down on me and could now begin to discover who I was, what I wanted and what was important to me.

I made many lifelong friends at Oxford but my five best were Danny, whom I've already mentioned, Alan Gordon Walker, Michael McIntyre, Justin Cartwright and Thomas Kuhnke. I loved these guys and each have played important roles in my life. Alan, who went straight from Christ Church into book publishing and very quickly became managing director of several top firms, has been the most enduring of all my friends and we have been continually in each other's lives for the last fifty years, whether through him publishing my first book, coming to stay with me in Ibiza, Mallorca and California or, over the last ten years, letting me regard his beautiful home in Putney, London, as my 'home from home'. The generosity shown to me over the years not only by Alan but also by his wife Louise, a therapist and Good Samaritan, whom I am also very close to, has been extraordinary.

In fact, I think it true to say that I don't know how I would have got through certain periods of my life were it not for Alan, who, being steadiness personified, has on multiple occasions, prevented me from making rash decisions. While I have tended at times to scamper about a bit like a headless chicken, Alan has filled in forms for me and done my accounts and attended to the nitty gritty of life for me. What greater love can anyone show you but that they doeth thy nitty gritty! I married Martina when I was seventy, and I remember him laughingly telling her that he was relieved he could now pass his unpaid heavy workload on to someone else!

Yes, dearest Alan has always been aware of my many faults and vulnerabilities, and while at times he did not hold back from telling me what he thought, I have to honour him for this and all in all he could not have shown me greater love or friendship. I have always loved hanging out with 'Finkel' (this being the nickname I gave him; I can't remember how or where it originated) as we knew each other so well, we could always say what was on our minds. Alan married Louise in his mid-twenties and they have two lovely children (I am godfather to their daughter Emily, now a top barrister). I am happy to report that Alan is still going strong.

After leaving Oxford, Justin came and shared my London flat with me for a few months. A very capable man, a great athlete (he was in the Oxford polo team), with a terrific dry sense of humour, Justino (as I called him) started off in the advertising business and became a documentary filmmaker and then went on to become one of England's best-known novelists. He published seventeen novels in all and won numerous extremely prestigious awards. Sadly, he died a few years ago—he had had dementia and went downhill very quickly. The last time I saw him was in hospital and he barely knew who I was. I miss him a lot.

Dearest Mikey McIntyre, like Finkel, started off as a book publisher, and then trained in China as an acupuncturist and

Chinese herbalist and opened his clinic just down the road from where I ended up living in Gloucestershire, so we have always stayed in touch. Mikey is a real fighter for truth, and for many years has been one of the most ardent activists on behalf of complementary medicine. A real spiritual warrior.

I have never known anyone as hard-working and conscientious, which is perhaps why, just recently and very sadly, probably due to his overdoing things, he had a stroke that has left him semi-paralysed down one side, but has taken nothing of the wind out of his sails. His spirit is as indomitable as ever; he still works helping people from his wheelchair, and has the same old cheerfulness that he always had.

My friendship with Thomas, who was German, started through our both being in the Oxford ski team—he was captain—and progressed through the Bullingdon Club. After Oxford we saw a bit of each other in London, but then he moved back to Germany and in all the years I was in California, I didn't see him. In the last ten years he has come back into my life. He has a wonderful son called Johannes and both of them came and stayed with me in Mallorca a few years ago and we became very close again.

Sadly, our friendship has completely collapsed. Because of this book! I thought he'd be sympathetic to my story and I had sent him a draft for his comments and he rang me back laying into me with such fury that I could hardly believe it. I felt very hurt.

Thinking about what happened a little later, I realised that I should never have sent it to him and the fault was entirely mine. There is an inherently strong puritan and conservative streak to him—Thomas is very proper—and he married someone who was a fundamentalist Christian, and I guess that combination does not make one especially open to the story that I discuss here. I am sad about this as I am very fond of Thomas, but it gave me a deeper understanding of how essentially large the gap is between those on the kind of path that I am on, and those who are wedded to more 'conservative mindsets'. So, Thomas, I say this to you, 'I have enjoyed our friendship and I thank you for having been in my life and for the contribution you have made to it on many fronts. You're a great guy and I understand where you have come from.'

Making close friends with someone when you are young is very important as I feel that truly to be intimate, one needs not only to have gone deep with a person, but you also need to have known someone for a long time. This is why I so treasure all my old cronies. In my last book, I had a chapter on friendship and here's a summary of six requests that I ask of my good friends and that I would wish them to ask of me. Here they are... I ask that my friends:

- Love and accept me for who I am (and for who I am not) and allow me to enjoy their company without my feeling I have to put on a special face.

- Are fond enough of me and know me well enough to always tell me the truth as they experience it and that if they feel I am going off course, that they don't hold back from challenging me, only that they do so in such a way that I am always elevated and never diminished by their insights.

- Always encourage me to be me and to be a space enabling me to share my innermost thoughts and craziest ideas without feeling silly.

- Not only enjoy the good times with me but won't desert me and stop being loyal and supportive if the going happens to get tough.

- Have the courage not to turn away from working through difficulties if any arise between us, as very often in close relationships, big Shadow issues can emerge.

- Can always be relied on to feed me the food of imaginative sympathy so that my heart and soul may blossom in their presence.

As you will be seeing, not all my friendships have satisfied these requirements, but then, if I am completely honest, I haven't always honoured them either!

Chapter 10

New Beginnings

I now had my degree; my father had died, my mother was living abroad, happily married to George and dividing her time between Gstaad in the winter and Venice in the summer. She now also had two more children, Anna and Geordie. I was twenty-three and London-based, and the question was: What am I going to do with my life now?! What I felt was a significant omen was the fact that when I'd attended my father's memorial service and had my hand shaken by some of the more prominent members of the 'great and the good' brigade, not one person made a step towards me to offer me any support or to say: 'You are a young man and your father has just died. Can I help you in any way?'

Now that my father was no longer there to be of use to them financially, I was of no use to them either. It somehow confirmed for me that while my father was certainly a generous person and I will always honour him for that, the world he moved in was not especially so; but then, it was not one in which I felt particularly comfortable anyway, and I am sure they intuitively also picked that up and realised that I was not 'one of them'. I found that world overly materialistic and uncompassionate, and I realised now that I was on my own and needed to find my world, or rather, discover what 'tribe' I really belonged to and felt comfortable with. And my father having died when he did, I now had financial resources so I didn't immediately have to get any old job. It is only looking back that I realise how precious this was and how privileged I was.

What transpired over the next year was that I found myself naturally becoming interested in spiritual things. I never said to myself, 'Now I am going to embark on a spiritual path and become a spiritual seeker.' It was more that I intuitively found myself gravitating towards certain ideas, certain books and, in particular, certain people who were very, very different from those I'd spent most of my time with up until then. These new people were interested in things like alternative technologies, in 'expanding one's consciousness', and generally in operating in the world from a more honest perspective. They didn't have any of the snooty qualities that my old friends seemed to have had. And I found this both inspiring and refreshing. Many were vegetarian and talked about the need to love our planet more and how we should meditate and eat organic food. And remember, this was still the sixties, before global warming had begun to be a real issue and before we realised that icebergs were beginning to melt.

This 'other world', however, was not wholly unfamiliar to me. Indeed, echoes of it had resided inside me ever since I went to Harrow—viz., my interest in Zen and beatniks and Allen Ginsberg—but until now, it had never had a chance to come out into the open. But now it did. It felt like a vast breath of fresh air and I realised how essentially false, narrow and uncompassionate my life had been until then, as if I had lived with blinkers around my eyes and so had only seen what I had wanted to see. But now these blinkers were starting to fall away. I began to want to know more about how the universe worked. I wanted to pull back the veil on life's great mysteries. If I was not especially adventurous externally, I certainly was adventurous internally.

One of the most interesting guys I met at this time, through my friend Alan, who'd just published his great book *Supernature: A Natural History of the Supernatural,* was Lyall Watson, a man of incredible knowledge about virtually everything. When in his company, I would just let him talk and I would listen. I also became good friends with Lawrence Blair, a very charismatic guy who looked just like the late pop star Marc Bolan, and who had just done the first ever PhD on esotericism, which he made into a best-selling book, *Rhythms of Vision*. A filmmaker and adventurer with a base in Bali, some years later, Lawrence came and lived with me in my finca in Ibiza. He had a wonderful mother, Lydia, who had been on a spiritual quest all her life and who lived nearby and beautifully mothered us both. A truly wonderful and compassionate human being, I learned so much just by being around her and being included in her radiance. Yes, my friend, something very slowly was beginning to shift in my life.

I began to devour all the many books by Carlos Castaneda, which explored his relationship with a Yaqui sorcerer called Don Juan who was teaching Carlos how to be a spiritual warrior. This idea resonated strongly with me. 'What matters,' Don Juan told him, 'is that a warrior must be impeccable.'

> *A warrior knows how to wait. A warrior learns without any hurry because he knows he is waiting for his will. And one day he succeeds in performing something ordinarily quite impossible to accomplish. He may not notice his extraordinary deed. But as he keeps on performing extraordinary acts, or as impossible things keep happening to him, he becomes aware that a sort of power is emerging. Sometimes the pain and discomfort of this power is very acute but the more severe the better. A fine power is always heralded by pain.*

These words proved to be very prophetic for me as later in my life, one or two extraordinary things happened to me and I discovered that in a small way, I seemed to possess certain healing capabilities.

But I was still young, and when we are young, our egos always play a disproportionately dominant role in our lives. The problem was that I didn't have a very healthy one. Yes, folks, we can have healthy egos and unhealthy ones. Our egos can be too big or not big enough, and as I later learned, the way to become less controlled by this part of ourselves was not to try to pretend our egos weren't there and think we can just skip over or transcend them.

On the contrary. I learned that we need to acknowledge our ego selves and work with them to help them become healthier, as the more this occurs, the more willing they are to stand back and gradually play a less dominant role in our lives and so allow an 'us' with a more expansive view of the world to begin running the show.

But I was still light years away from this being possible. At this stage in my life, although I was beginning to connect to a more expanded understanding of what constituted reality, and although little sproutings of a 'self' that was not wholly egoic occasionally showed its head, my ego still primarily ran the show. I discovered I actually had quite a bit of my father's ambition in me, only instead of wanting to advance up the corporate ladder and become a big corporate noise, I wanted to advance up the spiritual ladder and be a big spiritual noise, so the world would know what a fantastic holy bloke I was. I wince as I write these words but they are absolutely true. At that stage I thought that knowing one or two things in my head meant that I also lived them in my life. I didn't know that I was then a great example of what my teacher Ram Dass (whom I worked with much later) meant when he talked about people being 'phony holies'!

I would go to lectures by people whom I admired and feel wistful that it was not me standing up there spouting spiritual truths and having everyone be bowled over by my wisdom! It took many years for me to become a serious lecturer and even then I don't think anyone ever got bowled over, but the good thing was that by that time I didn't mind as it was no longer my aim. Yes, looking back, I realise that I had very quickly subscribed to being a spiritual seeker and thus being on a spiritual path, but I had as yet little idea what this entailed, and very much wanted to run before I could walk. In the past, I had been rather seduced by the glamorous life and I saw that I was now wanting to project that into my spiritual life, be a cool spiritual guy instead of a cool dandy man-about-town! I continued to read all the good old books that hippies read at that time, like Ram Dass's *Be Here Now*, and the great classic *Autobiography of a Yogi* by Paramahansa Yogananda. I didn't yet know that there was a huge difference between reading books, talking about spiritual truths and being able to embody those truths, and that it was possible to understand things in your head yet be nowhere near to practising them in your life.

It took me some time to learn that making progress in this area—that is, trying to wake up and become a tad more human—was not something you could do quickly and that it involved more than just reading spiritual books. I discovered that it also took a lot of inner work and very much required that we confront the darker, more subterranean side of our nature, which in my case, as I was soon to discover, was both unpleasant and extremely dark! Basically, then, I had to learn that the emergence of a 'deeper us' doesn't just 'happen' in the way that, say, an acorn morphs naturally into an oak tree, but has very much to be 'worked for' and that this constituted the whole challenge of what being a human being was really all about. I didn't yet understand Gandhi's wise words to the effect that if we want change to happen, we needed to 'be that change', i.e., meaning that there was a huge difference between actually embodying a state of being and merely talking or writing about it. I was starting to talk the talk in a superficial kind of way, but was light years away from any pretence of being able to walk it.

The truth was that I was both a slow learner and a late developer and the more I began to delve into myself, the more aware I became of how much work was needed. Yes, my friend, as you'll be seeing, it took me many, many moons and a lot of heartache and gnashing of teeth and one hell of a lot of workshops, seminars, teachers and gurus to become even vaguely balanced, as so many of my better human capacities had been squished down as a result of my upbringing. The homophobic, quasi-racist, patriarchal, macho and exceptionalist story that I had been raised to subscribe to meant that parts of me that were potentially kind and compassionate had not yet had a chance to germinate. I had a helluva lot of de-squishing to do!

Devouring all of Hermann Hesse's novels, such as *Siddhartha, Steppenwolf, Journey to the East* and *The Glass Bead Game,* as well as the writings of Simone Weil, Thomas Merton and Teilhard de Chardin, helped me realise that at this stage in my life, I was still much more style than substance and that there was something more than a little indulgent in the way I lived. I had a wonderful lawyer, Sir Percy Rugg (we called him the Persian rug) who dealt with all the legal business following my father's death, and I had also inherited wonderful Hansie, who used to work for my father and now worked for me.

Every morning dear Hansie would arrive at my flat, make me breakfast, clean the place, do my washing, take my clothes to the cleaners, often prepare me lunch, so I didn't need to lift a finger. The only cardinal sin she committed was throwing away two precious pairs of jeans that I had got girlfriends to sew patches on. One girl, Jill Purce, stitched in a spiral—she'd just written a book about spirals—another a sun and moon, another a Buddha, another a beautiful tree, etc. These jeans were fantastic sixties memorabilia. If I'd have hung on to them, they could have gone to the V&A Museum and hung there. O well…

Scanning my diaries from that time, I see they were dedicated to asking questions such as: how can one prove the existence of God; what does it mean to love? Do good and evil exist? I was also seriously questioning the enormous split that existed inside me between spirituality and materiality. Were they *really* that incompatible?

While the new friends I was starting to draw into my life had introduced me temporarily to vegetarianism and increasingly to value the quality of simplicity, I cannot pretend that the worlds of glamour and glitz didn't still at times exercise a strong pull over me. Leopards take time to change their spots. Especially this one!

I think what pulled me back into these glitzy worlds was because this was where the prettiest girls were to be found, and, still having strong vestiges of insecurity—though I hid it well—and vanity, it was important for my image that I be seen with an attractive woman on my arm, as that, I felt, said something about me. It made me OK! On the surface, I was this big, friendly guy who seemed to ooze confidence, underneath I was really a timid little boy afraid of growing up and becoming a man! Deep down I think I also felt ugly. I was on a quest to find the right woman, who would, I secretly hoped, rescue me from my ugliness and isolation and somehow save me from a gnawing sense of 'being separate' that had been with me, this 'only child', for all of my life. It was not until many years later that I came to realise that the despair I so often felt was not because I didn't have the right woman, but was because I was so distant from my own divinity. Women, I was to discover, far from being the solution, often only served to aggravate my issues.

Having time on my hands—being on a spiritual journey was not a 9 to 5 occupation—I nonetheless had plenty of time to pursue women, and I discovered from reading my old journals that I would often feel just as lonely even when I had two or three girls on the go all at once and even with them professing real fondness for me! The sad thing was that it was many years before I could truly begin to let love in. If we feel we are not 'good enough', as so many people feel who don't receive the right kind of love when they are a small child, we secretly believe that we don't deserve love and so there must be something wrong with someone who tries to give it to us! Thus, a lot of healing was needed in this area of my life. I saw that I was trying to integrate my burgeoning 'alternative' side with the 'swinging London' culture that was also happening around me. And it didn't happen too easily. Most days I would go and have lunch in the fashionable Casserole restaurant in the King's Road or maybe meet up with all my 'Chelsea set' cronies in a coffee bar called the Picasso. Many evenings I would dine at Alexander's, my favourite restaurant, which belonged to a wonderful couple who always had my favourite table reserved for me. Here's what I wrote in my journal at this time.

> *I feel I am a dharma bum kind of pseudo spiritual warrior, someone interested in alternative technology, a ski racer* (I still continued to do competitions and represented British Universities against European ones), *a girl chaser, a person who loves being solitary as well as being social and I'm not quite sure where I belong and how all these parts of me fit together.*

Truth was, in those days, they didn't fit together. I played out each of these identities serially.

One girl I became besotted with was Penny Cuthbertson, but our liaison was very short-lived as she soon deserted me for the painter Lucian Freud. Whenever I would hear that old pop song that has the line 'the purpose of a man is to love a woman, the purpose of a woman is to love a man', I would think of Penny. I never saw her any more except in Lucian's lewd depictions of her on canvas, which I came across a few years later as I happened to be walking down New Bond Street and peering in at the art galleries.

I also became very close to Annunciata Asquith, who was still at Oxford, and many weekends I would drive back up to see her in my cool little, black-windowed Mini Cooper S. She would invite me up to stay at her parents' great country manor and I needed to be on best behaviour. Dear lovely 'Ciata never married and I didn't see her again until many years later at the memorial service of another old girlfriend of mine.

I later began going out with Suzy Burton, who had just got divorced from her husband (he had the same name as the actor). She had been introduced to me by my old skiing friend Piers von Westenholz, and I found her amazingly beautiful. She had a little child and I thought after meeting her that I would be happy for life, as she was a very sweet, gentle and gracious lady. Suzy and I did a lot of things together and we had many of the same friends, and I remember taking her to celebrate Piers' second marriage and taking a cine film of the wedding. (It took another thirty years for video cameras to be invented.) All the 'in crowd' people were there who used to be so important to me in my deb party days. I don't want to namedrop just for namedropping's sake, but I will ask myself why we are inclined to do so... The answer is quite simple. It comes out of insecurity. We feel—or, more accurately, our ego self feels—that our status will be added to if we can somehow link ourselves with a person who is well known for some reason. In other words, we must be a helluva person if Person X sees us as their friend! Crazy, isn't it! My ego preferred to link me with pretty-looking ladies!

Sadly, my liaison with Suzy only lasted about six months as she didn't quite fit in with some of those 'other Serges', especially the one who was searching for his soul and who liked hanging out with the alternative technology crowd.

A little later I had a liaison with a lady called Pauline Brett, who was an artist and with whom I remained friends for a long time. She embraced both my social and alternativist worlds but sadly not the spiritual seeking one. We went out together on and off for many years. When I moved to live in Mallorca in my mid-sixties, we somehow lost touch. I hope you are well and thriving, Pauline, and that the son you had with another old Oxford friend of mine, Micky Astor, is also thriving. After Pauline, I dated a very sweet woman called Sarah Janson, who was also an artist, and I wonder what has happened to her.

Another wonderful woman who came into my life at this time was Francine Schiff. She was American and she knew everyone, a great party girl who was continually introducing me to my own friends. She was tall and slim with long blond hair, and we only stopped dating because she left to go back and live in the States. Ten years later, when I was living in California, we reconnected and very briefly rekindled our relationship. I recently googled her and found she had died about ten years ago and for the last years of her life had lived a very solitary nun-like existence and had written a book on how to nourish oneself spiritually. How people change!

Rereading my diaries of that time, which I'd not looked at for fifty years, I am a bit ashamed of myself as so much of them were simply chronicles of craziness concerning my relationships—or more accurately my entanglements—with women. Some were truly dangereuse, some were not, some lasted a few months, some a few days. But no one was right/good enough for half-Princey Serge! Or, conversely, I wasn't right/good enough for them. From my correspondence I'd see that I'd either be in agony over a woman or she would be in agony over me, and often we'd both be in agony together! What an old drama queen I was! Often the girls I fell for didn't fall for me, or didn't see me or let me in—my pattern with Moonie—while the girls who did see me and let me in, I'd often feel indifferent towards. But despite all this craziness, my sense of loneliness remained. That old song by Paul Anka, *I'm Just a Lonely Boy*, might have been my signature tune. Even today, I remember all the words...

I'm just a lonely boy
Lonely and blue
I'm all alone

With nothing to do
I've done everything
You can think of
But all I want
Is someone to love

Many, many years later, when I was in my mid-thirties and living in California, and had started therapy with my dear friend and mentor Larry Spiro, he told me that I used women in order ritually to prove over and over to myself that I was potent. This seemed pretty logical given the way my father had unconsciously conspired to take my potency away from me for all those years. The ritual went like this: once I had proved I was potent and, as it were, 'got' the woman and she became fond of me, the ritual was over. I would then be propelled to move on to find another woman to re-enact this same drama with. While this pattern was worst in my twenties and thirties, it took a great deal of psychotherapy over many years for it finally to be exorcised.

I never used my wealth to draw women to me—I never had big cars or fancy art on the walls and there was nothing flashy about me. I suppose I knew how to present myself in a simple way that I felt was genuine and likeable, and I often tended to connect with those with a similar kind of emotional wounding. As I said, I had a big issue around being abandoned, going right back to Moonie always having to leave me to go off on business trips with my father just when I was happy and felt secure with her. So, as I said, in order to protect myself, I would often have to do the abandoning first; thus, I tended to draw women to me who like me, had the 'abandoning gene'.

This pattern was spectacularly played out with the delightful Linda Estall-Cole, who was an actress and whom I absolutely adored. She was bright, fun, sassy, sensitive. Crazy lady, she wanted to leave the man in South Africa she was due to marry, for me. We had the most beautiful and romantic ten days in Paris and I had never felt closer to anyone. On the bus back from Heathrow to central London, I heard myself telling her it was over and she needed to return to South Africa and marry this man. Which she did, and in retrospect I am very happy for her as it was a very successful marriage and she had wonderful children.

But what a thing to have done. We had become so close. As I dropped her at the airport a few days later and saw her walking away, I felt a sense of relief: 'Ah, I am free again. Free to feel lonely and blue once more.' Absolutely bonkers! Many years later, I reread the sweet and sad letters she had written me and I wept.

I often felt guilty at being better off than my friends, and the result was that I found myself generally paying for everyone whenever we went out, and often giving away large chunks of money, not always to the worthiest of causes. Much of my 'giving' was therefore not done from a particularly generous place, but more from a fearful place: 'They might not like me if I don't give!' This all came from this insecure and rather timid little person inside me who deeply wanted to please people so they'd like him. Nowadays, I often describe myself as a 'please-aholic in recovery'!

There was one gift, however, that I am delighted about and where the universe has paid me back a thousandfold. I have already told you about Gwennie and how, after my father's death, I very much continued to need her counselling and spiritual healing. From my journals, here are two wonderful pieces of advice she gave me.

> *Who you are will flower in good time. When you are older. Be patient. You want recognition and as long as you want it, you have a target and your material self will dominate your spiritual self. You must be natural and not show off.*

On another occasion she told me that my role in life was to serve others and that the more I did so, and the more I took my attention away from myself, the happier I would be. Again, wonderful advice.

Well, I felt a strong impulse to help Gwennie and pull her out of the miserable little bedsit in Muswell Hill where she lived, so I sold one of my father's Kokoschka paintings that I had inherited, and with the money bought her a lovely spacious flat, furnished it with a grand piano (she played very well) and she lived happily there for many years. I remember her telling me that my act of kindness would reverberate back to me, and many years later what she said came to pass.

I had gone to America and as it were, had moved away from Gwennie and forgotten all about the flat. However, when she died, she left it to me and I sold it and, with the proceeds, bought a tiny wreck in Mallorca, which I did up nearly forty-five years later, and went to live in when I got divorced from my first wife.

If I hadn't bought that flat for Gwen—I am sure the money would have vanished somewhere—I would never have bought the little finca in Mallorca and in all probability I would never have met Martina, whom I married when I was seventy. This story comes later. But it is events like these that again remind one that there really is a tremendously intelligent purpose or an amazing grace being played out in the way in which our lives unfold. Dear Gwennie played a very important role in my twenties and I am ever grateful to her.

Chapter 11

The Blessings of Findhorn

A very important breakthrough in the arena of my spiritual development came when a friend suggested to me that I should go and visit the spiritual community of Findhorn up in Scotland. This felt very right and a few days later I was on the train to Edinburgh.

In fact, the three months I stayed there absolutely revolutionised my life, as it exposed me for a long period to people who concretely embodied the type of *human,* human being that I aspired towards. It made me realise that if you really want to change, it's much more than just reading spiritual books and meditating. *It is also about being in the physical presence or atmosphere of people who already are the change, who are further along than you, as they can carry you along in their slipstream.* After being at Findhorn, I understood why the master potters of old would insist that their pupils live with them for six months before ever touching a pot. They first needed to breathe in the atmosphere out of which great pots were created.

I arrived at this community not quite knowing what to expect and not really knowing anything about what a spiritual community was. I was greeted very lovingly by the Findhorn founders, Peter and Eileen Caddy—who subsequently became lifelong friends—and they made me feel very at home. I sensed they were genuinely pleased to see me, not because I was particularly 'special' (the story drummed into me by my parents for no other reason but that I was their son and so must be), but because I was a fellow human being, and for the Caddys, all human beings were special and precious and so needed to be honoured and respected.

In fact, the way they treated me was the way they treated everyone and I began to feel as if I was being enveloped by what I can only describe as a warm field of love. Within this field, I observed myself experiencing a deeper kinship with my new little 'family' than I had ever felt with my own family. Here, at Findhorn, I began to have the experience of what I can best describe as 'abundant being'—an overall feeling of wellness, affection for the world around me and cheerfulness, and the realisation that to feel this way is our true birthright. I felt so strongly that in no way are we the miserable, separate, lonely 'islands unto ourselves', that we are told we are by the stories we are initially indoctrinated into about how life is. I had no girlfriends during my time at Findhorn, but not once did I feel lonely. For the first time, I began to have direct experiences of higher states of consciousness and that a divine presence pervaded all of existence and was inside of me as well as external to me. The Sufi poet Hafiz, who refers to God as 'the Friend', expresses how I often felt:

Like two lovers who have become lost in a winter blizzard
And find a cosy empty hut in the forest,
I now huddle everywhere
With the friend.
God and I have built an immense fire together
We keep each other warm and happy.

One of the prayers of Bulgarian spiritual master Peter Deunov also resonated with me:

O boundless Supreme Being, I beseech you to allow me to come close to you so that I may feel myself to be an essential part of the wholeness of existence.

It was an incredible breakthrough to find out that the solutions to so many of our problems lay in working to deepen our relationship with 'The Friend' or the boundless 'Supreme Being', which I was gradually starting to see as being the same thing as that mysterious 'helping force' that at different times in my life seemed to have intervened on my behalf. The good thing was that you didn't necessarily have to find the Friend through religion and what I began to learn was that the Friend/Supreme Being couldn't give a stuff how one connected with it, only that one managed to do so. For me, the best way at this time was to quieten myself through meditation, which greatly improved over my time at Findhorn, and continually to be grateful for my daily bread and for the friends in my life and for the many blessings that life had delighted in showering on me. If there was only one prayer we'd be allowed, it might be 'Thank you, Friend' or 'Thank you, Supreme Being for your amazing grace'!

Eileen saw my challenges very perceptively, and wisely thought that I needed to learn practical skills to be helped down off my high horse, so my daily morning job before washing the vegetables for lunch was cleaning the toilets. At first, I couldn't believe it. What an insult. Half-prince me clean bloody toilets!

But as I gradually got into it, I saw it as a service and I actually came to enjoy it and put my heart into it and saw how important it was that I do this job well. In fact, I would get people to see how much the toilets gleamed as I became proud of my handiwork. No longer did I regard this kind of work as menial. Not if done with love. I realised that what constituted menial work was work *not* done with love, and that any work was holy work or good work if the spirit behind it was right. In other words, I discovered that it is not so much *what* we do that is important, but *how* we do what we do, and that if there is a good spirit behind our activities, our handiwork is much more likely to be aligned with what is appropriate or wholistically healthy.

Meanwhile a miracle was going on in the Findhorn gardens. Huge vegetables were being grown on only a tiny bit of topsoil on an otherwise sandy base. 'How is this possible?' I asked those who worked in the gardens. 'It is possible because we, the Findhorn gardeners, tend our garden with love,' was the reply.

'And so, the vegetables feel it and feel moved to grow more abundant?' I asked.

'Absolutely so,' was the reply.

Equally astounding was me being taken to where the printing machines were kept. Paul, who looked after this section, told me that he had an affinity with the spirit of these machines, and as a result, he could overrun them, have the lever move into the red, and the machines would still go on working. 'If someone who does not have an affinity with them, tried to work them the way I do, they would soon break down,' he told me. I believed him. No wonder technical things always worked rather badly for me. I had very little feeling for that world!

Essentially what the experience of being at Findhorn was also confirming for me was that humanity was one family, composed of different races, and that each of us are joined together as part of that family, intricately linked with our brother and sister human beings. From this perspective, what class or colour or religion or nationality or sexual affiliation someone was—all things which in my upbringing I had learned to deem so important—in actuality were wholly unimportant.

Essentially what makes us most unhappy, I learned, is believing in the lie of our separation. Conversely, what makes us most happy is realising the experience of our interconnectedness and that it doesn't matter a stuff whether one is well educated or not, rich or poor, black or white, gay or straight, fat or thin, pretty or not pretty, Muslim or Christian. First and foremost, we need to remember that we are human beings. Once I began to 'get' that, not just with my mind but with my deeper being, the new world I was starting to move into began increasingly to open its gates for me.

I learned that the way forward was not to try to crush, repress or feel guilty about those aspects of myself that behaved a bit weirdly, but rather to try to understand what the wounds were inside me that made me operate the way I did. Dear Eileen Caddy—what a beautiful soul—told me I should allow my womaniser sub-personality self to start 'dancing' with my more scholarly and mystical self. She felt a little cross-fertilisation was required. Genuine spirituality, I came to see, was not about repression and denial—we don't evolve (or most of us don't) by lying on a bed of nails and castigating ourselves for not being perfect (the kind of theology rammed into me at Harrow). Rather, we need to allow ourselves to feel fully alive and become increasingly more conscious that life is given to us as a great gift to be savoured and celebrated.

I realised that I was someone with lots of different sides and different impulses, and that some parts of me were a whole lot healthier and more evolved than other parts. The more evolved parts, I learned, could help the less evolved parts of me to grow. I also got to see that any part of ourselves that we hold negative thoughts about, dismiss or deny, we simply turn into our enemy. And enemies want to fight us.

So that was why I so often felt so conflicted. I was not accepting myself for who I was. I came to see that I was not a bad person, just a wounded and conflicted person. I saw that alongside my self-indulgent side, I had also been pretty hard on myself, and I realised that if I truly wished to make progress, I must learn to regard myself in a more loving and compassionate light. This didn't mean that I could let myself off the hook and do anything I wanted, rather that I not forget to honour what is deep and true and good about myself as *that* was what would fill the gaping hole inside me. I started for the first time to have faint intimations that women were not going to fix me. I was.

The more I honoured myself and learned to acknowledge my own deeper soulfulness, the more my inner hole or my soul wound would start to heal. This was an important revelation.

Being at Findhorn made me realise ever more poignantly that all my life I had worn a mask; that is, had put on a face that I wanted to present to the world that was not really mine but one I'd taken on, and that it took a huge effort to keep up the pretence. Here, in this community, it was possible to drop my mask because everyone else around me was doing the same thing!

What was also wonderful about Findhorn was that the wisdom of children was both respected and invited. They weren't shut away 'to be seen but not heard' as I had been; their voices were listened to. And the same also applied to older people. Just as in tribal communities where they were venerated as 'elders' and their wisdom was respected. In the world I had come from, people over a certain age were all too often shut away in care homes as ghastly and embarrassing nuisances!

Here at Findhorn, young and old, educated and uneducated, gay and straight, black and white, rich and poor all mixed together and in this environment, my elitism, thank goodness, was not given a chance to breathe. I felt little bits of it melt away every day! I shared a caravan with the most delightful man called Fred, who was a plumber. We became good friends and stayed good friends over the years and I picked up a lot of his gentleness and wisdom. I discovered that just as we catch colds, we can also catch good qualities from other people. I was starting to touch into what life really ought to be about and how, if humanity learned to relate together in this way, our lives would change and so would our planet.

I stayed there for three months. No longer. I realised that I had accessed something very precious and that I now needed to try to put it into practice in the real world and that I should probably try to do something vaguely 'grown up': go and get a job!

The Half-Princeling on his royal cushion

Baby me and Parents at Abinger

William, our wonderful guide, Chappie, Coco Chanel, and Moonie at St Moritz, 1947

Me and Moonie

Chappy and me in Zermatt

NO DEDICATED FOLLOWERS OF FASHION?

Cherwell fashion editor Mary Ensor attacks the dowdiness of the typical undergraduate — and contrasts it with two of Oxford's better dressed peacocks

Are you

A Dandy at Oxford

Engaged to Pamela

With Chuchie at my stepbrother Steve's wedding

Dining with Uncle Misha

Winning the Oxford Cambridge Giant Slalom, 1966

Just having finished Finals (with David Kirk on right)

With best friends Johnny Reed and Alan Gordon Walker

George and Moonie at Julian's hippy party, Gstaad, 1968

The Benirrás, Ibiza Beach Bums

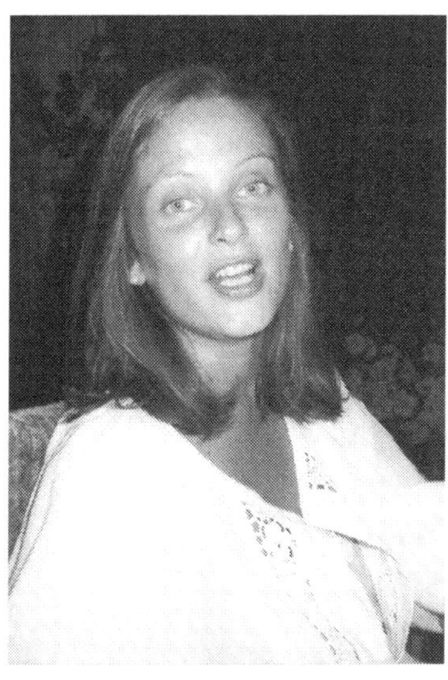

My wonderful half-sister Anna

Mustachioed in California

Having Coffee with Linda

My dear friend
David Lorimer

With lovely Sophia

With Uncle Misha and Sima

With Marcus, Two Mad Hatters in Gloucestershire

With my good friend Lawrence Blair

Celebrating my Fiftieth Birthday with Justin, Johnny and Mike

With participants at my New Year retreat

Chapter 12

Working Out in the World

My two great friends from Christ Church, Michael and Alan, both had jobs in book publishing and so I thought that this might be something that I could do. I felt I needed more of a structure in my life. Perhaps, as I'd read English literature, this could be my metier. I applied to many firms and received many rejections, but was eventually accepted by Secker and Warburg as its head, Fred Warburg, had known my father.

While, at one level, I felt 'grown up' in that I had gone and got myself a 'real job', the truth was that I wasn't very good at it. My ADD (which I still didn't know I had) began to kick in again and I found it hard to concentrate or read books that didn't interest me, and I gradually found that I did less and less work. I would arrive at ten, go for a long lunch and leave at five. I became very friendly with old Fred's wife, who, bless her, was a bit of a snob and knew and liked Moonie, and also with Mary the receptionist, and consequently I found I could get away with murder.

At the same time as being a publisher, I also became director of an art gallery run by a delightful man who was also a very good artist and interestingly was also called Lyall Watson, like the author. Though there was a forty-year age difference between us, we became good chums and I enjoyed spending time there and meeting some very interesting artists, many of whom, like me, seemed to possess aspects of the 'outsider gene'.

One thing I discovered was that the people we put on exhibitions for who took charge of their own publicity, and didn't just prima-donna it and leave it to us to bring clients in, were not only much better artists but were also much more successful. From this, I learned that there are two equally important areas that we are all challenged to be creative in: the area we have chosen as our specific field of work, and, as I had learned at Findhorn, the actual living of our daily lives. As my transformational journey began to open up more, I realised how important it was that these two areas fuse together, and that we cannot effectively develop or start opening up to our deeper humanity unless we also begin doing things like bringing more awareness into our daily living and trying to treat others as we would wish them to treat us!

I had a friend, William Bloom, who today is a well-known spiritual teacher, but in those days was better known as a novelist and an angry young man, angry at societal injustices, angry at racial discrimination. William persuaded me to join him in starting a legal aid centre for Black people who were being hassled by the police, which back in the sixties was a huge issue. If you were Black and lived in certain parts of London, you could expect, just walking quietly down the street, to be stopped by a policeman and searched. That was the mindset in those days. It has changed a bit today but not as much as it might have. Our organisation was called Advise and Black people who were getting hassled could call in and get free legal advice. It was very successful and many people used it and it was a real service to the community.

I felt very privileged when I, a pipsqueak guitarist—a master of three chords—was allowed to join in at some of their jamming sessions as a lot of these guys who used Advise were professional guitarists. In my diaries I noted what fun these gatherings were, and how much I preferred them to most of the smart parties I used to attend but which I actually found myself going to less and less. My experience was that as certain activities and habits became less relevant to me, they gradually fell away of their own accord. There's an old Hindu saying that goes, 'When the fruit is ripe, it falls from the tree.' So true!

I was also spending a lot of time with my half-sister Chuchie, whose spirit was so sweet and generous. I loved her a lot and when she'd come down to the country for weekends when I was a little boy, she'd always play with me. As her job was teaching music, she could play a lot of different instruments (she had a favourite French horn she called 'Hubert') and I would go along with her sometimes and observe the huge difference she made to so many people's lives.

Through her I got to meet and become close friends of Alan, who had MS and used a wheelchair, and Butch, who had been a Thalidomide baby and had some profound disabilities. Immensely handsome, he had the most extraordinary and genuine self-confidence, which I very much envied. Born without legs and only having a flapper as an arm, he rolled himself around everywhere, taught me how to play the harmonica, and there seemed to be little I could do that he couldn't. What an inspiration he was. I hung out with these two guys a lot and being with such positive people, who never complained about their lot, always made me feel happy. I was gently being indoctrinated into the idea that one of the best antidotes to a narcissistic personality disorder, which I was increasingly realising I had big time, was to a) hang around good people who didn't have that complaint and let their goodness rub off on one, and b) try to be of service to my fellow human beings. I was increasingly finding, in my small way, that it was also the way to be happy. I found I'd written in my journal this quote by a character in a play by George Bernard Shaw:

> *This is the true joy in life, the being used for a purpose recognised by yourself as a mighty one. I am of the opinion that my life belongs to the whole community and as long as I live, it is my privilege to do for it whatever I can.*

I hadn't yet found such a purpose but in my own slow, bumbling way, I was starting to move in that direction.

My time in the world of publishing eventually came to an end in a rather curious way. I had also started practising yoga and had found a young Swiss swami called Swami Jotyananda, who began to teach me kriya yoga, which I threw myself into with great relish; early every morning and then again in the evening, when I got back from the office, I would do the practices.

My teacher, however, was not experienced enough to know that I was far too immature and unready to take on the very advanced yogic techniques he had given me. After a few weeks I began to experience a huge amount of light around me and to feel very euphoric, and what was happening, I realised much later, was that my ego self (which, despite Findhorn, had increasingly clawed its way back into my life) was grabbing hold of this experience of expanded awareness and using it for its own inflated agendas. Within a short time, I began to believe that I was some super-enlightened special human being, superior to the rest of humanity, and that I had a unique mission to save the world. Help! In short, I was starting to suffer from what Carl Jung called a Christ Complex!

Actually, I was beginning to go a little crazy. I met a girl who took a fancy to me. I went back to her flat with her and sat beside her bed meditating all night! A wee bit strange, n'est-ce pas? And then, when asked to help in the editing of the manuscript of a world-famous author (I am too ashamed to mention his name), I insulted him by telling him that his book was not spiritual enough and of no value and needed to be wholly rewritten. I bumped into him forty years later at Paddington station and was able to apologise.

Things soon came to a head. I became less and less able to process the high-frequency energy that this spiritual practice was unleashing inside me and I thought I would explode. And I did. Like Icarus, I had sailed too close to the sun, and like him,

I fell. I awoke one morning in abject darkness and went into a deep depression that lasted several weeks. Friends who knew me well saw that I was close to going right over the edge and suggested that I stop my kriya practice at once, go to a gym, pump some iron and eat some good old beefsteak. Very sound advice and I took it—and everything quietened down.

I realised that had things gone on that way, I may well have become psychotic. The fault was not with kriya yoga. It is a valid yogic practice, but only for experienced meditators. The fault was me again trying to run before I could walk. I didn't then have enough structure inside me—enough scaffolding, as it were—to 'hold' this very high-frequency energy that my practice was generating. But it was a very valuable lesson on the potential dangers that lurk if you try to do things that you are not yet ready for, and ever since that experience, when I work with people doing particular spiritual practices, I always take care to see that they don't do something for which I sense they are not qualified.

But by then, my copybook at the publishers had been well and truly dirtied and dear Fred Warburg was very gracious (and I am sure relieved) when I eventually handed in my notice. At least I knew that sitting in an office in a suit and tie and editing books was not my forte. But I wasn't any clearer to realising what was.

Chapter 13

Spreading My Wings

Another agenda, however, was surfacing for me: I felt moved to put down some roots and buy a house in the country. I didn't want to stay in London for ever. Initially, I found a wonderful place in Norfolk, nestled deep in the countryside miles away from the nearest town and hours from London. It was a small castle that had a moat and drawbridge around it and, even better, dungeons. I was very excited—or rather, Lord Snooty inside me, who had been dozing for a long time, was, and suddenly began to wake up! This was right along his lines.

In my impetuous way, I was about to sign on the dotted line, when my lovely wise friend Alan—at one level, I see him as my conscience or the Sancho Panza to my Don Quixote-ness—suggested that I should first get it surveyed. 'When you get this done, then you can also negotiate the price. Also, remember, Serge, it's very big and a long way from London where most of your friends live.'

Well, I did as Alan instructed me (ADD, among other things, makes one very impulsive) and I could have wept when the survey revealed that the whole place was riddled with dry rot and about to collapse. Actually, it was a blessing. What would I do in a damp, collapsing, nine-bedroomed castle miles away from anywhere? Hang out in one of my dungeons?

A dear friend of my mother and my stepfather George then alerted me to a lovely little seventeenth-century cottage in Gloucestershire. It had an old haybarn in the grounds and was an hour and twenty minutes' drive from London. I went to see it and fell immediately in love. I noticed that the bushes in the garden were full of butterflies and this seemed to me a good omen. The lady who was selling it was a well-known painter of horses. She loved animals and had a veritable menagerie that shared her house with her—pet rabbits, cats, hamsters, stoats, chickens, geese and horses. I turned up at the auction and found I was the only one there, so I got it, and I have to say that the Old School House (it had been a school in the nineteenth century) has been a loyal and generous friend to me over many years. I knocked out the floor where the hay had been stored, and created a little mezzanine terrace for a bedroom, and what used to be the tack room I had made into a kitchen and bathroom. However bad my finances might become because of my financial promiscuities, I always knew that I possessed a good solid asset that would never let me down. And it never did.

I need to make it clear, however, that despite my starting to country-bumpkin it, I never once engaged in huntin', fishin' or shootin'! None of these 'country sports' had any appeal to me and the idea of killing animals for fun I found quite abhorrent. From time to time, the local hunt would meet in the field outside my house and I would take pleasure in placing my loudspeakers on the Cotswold stone wall surrounding my house and on full volume blasting out silly records like *Does Your Chewing Gum Lose Its Flavour on the Bedpost Overnight?* by Lonnie Donegan or the one about a girl wearing an *Itsy Bitsy Teeny Weeny Yellow Polka Dot Bikini*. I guess this sums up the rather pathetic Serge sense of humour. Whether the guys in the red coats and bugles found it as funny as I did, I have no idea. I presume not. But it was my protest about making the killing of an animal into a sport.

The important point was that I found it terribly funny. I've always felt a bit of a joke man and loved bringing humour into things, although to be honest, what I often found hilarious has not always been reciprocated. My Austrian wife today, for example, thinks my Monty Pythonesque/Fawlty Towers/Dame Edna Everage sense of humour to be both ghastly and outdated, and I guess she's right. But I have an aversion to being politically correct, and as I see it, so long as your humour is not nasty—i.e., you don't call a fat person fatty or a bald man baldy—no damage gets done. I think that over the years I have intentionally created a bit of a caricature character around myself, as a lot of people don't get what I'm really about, so if we can all have a laugh at me together and all have a bit of fun, I'm all for it.

I made some wonderful friends in the little village, which was called Hampnett, in particular Chris Dreyfus, his sister Coralie and their wonderful mother Daphne, who bred macaw parrots in captivity. Later, when I began doing shamanic retreats at my house, the parrots would always fly over and drop a feather or two as if to acknowledge that they too felt included in my work.

I was also expanding my terrain in more far-off lands and I felt a side of me wanting to hippie it a bit down in Ibiza and I found a small finca to rent that had no electricity or running water, which I felt would allow me to come closer to nature. I would stay there for weeks at a time, armed with my spiritual books and journals, and every morning I would get up early and go for a long run before breakfast. Often girlfriends or other friends would come and stay and every afternoon we'd all go down to Benirrás Bay just near my finca, which was a beautiful protected little beach where I kept a speedboat and we'd do a lot of water-skiing.

In those days, this beautiful bay just had a small hut on it, where the local fishermen would cook their meals, and they would turn it into a restaurant just for our little gang; for lunch we'd enjoy whatever was the catch of the day. There was something very special about this place. I felt it was a secret hideout for me and my buddies. In my diaries of the time, I wrote:

> *Ibiza is a kind of teaching centre. It brings to the fore in people exactly what needs to be brought to the fore. It is an island of magic and mystery. It takes you on exactly the right trips that you need*

to be taken on. Events that normally would take six months to happen get concertina'd down to two weeks!

So true. However, I visited Ibiza again a few years ago to see my dear old friend Peter Adler, whom I've known since I was fifteen and who now has a beautiful house in the old town, and I found that the place I once knew had become totally unfamiliar. A lot of Ibiza's old charm had been well and truly syphoned away. I went down to revisit 'my beautiful bay' and discovered that as with so many special places, commercialisation had won its battle over beauty.

But Ibiza back in the early seventies had a simplicity and an untamedness to it and it was a very important teacher to me. It took me into its heart. It helped me begin to develop the 'being' side of my nature. As I had no television or telephone to distract me—mobile phones weren't going to be invented for another thirty or so years—I started to develop my relationship with nature which has grown steadily over the years. I found that one of the best ways to connect with the 'deeper me' was through physical activity: to swim in the sea or go running in the hills, where I could then quietly thank the trees for their wisdom and beauty. Here is an extract that I found in my journal:

I have just gone on a long walk and I climbed to a high point on a cliff and sat looking at the sea and the mountainous terrain around me and I felt great joy creeping into my heart. I felt the power of the earth, the warmth of the wind, the light of the sun and the softness of the ocean and I felt so grateful for being alive, for being part of the miracle of life. I felt humble and somehow blessed and utterly free from that nagging feeling that would often at times dog me, namely, that I had somehow to justify my existence.

I felt connected to joy because I felt grace all around me. I was graced and we all are graced only we don't realise it and I felt that despite all my struggles and mistakes and difficulties, that deep down I am OK and always have been OK and like the rocks and bushes around me, I was growing out of the earth. Hallelujah!

As islands are unique places, it follows that they produce and attract unique people. I made a bunch of interesting new friends with rather cuckoo names like Blind George, Dutch Peter, Moe Joe, Li'l Annie Fanny, Rich Frank and Nude Yanny. (He was an erotic sculptor and did all his work outdoors and, of course, in the nude.) I particularly learned a great deal from Dutch Peter. He was a painter; missing a few front teeth, and generally always broke. I had to buy plenty of his paintings, pay his rent and give him money else he would have died of starvation. But he was one of the most honest human beings I have ever met and was always giving me wise guidance on how to conduct my life. When I told him I was going to a lawyer to draw up a proper contract for the finca I was renting, he flew at me. 'This man has been an honest farmer all his life. Do you not trust him? How dare you have a contract?'

I took his advice and I didn't and the farmer, Senor Torres and I had a good relationship for all those years that I rented from him. Ever since then, whenever I have rented out places, if I have felt the people I was renting to were good, honourable people, I have followed Peter's advice and I've never had contracts; and I've never had anyone try to cheat me. I really give Peter credit. He realised I was doing a lot to help him and was certainly grateful, but he never tried to ingratiate himself with me or tell me things I'd like to hear. On the contrary. He always spoke the truth to me and was forever confronting me with the many inconsistencies in my behaviour—and he was generally right. You only find people like Peter on islands like Ibiza. I wonder if he's still alive and if he has any teeth left!

I also had a good friend called Larry, who, when I first knew him, had hair down to his waist, played beautiful guitar, knew all about herbs and painted mandalas. He was an integral part of our little Benirrás Bay beach tribe. I also learned a lot from him. Twenty years later, I met up with him again in California and he'd transmogrified into a 'suit' with a short, back and sides, and worked for a petroleum company. He had none of that old zest for life anymore. All the old swagger had gone. Poor old Larry. I felt sad for him. 'I had to do something to earn money,' he explained somewhat shamefacedly. I realised once again how blessed I was that this was not my fate and I didn't need to make compromises but was free to follow my heart. Apart from my short stint as a publisher, I've never worked for anyone and have always been my own boss!

So, my time from early to late twenties was spent mainly in Ibiza and Gloucestershire and a little bit in London. But I'd also go and spend time with my mother and George. They lived, as I said, in Gstaad in the winter, and over the summer in their palazzo in Venice. During this time, I began to get closer to my little half-siblings, Anna and Geordie.

I had a particularly strong connection with Anna, which grew over the years. Anna was quite a rebel and didn't conform to Moonie's ideas for how her beloved daughter should turn out. No deb parties for her. Anna was a traveller, not a fashionista. There were no compromises for her. She loved seeing the world and eventually got married about the time I first married, after our mother's death; not to a Hooray Henry, as Moonie would have liked, but to an Afghan musician she'd met in Afghanistan. He had beautiful blue eyes and long dreadlocks, and was a truly lovely guy. Sadly, the marriage broke up.

In the last years of her life, when she was dying of cancer—she, like Moonie, had been a heavy smoker—Anna's partner was another musician, a Black American jazz pianist from Brooklyn. I mourned Anna a lot. We were very close. She met my daughter Irena just before she died. Annanie (my nickname for her), I loved you a lot and I miss you. You left this world much too soon. As I sit writing this, I have a big lump in my throat and

I'm looking at a photo of you I have in a frame in front of me. You were very beautiful and you are always in my heart. I'm so, so sad you're not around now. We would have so much in common today and you would love Martina and Irena.

I enjoyed visiting Venice in the summer, and my mother and George would often give very chic parties (my mother told me once that they'd managed to poach the head chef of the Aga Khan!). I preferred being there to being in Gstaad, which was more a place where you *après-skied* as opposed to skied. Now that I was starting to make inroads into a whole new simpler, more authentic lifestyle, one side of me would always feel slightly uncomfortable mingling in that world of multimillionaires, where people would have a fit if the stock market went down and for a few days they'd only be worth thirty million instead of thirty-three.

But Gstaad in those days was where lots of pretty girls from all over the world seemed to congregate, and this always stirred me to tiptoe back into that world from time to time. My old Harrow school friend, Julian Moulton, made Gstaad his main base, setting himself up as a professional playboy, having shipped in his E type Jags and Ferraris to confirm his credentials.

The truth was that I actually quite liked contrast in my life. Gstaad was the world where the chic ladies hung out and my little finca in Ibiza was the place of calm, but as yet I had not learned to integrate these different realities inside myself and in my mind I kind of labelled the world of Ibiza 'good' and that of Gstaad 'bad'!

Chapter 14

Expanding My Consciousness

But something new inside me was definitely beginning to awaken. I could say that a 'deeper me' was beginning to emerge out of my closet. I became a student of the Alice Bailey esoteric teachings, which, so the story went, had been directly channelled through her by a Tibetan Master named Djwal Khul. Through these books, I came to understand that all the great world religions had a deeper esoteric dimensionality that could only be accessed by those who were evolved enough to be able to understand it. I also learned that the name of the spiritual game was about how we might awaken the soul part of our nature, and that the more this dimension of ourselves came into expression and the more aspects of ourselves it infused, the less control our egos would have over us.

I also found out that most of us live most of the time on what is known as the 'astral plane', which is essentially a plane of illusion, where we are strongly motivated towards desiring things that are big and glamorous but which are not necessarily in our own best interest. 'The glamour of materiality,' Alice Bailey wrote, 'is the cause of all the present world distress, and what we call the economic problem is simply the result of this particular glamour'. Written nearly a hundred years ago, these teachings are still eminently relevant today. I think my dear papa succumbed to this particular glamour.

I also began reading books by George Gurdjieff and Peter Ouspensky, whose angle on life was very similar. Their thesis was that most of us are very unconscious. We don't have a clue who we really are, and only by working very hard to try to come to know ourselves do we have a chance of remedying this situation and thereby breaking out of the prisons we live in! As we do this we start to realise that we are not the person who we think we are, and that our true purpose in life is actually to help in the evolution of our planet, or, in Alice Bailey's words, to be 'a world server'!

For a short time, I was also part of a Sufi community near where I lived in Gloucestershire, called Bashara. There I studied the mystical teachings of a twelfth-century sage called Ibn Arabi, and I have spent many years puzzling out what he meant when he said, talking as if on behalf of God, that 'I was a Hidden Treasure and I loved to be known, so I created the world that I might be known.' I think only now, fifty years later, am I a wee bit closer to solving this riddle (my attempted answer appearing in chapter twenty of my last book!).

I was also a very active member of an organisation called the Wrekin Trust, which was the brainchild of a wonderful man, Sir George Trevelyan, who was to play a very inspirational role in my life. He seemed to be the 'father' of the spiritual movement in England – in those days called the 'new age' movement. Through him I got to meet and become a close friend of Baroness Edmee di Pauli, whose London house I would later on use to give lectures, and who was a wonderful aristocratic old lady who had dedicated her whole life to the spiritual edification of humanity. Even in her nineties, she was organising seminars and on different themes relating to 'saving the world'. What a gem she was.

George had a wonderful presence and also a great sweetness to him and was a very inspirational lecturer. He was a few years younger than I am now when I first met him, but he seemed terribly old as he suffered from severe arthritis. I would attend weekend seminars put on by his organisation on all sorts of 'alternative topics', all given by the most interesting people. I loved being at these conferences as I felt I was learning a lot and experiencing being in the company of kindred spirits, where it was safe to allow myself to be myself and where there was no need for me to put on any kind of false face. At this time, I became particularly fascinated by UFOs. Did they actually exist or were they, as Jung believed, projections from our own unconscious or perhaps stories invented by people who wanted to appear more interesting? Or did they perhaps come from inner and not outer space, or were they perhaps special craft created by the military? While my interest has continued to this day and my mind is still open, what I do feel is that to believe that we are the only intelligent species not only in our galaxy but in the billions of galaxies that exist, is certainly cosmic provinciality at its most extreme!

Another of the important people who came my way at this time was John Whitmore, a baronet and ex-racing car driver, like me a trust-fund hippie and who had had a not dissimilar upbringing. John was fervently—almost fanatically—on a path of self-discovery. He was a real adventurer and had just made a breakthrough film called *Here Comes Every Body* about group therapy sessions at the Esalen centre at Big Sur, California. A few years older than me, I saw him as a kind of kingpin in a new world that I was becoming fascinated by and he kind of adopted me as his sidekick. I would accompany him on some of his lectures and through him got to meet many more interesting people.

Later on, I felt that things became a bit bizarre with John. He teamed up with a psychic called Phyllis Schlemmer and a scientist called Andrija Puharich and financed by John, the three of them toured the world, meditating in certain areas selected by Phyllis and believing that what they were doing was 'saving the world'. Maybe they were. Who is to say! Then a tragedy happened and John's rogue trustees ran off with all his money, and John who had owned a wonderful country estate, was now rendered virtually penniless. However, being extremely resourceful, he quickly reinvented himself as a corporate coach and became one of the best-known coaches in England and wrote several best-selling books on the subject. We lost touch for a long time, until he came back into my life about ten years ago and agreed to give a talk at the launch of my first book. He died two years later. A good friend and a great guy. You had real chutzpah. Bless you, John. You were a really important figure in my life.

Among the many interesting people whom I met through John was Brendan O'Regan of the Institute for Noetic Sciences in California.

Brendan once took me with him to visit the famous spoon-bender, Uri Geller, who was visiting London and who worked very closely with Puharich. Sitting in Uri's bedroom in the Hyde Park Hotel and talking to him—Uri on his bed and the two of us in chairs in front of him—I had quite a shock when suddenly there was a terrific crash and a washbasin landed at our feet and broke into little pieces. Uri apologised. 'Excuse me. These kind of things always happen around me. I don't have a lot of control.'

Looked at logically, why would Uri have arranged—or indeed, could he have arranged—to have had a washbasin hanging up suspended from the ceiling as we entered the room? And if he'd done so, how could he ensure that it would fall at a particular moment? And surely, we'd also have seen it when we came in. But if this was not the case, how in hell could it have 'flown' through the wall from the bathroom into our room? The bathroom door was closed all the time we were there. I went into the bathroom and there was a big gash in the wall where the washbasin had been. It must somehow have teleported itself through the solid wall!

At that time, Uri was quite famous and many people wanted to debunk him and show that he was just an illusionist. OK, there are many magicians today who perform the most extraordinary feats like seeming to hang in the air, walk on water and step through glass windows, but the purveyors of these conjuring tricks admit to them and later show us how they are done. I don't think this was the case with Uri. Or maybe some of what he did was genuine and some not. Certainly today, the whole field of parapsychology is opening up more and more and there's no doubt that certain people seem to have extraordinary powers. Let me give you another example.

A few years later, I flew to Oregon to attend the marriage of dear Peter Caddy who had left Eileen and gone to live in the States. The event was happening on Mount Shasta and it was being orchestrated by an old shaman and all us guests were invited to go into a sweat lodge to prepare themselves. (It is like going into an intense Turkish bath where you take off all your clothes so you can sweat out your impurities.) Yes, my friend, no grey tailcoats and top hats and carnations in the new worlds I was now entering! Nudity was the name of the game! Well, with my own eyes, I saw the shaman reach into the fire he'd built to heat the stones to put into the sweat lodge, and drag them out white-hot, and carry them slowly one by one in his hands without a single burn appearing. How do you explain that?

At this time, I also became friendly with a very materialist-oriented scientist also called John, who had been an ardent 'debunker' and sceptic and had been engaged in a project to prove that children who felt they could bend spoons like Geller, were all charlatans. Over lunch one day, he told me this story:

'I was just finalising my research to show that all this nonsense didn't exist, and my final visit was to a child in Kent, and I had just finished my work with him and was leaving the room delighted that I'd been proved right, when my attention was directed towards a doll's house on the right of the door. I had observed it as I first came into the room, and had happened to notice that a heap of paper clips were lying on the floor in front of it. Now, as I glanced at it on leaving, I was shocked to observe that the paper clips had suddenly rearranged themselves as lots of little stick figures inside the house. Nobody had touched them—and I know that, as I was in the room with the boy all the time. It felt as if the universe had done this to try to snub me, as if to say "See, matey; you aren't as clever as you think!"'

A few months later, I met up with John again, and he told me that this experience had turned his whole world upside down and that he was having to unlearn many of the core assumptions he had acquired during his scientific training. 'Yes, Serge, I think the universe is very, *very* clever and that whenever we feel we have a final explanation for something, it will often pull a joker out of the pack to confuse us. But perhaps this is good as it means that we will never ever be allowed to close the book of our inquiries into trying to find out how the cosmos operates.' I told John Whitmore this story and he quoted me something that a Nobel prize winning scientist had written, namely that 'Science evolves through the death of those who oppose new theories!'

I understand this. It is pretty traumatic if all your life you've been educated to believe that the universe is one way and suddenly you discover that it's not. You want to close off your mind! In a lesser way, this was happening to me as well as I was increasingly discovering that the rather conventional world I had been brought up to believe was the real and only world, was actually very far from being that.

In this context, I can also share an experience of mine when I was fifty-two and had just been diagnosed with a rare form of leukaemia, the same kind that my dear friend Danny eventually died of. I had a good Chinese friend, Zerzing Wang, a young man who was a qi gong master (qi gong being a millennia-old system for coordinating body posture and meditation for the purposes of health and spirituality), and on hearing of my predicament, he arranged for me to be the guinea pig in a class he was teaching, where he had invited the greatest qi gong Master in all of China to work with him.

This great Master began by demonstrating some of his powers to the class. This involved him first pointing his finger at a piece of paper and setting it alight. He then unplugged a light and, holding the plug in his hand, made the light flash on and off. We learned that all this was the power of what in China is called qi energy. My friend Lawrence Blair wrote about a man who also had very similar powers and who was called Dynamo Jack! He could point his finger at a tree and bore a hole right through it!

But the important thing – at least for me – was not all this seemingly magical stuff. The important thing for me was that this qi gong master worked on me to draw the cancer out of my body. I don't know what he did or how he did it, but all I know is that ever since then, I have gone five times a year for over twenty years to have my blood checked at the Royal Marsden cancer hospital in London, and my leukaemia has never worsened. I have never had any symptoms or required any treatment.

So thank you again, dear 'Friend', for putting me in touch with Zerzing and thank you, Zerzing, for having connected me with this great Master.

I tell you these stories not because I view these phenomena as necessarily being spiritual, but more to inform you that I was being gradually taught to question the very materialist worldview that I'd inherited, whereby nothing is allowed to exist beyond what our three-dimensional space/time reality and our five senses tell us exists. My friend, this is nonsense. I was gradually coming to realise that we not only have many more than five senses but that many different universes or realities exist and that it may well be that at certain times some of these realities interface with our own reality enabling certain things to take place that otherwise could not. It may well be, for example, that what we call a miracle is a normal event taking place in a non-normal reality. I wrote about this in my last book on the soul and have more stories on this theme coming up a little later on.

What I was also starting to become aware of was that each new 'step' into a slightly more expanded universe, was making me become increasingly aware of how enormously 'unfinished' I still was as a human being. The truth was that my emotional world was in more turmoil than ever. Here are some notes from my journal at the time:

I think I avoid looking at myself honestly by always being on the move. I feel like the 'fool on the hill'. It makes me feel weak as I realise that all my many blockages that I've not worked through, are now coming to the surface and demanding that I confront them and I think there's a lot of very dark stuff lurking around.

I realise that if one tries to be honest as I acknowledge I am trying, one inevitably pays a price, although I also realise that not being honest is to pay an even bigger one. I laugh as I watch the somewhat crazy way I go about living my life and especially all my ongoing dramas with women. I also observe that while I think I am growing at one level, the snobbish part of me is not nearly as dead as I had thought and I can still have a tendency to undervalue people if they are not witty, attractive and classy, and similarly, I can overvalue girls if they happen to be pretty. As I see these things about myself, my superficiality utterly appals me.

I also see that I often don't give people enough space to 'be', and still have a terribly critical side to me and I feel saddened and ashamed. I see that I am still incapable of forming a genuine and enduring relationship with a woman. I think I am afraid of a girl knowing me well and so seeing all my many negative traits.

A little further on I wrote:

As if all my personal efficiency has totally blown to the winds. I am a kind of floating, amorphous, desperate kind of fleeing away

> *creature, rushing here and there in taxis, guilt hanging around his neck like an iron collar, half doing a number of things and my spirituality lying around like something crushed and forgotten. I feel very stuck and that I've somehow lost my way...*

Yikes! The idea of possibly going into psychotherapy was not yet something that had occurred to me. As was usual, however, the universe arranged it very neatly for me. Of course, it used my relationship with a woman! I was now twenty-six and in Gstaad had just met a French girl, Nicole, whom I had grown quite fond of and in my endeavour to bridge these two worlds, I'd invited her to relinquish the world of chic and come and hang out in my simple little Ibizan farmhouse. It felt as if we were getting on well as she was also interested in many of the same things that I was.

After a few weeks, I had to go to London for a sinus operation. It was successful and I was able to return to Ibiza earlier than I thought. I decided not to let Nicole know and just come back and surprise her.

However, when I returned to my finca and opened the door, I had a big surprise. There standing in front of me was a man with blackened, broken-off teeth and nicotine-stained hands. A pungent smell of bad breath wafted towards me.

'Who are you?' he said aggressively in a strong German accent.

'Who am I? Well, I am Serge and I have returned to my finca to see my girlfriend. Who are you?'

Nicole then arrived on the scene and I gathered from her that she'd met him shortly after I'd left, had invited him to stay as he had no abode and one thing had led to another.

A more frightful fellow I cannot imagine. And I later learned he was a member of the German terrorist gang Baader-Meinhof. Jesus Christ. No apology for living in my finca and having appropriated my girl.

But, and here is the point, instead of my confronting him by acting in a way that (Nicole later told me) would have been a show of my manliness, I squirmed. I was polite and got a bit victimy. I slept in the spare room that evening—in my own finca!—with my little tail between my legs.

The next morning, I managed to corner Nicole and asked her: 'Nicole, tell me. What made you fall for this uncouth, penniless, smelly, terrorist figure?' Here's the essence of her reply and it made me shudder.

'You want the truth, Serge. OK, I'll tell you. I like him because he is real, whereas you, Serge, you are often not real. You live too much in your mind and you don't walk your talk. You are always so nice, so polite and I don't feel it is genuine as you never really say what you feel. You equate being a man with how long you make love to me for. That's not what a woman wants. I'd actually been angry with you for some time and that's why a space opened up for me to connect with Wolfgang. Look, you never stood up to him. You never reprimanded me for doing something that, I admit, was not good, and I apologise to you now. But you could have fought for me emotionally. You're the big, tall one, in truth, you behaved as the little ferret that you described him to be!'

Why her words really got through to me was because deep down I knew they were true. I don't say what I feel; I don't tell people what I need. I don't like conflict. I had to confront the fact that there was something decidedly wimpy about me. Why did I not confront Herr Wolfgang? Truth is, I saw that I was afraid of my power. I equated it with my father's dominating ways and to not be like him I had shut down this side of myself.

It is all well and good to have a sense that you are connected to something bigger than you, like the 'Friend', but if you don't confront a man who is stealing your woman, if you don't know how to stand in your power and instead keep giving it away—as I saw I had just done—if you continue rejecting women who love you and allow other women to treat you shabbily, there's something mightily wrong somewhere.

Something new was needed. So just as a friend told me about Findhorn and I visited Findhorn, so, some time ago, John Whitmore had talked very positively about a particular psychotherapy called Psychosynthesis (his wife Diana was a practitioner of it) and informed me that its best practitioners were to be found at the Institute of Psychosynthesis in San Francisco, California.

So I decided to fly there. I gave up my finca to my old mate Peter Adler and I wrote a letter to Nicole to thank her and Herr bloody Baader-Meinhof Wolfgang for the appropriate kick in the backside they'd just given me! This marked the end of one phase in my life and the beginning of a whole new and very amazing journey. I often tell people that 'the moment my plane set down in San Francisco' was when my *real* education began...

Chapter 15

California Dreamin'

Yes, my friend, if the death of my father when I was twenty-three heralded one important new beginning, my going to California, where I lived for the next eleven years and became a US resident, heralded another extremely important one. Indeed, those years from the age of twenty-seven, when I left Europe, to thirty-nine, when I returned, were probably the most creative, transformative and adventurous of my entire life. During this period my life really took off. I really began to savour what being fully alive was all about.

I remember a character in a Thomas Mann novel saying: 'If a way to the better there be, it lies in taking a full look at the worst.' I heartily agree. I really wanted to do this—really look at all that craziness and darkness lying at the bottom of my heart.

Gurdjieff understood how difficult this was. 'Man being the lazy creature that he is,' he told us, 'he doesn't really shift unless he is hit by a shock greater than the sum of his own inertia!' So true. Well, in a small way, this had just happened to me. My vanity had come in for a sound bashing, and that was good. It needed it. Dear John Whitmore had arranged for me to stay with his ex-wife Gunilla, who lived in San Francisco, so I had somewhere to hang out until I found my bearings. She very kindly lent me her old car, which was a Mustang similar to the one in the Clint Eastwood movie *Gran Torino*, and I found that lots of fun.

Why at around this time did the physicist Fritjof Capra leave London and base himself in northern California to complete his seminal work *The Tao of Physics*? Why did the Israeli visionary Moshé Feldenkrais come to the Bay Area to live and develop his ground-breaking work with the human body? Why did Ida

Rolf, who invented Rolfing, Fritz Perls, the father of Gestalt therapy, and Roberto Assagioli, who created Psychosynthesis, which I had come to study—why did all these virtuosos leave their native countries and converge on northern California?

The answer: because culturally, there was something very special going on there, and I am sure that all of them must have intuitively realised that they could only develop something new and revolutionary—or more accurately, evolutionary—away from the creative restrictions of their native countries. I say this as certainly, when I arrived in California, I found it to be a hotbed of such visionaries. I was deeply privileged in that I not only got to meet some of my heroes personally, but also, when I became involved with the creation of the Institute for the Study of Conscious Evolution a few years later, I became friends with and even worked alongside some of them. This was so important. As the great Indian saint Ramakrishna put it: 'Seek spiritual advancement from one who is advanced. One should take some trouble to live in the company of the good.' I'd done so at Findhorn. Now I was to do so again—and boy, did I need to.

Yes, my friend, my arrival in northern California coincided with the emergence of a very important movement called the Human Potential Movement, which was little known outside of the group who constituted it and where it was located. While much more emphasis has been placed on the whole glamorous 'flower power', Haight-Ashbury, 'turning on, tuning in, dropping out' psychedelic revolution of the sixties, in terms of what was actually achieved, I think the Human Potential Movement, which got far less coverage, was of far greater significance.

So what exactly was it about? Well, quite simply, as its name tells us, it was about how we can realise or release our human potential, what we need to do to become the full person that we are meant to be, and thus both feel better and be better as we learn to wake up out of the sleep of our old conditioned self. Human Potential-ites' lives revolved around exploring what was needed to become more real, more creative, have more energy, be more healed and whole and effective in all areas of one's life—in one's work, in one's relationships and friendships—and, most importantly, to discover what were the most effective 'technologies of transformation'—that is, processes—to enable these things to take place. In other words, what were the best techniques to help speed up our awakening?

This was exactly what I most needed, because, as my diaries showed, I had very much lost my way. In retrospect, I think that too much had been going on for me and what I had lacked was any kind of external scaffolding, structure or discipline to 'hold me together sufficiently' to enable me properly to digest and integrate my experiences.

Which was exactly what I was now about to receive.

What especially interested me about this movement was that it stressed the need for a greater convergence between psychotherapy and spirituality, seeing how and where they interrelated and complemented one another, and Psychosynthesis particularly focussed on this. Roberto Assagioli, its genius creator, whom sadly I never got to meet, had originally been a psychiatrist and recognised that psychotherapy without soul lacked something very important. So, he put together a system that integrated the best of Western psychology, Eastern religion and esoteric Christianity. He too, had been a student of the Alice Bailey books.

He realised that we didn't have enough force to heal our personality wounds at a deep enough level if our soul life remained unexplored, and by the same token he also recognised that the more we confront where we are wounded, the more space we allow for our 'higher human nature' or our soul life to shine through. In a word, we can find our light by delving down into our darkness, by exploring what has become hidden away in the many nooks and crannies inside our psyches. Also, unlike many traditional psychologies, which regarded exploring the more transcendent realms of consciousness as being escapist, Assagioli recognised that learning to access these 'higher-order' realms and trying to centre ourselves in them was key if we were to live more harmonious and creative lives. Psychosynthesis therefore focussed both on 'height work'—helping us reach into the higher areas of our humanity—and 'depth work'—delving down and exploring our dark sides or what Carl Jung referred to as our Shadow.

Essentially then, what this Human Potential Movement was about, and particularly what Psychosynthesis aspired towards, was what was needed for us to become more whole as human beings. *It recognised that if our world was to work properly, more of us needed to work properly!* (Our planet was—and of course, still is—in a perilous state precisely because the vast majority of us human beings do *not* work properly, and so we are continually projecting our lack of humanity out into our society.) And being 'wholistically healthy' means having harmony in *all* areas of our lives. Just eating organic food and doing yoga and keeping physically fit is not enough if we are unhappy in our work, have toxic relationships, cannot deal effectively with love, and feel creatively unfulfilled. The name of the game that I was on the cusp of learning more about was not just about learning to feel better but also about discovering how to live a more balanced, creative, and meaningful life.

Initially, as I said, I came over to America just to have this kind of psychotherapy done to me, but this wholistic approach so intrigued me that I signed up to train as a psychosynthesis practitioner, and I have never looked back. Everything about psychosynthesis and the fantastic people associated with it resonated with me and, while today I do not call the work I do by that name, as over the years many other influences have also come in, there is no doubt that psychosynthesis definitely underpins everything I do.

So, this was the world that I had landed right in the middle of, and I found it enormously exciting. At last, I had found my tribe, people I could allow myself to be myself with. No more mask-wearing. I made some wonderful new friends among both my fellow students and the teachers. I became particularly close to Tom Yeomans, who was one of the main instructors, and we have stayed in touch ever since. I found it so refreshing to at last have friends all around me who were on my wavelength, who saw the world as I did, and who were interested in the same things as me, and, most importantly, to discover that I was not the only one to feel confused and to have emotional problems. Indeed, I learned that many of the most effective psychotherapists also had deep and difficult issues to work through in their lives and that there was a connection between where we are most wounded and where our potential strengths lie. Achilles, the Greek god who was revered as the fastest runner, I found out, had been wounded in his heel!

I didn't only train in Psychosynthesis. I also took part in many other human developmental programmes. There was a well-known motivational guru at the time who gave himself the name of Werner Erhard, whom I got to know and whom I liked, and when he taught large seminars I would always find myself standing up and challenging him. I think I liked to hear the sound of my own voice (and still do a bit!). But I got a lot out of his many trainings, especially as I was also learning the skills to teach seminars myself, which I was to begin doing in a few years.

I remember the first EST (Erhard Seminar Training) I did, just a fortnight after arriving in California, happened to be a weekend called 'About Sex'! I felt very honoured when a dark-haired girl with a huge Amy Winehouse beehive hairstyle and oodles of black around her eyes approached me and said in a Texan drawl, 'Dude, you're real weird; you've got a funny accent. Are you a cockney by any chance?'

What a relief. To be thought a cockney. Far away from all that wretched British class stuff that somehow I could never quite escape from in England. I answered very affirmatively, 'Yes, ma'am, I am a cockney, born within the sound of Bow Bells, a cockney who has just arrived in California and doesn't really know his way about.'

Well, Miss Texas (she'd actually been that some years ago) could not have been more gracious and she showed me around and introduced me to her friends and made me feel thoroughly welcomed in the new world I had just entered. Through her, I found a small cabin to rent in Mill Valley in the Bay Area, which you got to by going over the Golden Gate Bridge from San Francisco. So yes, the helping spirit was still very much with me, always connecting me with what I needed; and again, so many of my important connections came, in one way or another, via women.

I was continually attending seminars and going to conferences, but it was all interesting work, not hard work, and I was so fascinated with what I was studying that I could not wish to have been doing anything else. One thing I found, however, was that I was learning increasingly to disagree with those pundits who told us that we should all have a good 'work/life balance', as if to suggest that work and life are separate.

That had been my problem before. I would put all the various things I did into separate compartments. Now I could open them all up and view them as being interconnected, and in that context it was clear that life and work were very much integral parts of each other. On the one hand, I saw that we needed to put work into the everyday living of our lives in order to bring more fullness and harmony into it, and on the other hand, given that many of us spend a large part of our day engaged in what we do to earn our living, to say that it should not be seen as being part of 'the living of our lives'—implying that we are somehow not 'living' when at the office or doing whatever we do—simply did not make sense.

Today, this is even more true for me. The vaster part of my life is centred around my teaching seminars, writing articles, conducting retreats, working with individuals and doing research, and I celebrate this as a very integral part of my creative living!

Because being in California I now resided in a culture where, just like at Findhorn, I felt given permission to be 'me', it was again much easier to allow my genuineness out of my closet and to start living in a less clenched and more surrendered way. This meant I could allow certain aspects of my personality self that were never really that true to me, and which, for example, I had needed to utilise for 'Gstaad society', slowly to fade away through underuse.

Contrary to what many believed, however, it was not all love and light in the Human Potential Movement! There was a strong flavour of what in those days used to be known as 'new age' spirituality, which had a distinctly dark side to it and that attracted its fair share of snake-oil salesmen. Many of them were teaching courses on what they called 'prosperity consciousness', which was basically about how to use your spirituality to grow financially richer and attract more partners to you.

I found this to be hugely manipulative. Unadulterated spiritual materialism. I remember one cowboy charging a fortune teaching a seminar called 'Learn to Be a Millionaire in Love'. Yes, of course I liked girls, but I was certainly not going to use any hocus-pocus in this arena as this was not what being a wholistic human being was all about. This for me was out and out manipulation. I took a strong stand on this topic and challenged quite a few of these snake-oil guys (there were also gals involved) and in certain circles I was not Mr Popular!

Talking about shysters, a rather funny story concerned a very tall, thin Black guy who purported to be a 'breatharian': that is, someone who doesn't need to eat but survives solely by drawing in the prana from the air. While there are people who can genuinely live this way, just as there are yogis who can stop their breath and survive for weeks buried underground, this fellow was a true cowboy. Once, after having given a performance where he lifted very heavy weights and people paid quite a bit of money to see him do so, a film crew secretly followed him afterwards—all the way to a McDonald's, where he was photographed holding a quadrupled-sized Big Mac to his mouth with an expression of surprise and terror. Actually, I felt a bit sorry for him.

That said, the light side of this great wholistic movement was very considerable. I would take myself to many conferences and, after a year or two, would be asked to give the odd talk at them myself. I also met many fascinating women who were all much more developed than me, and while I still continued to have a few liaisons dangereuses, I found that those women with whom I had serious relationships had a huge amount to teach me.

Here in the Bay Area, the feminist movement was very strong. I had a very loving connection with a woman called Dianne Morrison who was very high up in Werner Erhard's organisation. Our relationship lasted a year and she taught me to be both softer and stronger as well as showing me that she was unwilling to deal with my old macho posturings. Bless you, Dianne, and thank you.

Emotionally, I was being forced to grow up and take much greater responsibility for my life and, in so doing, begin gradually to release my 'puer aeternus' fixation! (You can't do something like that too quickly, especially if the complex has been stamped into one for many years.) I realised that I was not only going through a psychological training to help heal my many emotional wounds, but I was also undergoing an important real-life training to try to become a more authentic and caring human being.

Chapter 16

Treading the Path of Heart

A seminal experience in my new Californian life was going on a two-week 'Awakening the Heart' retreat with a doctor who had the interesting name of Brugh Joy. My English chiropractor buddy, David Tansley, had said to me: 'If you are going to San Francisco, Serge, be sure not only to wear flowers in your hair, but also go and do some work with Brugh. It will change your life.'

And it did. It was an epiphany. There were twenty of us present at this retreat and ten of them subsequently became friends. Its gift to me was to open me up to a deeper connection with my *inner* heart, with that part of myself that carried qualities like love and peace and joy and kindness and compassion. This is so important as essentially what is wrong with our society is that far too many of us have lost touch with our hearts and thus with those qualities, and the problem is that what is inside us doesn't get exercised, tends to atrophy or close down. This is especially true if we are a man, where we are trained only to live in our heads. Certainly if I look back at my education, that had been my experience. Our motto at Harrow was *mens sana in corpore sano* meaning a healthy mind in a healthy body. No mention of the heart. And similarly at Oxford. I saw that deep down I was afraid of opening my heart, not only because I didn't quite know how to, but also because it was not part of the story I had been conditioned to believe in. Men must be tough guys, I seemed to imagine my father saying. Not namby pambies with all those mushy feelings!

In working with Brugh I came to realise that so much of my mushiness (which incidentally, I was very prone to) was precisely because my heart was *not* open. Actually, I found that it carried a lot of fear. I also came to see that essentially what lay behind the dysfunctionalities in our world, starting with our obsession with materiality and our tendencies to overconsume, overwork and be prone to addiction issues and self-destructive tendencies, was essentially an impoverished, wounded and under-nourished inner heart. We'd go to gyms to train our body and universities to broaden our mind, but what about the world of the poor heart!

I had begun reading the books of Osho, an Indian guru (in those days he was called Bhagwan Rajneesh) and these words of his I found very important.

> *The mind is only a servant. The master is the heart because all that is beautiful grows in the heart, all that is valuable comes out of the heart – your love, your compassion, your meditation.*

So true. The two weeks I spent on retreat with dear Brugh, then, served to set the tone for the rest of my life. This beautiful and unusual man radiated a special 'heart energy' that had the effect of gradually awakening me to a dimension of my being that I had never intentionally connected with before. I began increasingly to feel compassion for myself and for other people and for the world, and I also came to realise how much we need to take responsibility for the thoughts we radiate out at any time as they have the capacity not only to affect those around us but also our environment. I learned from Brugh that when we are around someone and we feel uncomfortable or we sense that their presence pulls us down, that in all probability it is because their inner hearts are closed or are not in good working order and we may well be picking up how they feel about themselves!

These two weeks also brought up a lot of sadness because I got to see that in addition to often being indulgent with myself, I could also be harsh and judgemental, and that with so many of the women I had been with, I had never really opened myself properly to feel how they felt! In Brugh's words: 'without the heart, the human is sinister. To be able to feel is the great gift. When you feel for another, you become united with that person in an intimate way; your concern and compassion comes alive, drawing some of the other person's world and spirit into yours.'

I saw that I had never really done that properly. Yes, my friend, this fortnight heralded the start of a long journey into intimacy and my beginning to move further and further away from my narcissism.

Brugh told us his story. He had been a very successful medical doctor with highly paid and very prestigious jobs in various hospitals, but he began to feel something was deeply wrong with his life, and that somehow he was a fraud. He was very unhappy and had terrible pains in his pancreas that were getting worse and worse, yet all medical examinations found nothing wrong with him. He realised that his symptoms were telling him something important and that he had to take a very important step and honour his deeper truth, which meant that he had to give up his 'comfort zone' of well-paid status jobs with the medical establishment, and risk jumping into the unknown and start teaching people about personal transformation.

He told us that one day he woke up in such despair that he couldn't bear it anymore; he resigned from all his prestigious jobs and took steps to begin to do the work that his heart told him he needed to do. Almost immediately his symptoms vanished, his old joie de vivre returned and suddenly he was drawing lots of students to work with him.

I learned a lot from that story and it gave me courage a little further down the line, in my own little way, to do exactly the same thing—to follow my heart; and indeed, the central focus of my life has also been as a teacher of transformation with a special focus on the awakening of the heart. It also became clear to me why I had so many personal problems to contend with; I learned that we can best assist other people in areas where we've also struggled ourselves. I mean, how can we truly feel empathic with other people's pain if we've never felt confused or lost in similar ways ourselves! From Brugh, then, I learned that the condition of feeling lost in a dark forest (which was very much how I felt before coming to California) was actually an integral stage of all spiritual journeying and echoed the parable of the prodigal son. My goodness, I'd been a prodigal old creature for long enough and it was high time that I started coming home! And now I felt that I was beginning to do so.

Interestingly, one of the things I specialised in over the years was being a relationship consultant, and I would often tell clients who would come to see me that I had plenty of experience in this arena as I'd made all the mistakes anyone could ever make! It was true, and as you'll be seeing, I still had a lot more to make! Yes, I'd been lost for a long time, but now amazing grace was with me and I was slowly starting to find myself, and Brugh played a key part in this. I am happy to say that he became a friend and our buddyhood over the years was important to me and I would return to do two more groups with him over the next fifteen years. He died a few years ago, bless him. I loved you, Brugh, and was so grateful to you. You were a very unusual man. Thank you for your support and your wisdom and for having entered my life.

Working with Brugh, then, confirmed for me that we need to do a lot of work to get to know our inner heart and that the more we try to honour what we experience as being its truth—i.e., the more we follow what we deem to be real and listen to what feels right for us—the more we open to grace, and consequently the more empowered we will feel. I saw that there was definitely a connection between love and power, and that much of my wimpiness was connected to my heart having been insufficiently open. Writing in the 1940s, the great Teilhard de Chardin told us that 'there is more power inside an awakened heart than inside the atomic bomb'! I believe that. In a seminar

I taught quite recently, I referred to our heart as *our greatest weapon of self-construction*!

From that time on, I've never done work because I felt I *should*, but always because I felt delighted to do so. As I've said so already, I am such a lucky man in that I have always loved what I do, and so I have always felt my work to be easy. People over the years have often asked me, 'Serge, isn't it exhausting working with people and hearing all their woes? Don't you get depressed?' My reply has always been that because I enjoy people and seem intuitively to understand them and to be able, in small ways, to help them with their struggles, the answer is 'No, I don't.'

A few months later, again listening to my heart, I took myself with Dianne on another 'human potential' adventure: a Native American Indian vision quest that took place in Death Valley, California.

Here, the name of the game is that you fast for ten days, and all you are allowed to take with you is a toothbrush, toothpaste, a notebook and pen, a poncho to wrap around yourself at night and a large bottle of water. Fasting is very powerful. What it does is that it empties us. Not only physically but also mentally and emotionally. It therefore leaves more space for our deeper self to come alive inside us, which it often cannot do if we are all gunged up with our many psychological and social toxins. With Brugh, I'd done a kind of fasting or emptying of my heart; now I was adding to it a fasting of other parts of me as well.

It works like this. When we begin emptying ourselves of all the 'stuff' we ordinarily draw into ourselves and hold on to—such as half-baked ideas we unconsciously absorb, negative thoughts we pick up from other people, general anxiety and fear hovering in the atmosphere around us, plus personal regrets, anxieties and resentments—we become lighter psychically, and thus more open to connecting with life much more deeply.

The first three days were very difficult. A lot of resistance came up. I felt bored and tired and very hungry. I recognised how difficult I found it to just 'be', and saw a part of myself that liked to fill up every moment either with food or with doing things; and suddenly there was no food and nothing to do. Help!

But after those initial few days, I broke through to a new level and I loved the experience of feeling light inside myself. A certain 'clenchedness' which I saw had always been with me began slowly to waft off the menu. On my fifth day of not eating, I no longer felt hungry. I just observed how enormously awake and alive I felt and how much easier it was to meditate, as well as appreciate the extraordinary beauty of the barren terrain all around me. In Native American Indian terms, the aim of a vision quest is 'to dance your dream awake', that is, to clear away the inner cobwebs obscuring your deeper truth and so wake you up to what your real purpose in life is all about—what you have really come into the world to be and to do. These were questions that few of us ever ask ourselves. We just fall into whatever agenda we are told is right for us which was exactly what I did for many years. I was starting increasingly not just to sense but to know that my main purpose in life was to help others be more fully themselves. But first I had to learn to become more fully who I really was!

By day seven, I was experiencing a profound connection with the rocks and stones and sand around me, and was feeling increasingly at one with my environment, with the stars and the cosmos. I didn't just *think* that all of life was interconnected and pulsating with intelligence. I was starting to *know* this to be so, and as this insight deepened, my experience of life being my friend and therefore always on my side, became ever clearer. I had had fleeting experiences of this in the past, especially when I was at Findhorn, but now I was having the direct *felt sense* of this truth. I saw that all of life had an aliveness and beauty and purpose, and that I was a tiny part of that beauty and purpose. Great eagles would circle in the sky overhead and I would somehow feel them communicating with me, reminding me that

I, too, was powerful. (Later, in my shamanic training, I learned that they were power animals.)

At one point, in the distance I saw a sandy-coloured mountain lion climb onto a rock. But I felt no fear. I felt connected to it and I thanked it for its sleekness and for revealing itself to me. I felt this lion right in the middle of my heart and felt such love for it that I know that if it had come closer I would not have felt any fear and it would have picked up my vibes and also seen me as its friend.

I wrote pages and pages in my notebook as those scales, which were always around me and which prevented me seeing life as it really was, began quietly falling away from me. My time with dear Brugh had prepared me for what essentially was a direct experience of my heart's knowing. And I realised that my heart knew a lot and felt a lot and that I needed to trust its intuitions much more. Yes, as I sat there on a rock in this vast desert, I saw that the purpose of life is that we celebrate it, that we feel grateful for its many blessings, which all too often we are so closed off from ourselves, so clenched up that we simply can't appreciate them. I saw that if we can't feel the beauty of nature around us, if we have no inkling of the majesty of our own core nature, we risk being drawn to go for substitute 'highs' to fill the hole, with activities like being busy, gathering possessions around us or doing things to give us kudos—make us feel important—or in my case, pursuing women. I sat on my rock in great peace and there was nothing more I needed. I realised that I had a teacher inside me as well, whose voice I needed to listen to and that this voice could best be heard when I was in a quiet space. I realised how large swathes of my life had been lived so unconsciously and so disconnectedly and that for many years I had had little to no connection with the worlds of my unconscious. The name of the game, I began to see, was to make more of who we are become conscious so that we can become increasingly aware of all those many inner agendas that constantly drive us. If we are unaware of them, they control us. If we become aware of them, we can have much more mastery over the way we live. Yes, this was a very powerful twelve days for me and it provided me with the inspiration many years later to teach retreats with names like 'Living Life as a Celebration', 'Living with Joy' and 'The Art of Living Courageously and Outrageously'.

A little postscript. Often the sublime and the ridiculous go hand in hand. The naughty-boy part of me had managed to smuggle in under my poncho a little calor-gas stove to heat some coffee, a packet of the best Jamaica coffee, a cup and some powdered milk. I treasured my coffee and if no food was available, I damn well wasn't going to be deprived of my early-morning caffeine shot.

I had decided to sleep on my first night near the top of an old volcano and in the morning, I woke up to find that my packet of coffee had vanished. There had been a lot of wind in the night and it must have been blown over the edge. I went to the edge and peered over it, and there on a little ledge some twelve feet down was my packet, winking at me! 'I'll climb down and get it,' I thought, but after climbing down about six feet and nearly losing my footing—had I done so I would have plunged hundreds of metres down into the abyss—I suddenly caught myself.

I imagined a headline in the papers: 'Spiritual seeker loses his life retrieving a pack of coffee'! Not without difficulty, I pulled myself back up to the top—and thanked my lucky stars that I had climbed down where I did: a few feet to my right, the rocks were very loose. I might have fallen to my death. Thank you once more, amazing grace! 'You can survive without your damn coffee,' I told myself. A new value system—or should I say my own innate value system—was slowly beginning to emerge out of the shadows and come alive inside me.

The last night of my vision quest, something extraordinary happened. I told you that I'd become interested in UFOs and what they might signify. As it was growing dark on this evening, I saw hundreds of little lights hovering over a mountaintop a couple of miles away. They moved in a curious formation, winking on and off. I felt they were dancing a little dance just for me. OK, I was light-headed, but this was no hallucination. I sat down and meditated and tried to sense if they had anything to tell me. They seemed to. 'Go and teach workshops on awakening the heart. Your heart is starting to awaken and by teaching love, you'll experience more love and if you do so, you will help yourself and help many people.' Whether these lights came from UFOs or from other sources, I'll never know, but within a month of that experience, I had fifteen people sitting around me in a circle and I was teaching the first of many workshops on 'Awakening the Heart'.

Chapter 17

Putting Down Roots

As a few people began to come to see me as clients (I was still in training, so no one as yet paid me), I started to have the sense that maybe I was destined to stay in California for a long time. Maybe forever. So it felt right to put down some roots; and what better way than to purchase a property. So, I sold another of my father's Kokoschka paintings and bought a lovely, funky little redwood house built on a hillside in the woods with about an acre of land around it. It had high ceilings just like my lovely Gloucestershire barn, and beautiful stained-glass windows, and was situated in a little cowboy kind of town in Marin County called Fairfax. At the bottom of the hill was a stream, which was quite deep just where I was, so when it was warm, I had my own natural little swimming pool. I loved this place.

The guy I bought the house from, Jim Rashik, who was half-Cherokee and who had built it all himself, had never had real money before, and blew it all on a first-class trip around the world. The result was that a few months later he had nowhere to live and so came back and lived in a tepee in the garden and his rent was to look after the house. As I am not at all mechanical and had been brought up in a world where if you needed a nail knocked into the wall, you called a little man in to do it for you, Jim served a very useful purpose!

But there was nothing 'little mannish' about dear Jim, and he became a good friend and an integral part of a little community that gradually grew up around this house. I converted the garage into a two-storey flat and my friend Diana came to live there with her boyfriend John, who was a musician, together with her ten-year-old daughter Euella.

Around this time, I met a delightful German man called Marcus True, who was also a psychotherapist, even loonier than me and a veritable psychedelic explorer and close friend of the eminent visionary psychiatrist Claudio Naranjo, whom I had the privilege of meeting and learning a lot from. Marcus—or Marcusian, as I called him (I always like giving my friends little nicknames)—also moved into my house and we became very close buddies. He loved his food and, very sadly, fifteen years later, he fell over and died of a massive stroke. I had left California by then but I still mourned him a lot as we had stayed in touch and were always very supportive of one another. He would always give me good advice regarding how best to deal with the various women who were still entering and exiting from my life.

I was also great friends with two acupuncturists, Dianne Siegelman and Yola Jerzykowski, and with my fellow trainees Chuck and Larry and Phil Brookes, and Avon Mattison who started a wonderful organisation called Pathways to Peace, and with Naomi Remen, a wholistic physician, and Elisabeth Kelly, and dear old British Patrick, who ran the café-bookstore downtown.

The wonderful thing about living in the Bay area in northern California at that time—from what I have heard, things have changed mightily in the last fifty years—was that I felt part of a very creative community. All my friends were wholistic practitioners of one kind or another, either therapists or bodyworkers or psychics or acupuncturists or artists or musicians or self-appointed gurus, and there was always a beautiful creative energy present that felt very fresh. We all felt we were counter-cultural visionaries and explorers at the 'leading edge' of a new emerging society, and life was very stimulating and exciting. I saw these new friends as my 'soul buddies' and there was so much genuineness in the way we all communicated. And we all lived near to one another. There existed a little triangle between Berkeley, which represented the mind, San Francisco, which represented the body, and Marin County, where I hung out, which stood for the heart. I by now was beginning very much to identify with being 'heart man'!

If any of us had something we needed to decide about, we'd organise a 'decision circle'. This consisted of our ringing six to eight friends and inviting them round for a meal and, when everyone was quietly gathered, we'd briefly share our dilemma with the group, with everyone listening in silence. After we'd spoken, we'd ask everyone in turn to air their perspective on the issue, with the rest of the group listening quietly. When everyone had had their say we would have an open discussion, and it always led to a resolution.

Also, people brought a good spirit—a real desire to help—to these meetings. Earlier I spoke about not needing to have any separation between life and work. What I also realised was that work didn't necessarily have to be *hard*; it could also be *soft* and it could be fun and playful. I always felt this sense of play when I taught my workshops on Awakening the Heart, and the more I did so, the more effective they became. This sense is still with me as strongly as ever in my work today.

I felt I wanted to learn more about Zen Buddhism, which I had read a bit about when I went up to Harrow but hadn't connected much with since, so I elected to spend two months living and working at the Tassajara Zen Centre, situated in Carmel Valley. It was renowned for its breadmaking and so as a voracious bread-devourer—give me delicious, newly-baked bread over champagne and caviar any day—I was not only able to indulge my piggyness, but also learn something about Zen meditation. As this training required that one get up very early in the mornings—and I always tended to be more of a night owl than an early bird—I would often fall asleep meditating, and never much appreciated it when the Zen Master would pass by and whack me on the shoulders with his stick to wake me. But

I greatly appreciated the essential simplicity and beauty of Zen and over the years, in a small way, I have tried to integrate its worldview into my work and life as a whole.

Perhaps the most important aspect of my stay at the Centre was that it gave me both the time and the space to explore the philosophy of Chuang Tzu, whom Suzuki, the great Japanese Zen scholar, declared to be the greatest of all the Chinese philosophers.

Chuang Tzu, who lived around 300 B.C., espoused simplicity and humility and a refusal to embrace the aggressivity and self-importance needed in order to get along in society, and which in today's world, has so run amok. 'I always wanted to be intoxicated by the wonder and power of nature,' he wrote, 'not to have to work to attain high office.' Legend has it that he declined to be prime minister to King Wei of Ch'u, saying that he much preferred 'to live the life of a tortoise wagging its tail in the mud than a dead one venerated in a golden casket in a king's ancestral shrine!'

His idea was that there is a natural goodness inside each of us that simply needed allowing out, as opposed to our always striving to be good, which the moralists taught was the way to an honourable life. For Chuang Tzu, such a life was not attained through the accumulation of virtue and merit but through *wu wei* or not doing; not living one's life according to consciously laid-down plans, which, as you can guess, resonated strongly with me. I loved his ideas of wholeness. What he said about the *fasting of the heart* or the need to 'empty ourselves' put my time with Brugh and my vision quest in a much broader and deeper context. It also confirmed in me the kind of empty space that I aspired to be in when I sat in front of clients, trying to be of some assistance to them. In his words:

> *We need to hear, but not just with the ear... we need to hear with the spirit, with our whole being... This hearing is not limited*

> *to any one faculty... Hence it demands the emptiness of all the faculties. And when the faculties are empty, then the whole being listens and only then can there be a direct grasp of what is right there before you which is nothing that can be understood with the mind. Fasting of the heart empties the faculties... It begets unity and freedom... If you can do this, you will be able to go among men in the world without upsetting them... If they will listen, sing them a song. If not, keep silent. Do not try to break down the door, just be there among them because there is nothing else for you to do but be one of them. And then you may have success. If you follow official methods, you will deceive. In this way no deception is possible...*

This so resonated with me, in particular the need to move beyond always seeing the world through the lens of our intellectual biases. It allowed me once more to ask myself the most important question of all and which over the last years I had been increasingly trying to engage with, namely:

How may I live more appropriately?

Essentially what I learned from Chuang Tzu was that an innate goodness of being and an understanding of balance and harmony lies inside each of us, and if we can let go and access it, as opposed to struggling to attain it, then what we need to do or not do at any time will always be made clear. So, if say, it is time to act, we will act, and how we will express our activities will be both spontaneous and appropriate.

If, on the other hand, we are always striving for something—even if it is to be 'good'—it has a kind of self-aggrandisement about it and its objective is annulled. For Chuang Tzu, the truly great person is not someone who has all the answers or who, all his life, labours to accumulate a great fund of virtue, but rather the person who has learned how to align themselves with the Tao, which I also see as being the intelligent, guiding, grace-bestowing presence in life. Perhaps it is also Hafiz's 'Friend'!

Perhaps if it senses that we are ready to be open to it, it may even seek us out!

To sum up, when we align ourselves with the Tao—which is not because we *effort* it, but because we *allow* it—we find ourselves in a state of balance and appropriateness, either keeping our mouths shut, if this is what is called for, or, conversely, saying and doing what is the right thing to say and do. If we can allow ourselves to live in this way, it gives us happiness and great inner peace and power.

We need, then, to realise that both happiness and goodness are innate to us and are not to be found either by our looking for them, or by following a particular programme. *Wu wei* is therefore not about our being passive but, on the contrary, about our choosing to live in a more 'surrendered' and responsible and aware way, where our ego selves are less and less running the show. It also enables us to live more expansively. Because we are no longer driven by the need to impress others or be important and self-righteous, we are much more able to 'be a space' for grace to flow through us and to inspire, illuminate and guide us.

Today, so much pain in the world is because we live in a culture where people are obsessed with the need to stand out and be successful and be a certain 'somebody' and to feel a failure if we can't do this. That was the world of my father and was certainly what I was taught and I used to suffer because I felt I didn't stand out enough and that my somebody-ness wasn't good enough!

Imagine if we had world leaders cognisant of these teachings. Imagine if President Xi of China had been steeped in this philosophy as opposed to in one of needing to be continually in control. Certainly, if more of us were steeped in this worldview, we'd be much happier and our planet would not be in the terrible shape it is in today.

The other interesting thing that I received as a result of my sojourn in this Zen world was that I became aware of a very important paradox, namely that from a Western viewpoint, there is always something 'wrong' with us; we are trained to recognise that we are not OK the way we are, and so we need to investigate where and how we became wounded and the best approach or approaches to try to heal ourselves, and then and only then can we approach OK-hood!

From a Buddhist perspective, however, the scenario is very different. It recognises that we are the way we are and that there is an OK-ness about it. We don't need 'fixing' so much as we need to come to realise that the reason why we suffer is because our attitudes are wrong and we don't live a balanced life primarily because we have lost our connection to the Tao—or, in most instances, never linked up with it in the first place.

In other words, we are always striving to manipulate everything; always trying to engineer positive outcomes and avoid negative ones, always trying to acquire those things which we think will make us happy, but which Chuang Tzu assures us not only don't do so, but on the contrary, can serve further to destabilise us. Thus, we are continually clenched and find it hard to be fully present, and the result is that our innate goodness gets squashed down and not allowed space to emerge. Many of us also live a lot in the past and we fear the future and this also stands in the way of our connection with the Tao, which best occurs when we allow ourselves to exist in present time, or as my dear Ram Dass put it, 'To be in the now!' *Therefore, no matter how much psychotherapy we do, to expect that we can be happy and live harmoniously if our lifestyles are based on continually consuming and striving and trying to impress others with how wonderful we are, is like believing that cows can jump over the moon!*

1978, the year I turned thirty-three, was an important year for me. A group of us decided to organise a conference in Florence, where the first Renaissance was born, to celebrate what we called the second Renaissance that we saw happening in the world at that time. We called it the Florence Congress of the New Age and it was an enormous undertaking that required many months of planning.

We invited some of the foremost visionary thinkers alive on the planet at that time, and I had the great honour to become friendly with the great Buckminster Fuller, mathematician, poet, scientist, philosopher, architect and creator of the famous geodesic dome. Like so many truly eminent beings, 'Bucky', as he liked to be known, was extremely humble and gracious and you could sense that the Tao was with him. He was always ready to give his time to listen to the eccentric rantings of this young man who, as he was starting to find his creative feet, grow more confident and feel his way around in the world a bit more, would sometimes get very non-Chuang Tzu-y and a bit big for his boots.

A few months later, I took myself on a two-week retreat with the eminent mythologist Joseph Campbell, the author of the famous books *The Hero's Journey, Myths to Live By* and *The Hero with a Thousand Faces*. This was very important for me. Like my dear Brugh, he too was someone who followed his heart. He told us students the story of how when he was an undergraduate, he was in a café having lunch and noticed a couple sitting near him with their son. He observed that the father was haranguing his son to finish the food on his plate, which the son clearly didn't want to. The mother intervened.

'Aw honey,' she said to her husband, 'Can't you see that he doesn't want to eat it?'

This triggered something deep within the husband, whose face turned purple as he proceeded to stand up and scream despairingly to the whole restaurant that 'I've never ever done anything I wanted to do.'

Obviously, Campbell decided, the man has been caught in the system and has spent his whole life doing a job he disliked. And from that moment on, exactly as with Brugh, he decided that he would only ever do what his heart told him to. 'You must be willing to get rid of the life you've planned,' he told us, 'so as to have the life that is waiting for you'; or, as I would put it later, the story that our soul has in store for us, or in Chuang Tzu's lingo a way of living where you feel aligned with the Tao. One of the exercises Joseph Campbell made us do—and I've also used it with my students over the years—was to draw a map of our lives where we mark out the important areas where key things happened for us, and then continue this map into our future and write down what we see occurring.

What was interesting about this exercise was that I predicted that I would return to England, continue teaching, go from strength to strength in my work, meet the woman whom Gwennie earlier had predicted I would, as well as write a book, and that I would live well into my eighties. All these things have come to pass—only I've so far published two books not one—and as I am seventy-seven now and feel I am still going strong-ish, I have no reason to believe I won't hang around on this mortal coil for a good while longer.

I sometimes think that our 'future, fully awake or fully realised us' already exists in a different space/time reality, and is continually broadcasting intimations of itself back to the 'us' in our present time, and so could be said to be always trying to pull us up towards it—if we can only be a space to allow this 'raising of ourselves' to occur!

Put slightly differently, could we perhaps argue that not only are we potentially being pulled back into our past as a result of our old unhealed wounds or 'unfinished business', but at the same time we are also being 'propelled forward' or 'wheeled upwards' by our future self, and that the more we heal and let go of our past, the less resistance we will put up, and the more powerfully we will allow ourselves to be embraced by our future!

'A hero,' Joseph Campbell told us, 'is someone who has given his or her life in service to something bigger than themselves.' I thought back to the Castaneda teachings, where Don Juan tells Carlos that 'the spiritual warrior is the one who is not afraid to be themselves,' and that only when we truly become ourselves do we tune in to our deeper human collective identity. The true spiritual warrior, then, is both the hero and the future human, and the one living in harmony with the Tao, and thus the name of the game is surely this: how do we live in such a way as to allow this deeper dimension of ourselves to increasingly come forward and proclaim itself?

I've tried to live my life out of the asking of this question...

There was no doubt that here in California, I was encountering a new species of human being; I was connecting with men and women who were as different from the kind of people I had known in my past as chalk was from cheese. Essentially, the difference was that they were more awake, their hearts were more open and their minds were more illuminated, and if you are privileged enough to come into contact with such people, something deeper also gets ignited inside you. Just as in tennis, if you play with someone who is much better than you it allows you to 'raise' your game, so the same kind of 'raising' occurs when you are around people who are increasingly trying to live as heroes or spiritual warriors.

I am not exactly sure just how the wonderful Larry Spiro came into my life. I think I had been invited to teach a course at a centre in Berkeley that he had started. Anyhow, he first became my friend, then my mentor and later my soul guide and psychotherapist, and he not only helped me mature as a man more than anyone else, but he also set a whole new context for the way I worked.

So, while I owe a huge debt to psychosynthesis, vision quests, Tom Yeomans, EST trainings and Brugh Joy, etc, no one has been more instrumental than Larry Spiro in helping me understand how, in working with someone, one can assist them to heal their emotional wounds and at the same also draw closer to the divinity inside them. He not only helped me integrate Buddhist with Western psychology and thus inspired me to take my psychotherapy work to whole new levels, but he took me much deeper into my own healing process.

Larry was big. Nearly six and a half feet, stooping, a little pot belly, a bushy beard and a receding hairline. And he was one hell of a big soul. He was a true mystic. He was a Buddhist practitioner, a Kabbalah scholar, a serious meditator and a transpersonal psychotherapist; but above all he was a deeply loving human being, and I loved him a lot and got to work with him very intensively over many years, later on often popping back from England to California to see him. Larry was humble and gracious and he stood behind so many different people's success. I have opened so many books on themes of spirituality and consciousness where, foremost among the acknowledgements, would be Larry's name.

I once spent six weeks in Jerusalem with him. It was quite an adventure. He had gone there to study with his Kabbalah teacher and I wanted to work with him, so we rented a flat together. Every morning we would have a two-hour session, and then, when he would go off to his teacher, I would go out and explore the different religions. I would go to the mosque wearing a Yasser Arafat-style headband; I'd put on a skullcap when I'd go and pray in the synagogues, but my favourite place and where I felt most at home—because I so loved the music and the smell of incense—was the Russian Orthodox church.

For many people, connecting to all these different traditions would be confusing. It wasn't for me. For me, the important thing was being able to access the sacred and it didn't matter in what form it came, whether it was to be found inside a synagogue, a temple or a church—or, for that matter, on a mountaintop or in a forest. What particularly helped my own awakening process was if I entered spaces that had already been sanctified, and so much of my stay in Israel evolved around my discovering where these places were.

There was something very beautiful and noble about the Israeli people—I found them open, conscious, alive and very gracious—and I felt very at home in that country. How important it is always to separate the people of a country from its leadership and politics. I met an Israeli girl there who was a captain in the army and we would often have coffee together and have fascinating conversations. She was a deep meditator and I was touched by her warrior spirit. One day she told me that if she wanted to, she could kill me in twelve seconds. 'Wow, I hope that will not be necessary, Zahava,' I said.

Larry, as I write this, I don't know if you are dead or alive. I've tried to reach you via your email over the last five years, but I don't get any reply. The last thing I heard from you fifteen years ago was that you had married an Israeli woman and had gone back to live in Israel. Wherever you are, in this world or in the next, I wish you well and I thank you very deeply for all you have meant to me. You've been the dearest and wisest of friends. You've played such an enormous part in helping me straighten out my life.

Perhaps the central part of my living in California, where I had now become a resident and was starting to have a proper psychotherapy practice, was my becoming a co-founder, with five other friends, Barry McWaters, Susan Campbell, Barbara Marx Hubbard, Naomi Emmerling and my great friend Marcus, of what we named the Institute for the Study of Conscious Evolution (ISCE). It was located in a large house in San Francisco that Barry and Susan had recently purchased.

These were very exciting times; this institute was a platform that reflected all our collective visions, and it was a very great honour to play a small part in its emergence. We attracted some very eminent luminaries to be part of our organisation and sometimes I would find myself working side by side with some of my great spiritual heroes. We had a programme on consciousness research, on science and consciousness, on conscious relationships, ecology, climate change, personal and planetary transformation, studying how communities worked, transpersonal psychology, corporate transformation, parapsychology and what constituted enlightenment or self-realisation. Pretty forward-looking given that we're talking about the early eighties!

We managed to achieve accreditation and so students who worked with us did courses that contributed to their BA or MA degrees and in effect we were a kind of mini university. At ISCE, I taught courses on personal and planetary transformation, on relationships (yes, my friend, we teach best what we need to learn!) and on the psychology of healing the heart, but I still felt—indeed, I still feel today—very much the eternal student!

It was a particular honour to have become a friend of Barbara Marx Hubbard's as in every fibre of her being, she embodied the 'new woman' or the next step of evolution for women. She was deliciously and gently feminine yet also had a powerful masculine drive, a big, big loving heart coupled with a ferociously brilliant mind. I greatly respected her.

As I write, I have her book *Conscious Evolution* in front of me. Written over forty years ago, the ideas in it are as fresh as if they had emerged today. Barbara was one of the most courageous women I have ever met, and, later in her life, way before the idea ever occurred to Hillary Clinton, she campaigned to become the first female president of the United States. Wow. If that had ever happened, I tell you, America would not be in the perilous state it is in today.

I also became very close to Barry and Susan, who, both older and more experienced than me, became important role models. Sadly, their marriage broke up after a few years, and Susan and

I lost touch and Barry passed away. She went on to write many books ranging from how to 'do relationships' to how to succeed in business, to how to live a creative life, and we got in touch again a few years ago. For me Susan is also a terrific model of how an evolved woman needed to be. Now over eighty, she still looks youthful and works as hard as ever teaching all her courses and doing her online 'salons'. I am full of admiration for her as a human being.

At about that time, someone else came into my life who has continued to be a very dear friend to this day, and that someone was David Lorimer. When I first met him, he was a schoolmaster at Winchester and had just written a book on near-death experiences and was touring California to promote it. A mutual friend suggested he contact me.

David came and stayed a week with me, and we hit it off at once and our friendship over the years has grown from strength to strength. He is one of the most positive people I've ever known and, like me, was very close to Sir George Trevelyan. And also like Sir George, I have never heard David ever say a negative word about anybody.

Immensely erudite on many different subjects and author of many books, including one on the philosophy of Prince Charles entitled *Radical Prince*, he was a terrific example for me of how to integrate the world of his old school Eton with the higher echelons of consciousness. He later rented my cottage in Gloucestershire for four years and it was such a joy to have such a lovely human being live so close to me. He was a great runner and we would often do our keep-fit training sessions together. He had recently become a student of the Bulgarian spiritual master Peter Deunov and was learning Bulgarian in order to translate his books into English (that's the kind of person David was). His father was so angry at this that he decided to cut him off. David accepted this with equanimity.

He met his second wife a few years ago, and they fell in love when he came to teach at her spiritual community in France. It is a beautiful love story and it is fitting that it should happen to such a pure and beautiful man.

I had recently been inspired by attending a three-day conference created to honour the eightieth birthday of Joseph Campbell, and David and I decided to put on something similar in London to honour Sir George, who was also about to turn eighty. To our amazement, over two thousand people signed up to be part of our event and the problem was that we'd only hired a space for four hundred. Again the helping forces came to the rescue and the Vegetarian Society, which had booked the hall for two thousand, found that only four hundred punters showed up and so we conveniently shifted venues and the day was a great success.

Chapter 18

Intimate Relationships

I think I need to devote an entire chapter to exploring perhaps the most challenging and problematic area of my life, namely, my relationships with women. Indeed, this part of my life and the pain and struggles I often went through, has constituted a very integral part of my spiritual initiations, as trying to heal my patterns with women has required I not only do a lot of delving into my own personal Shadow side, but also into the Shadow side of Western man as a whole. As I said earlier, I often felt that I carried wounds that were not just 'personal to me' but pertained to splits in Western man's psyche as a whole.

I am also convinced that my ability as a psychotherapist to be intuitive and tender with my female clients (at least I hope they have seen me that way) has emerged out of my own personal struggles. If you remember, I shared with you earlier how, because of my mother's rigidity combined with her always being taken away from me by my father just when I would be feeling comfortable with her, I grew up with a fear of being rejected. Either I would reject a woman before I felt she would reject me or, conversely, they'd get in there first and kick me out! I also tended primarily to be drawn towards ice-queeny, drama-queeny, overtly sexy types, the femmes fatales who couldn't see the real me and wouldn't go deep and didn't know how to love or give of themselves. The result was that with many of the women I was with, I would not feel my soul being fed, and thus I often felt very dissatisfied. I guess, however, that at some level, I also enjoyed the dramas and the highs and lows of the chase. In some weird way, it perhaps served to balance the rather intense inner life that I was also attempting to live.

It was only a bit later, however, that I realised that in my relationships I was actually getting exactly what I was asking for. If the women were not seeing me for who I was, I was doing exactly the same thing with them, which was not offering my soul either, and I realised that we need to be much more clear as to what our unconscious intentions actually are!

So yes, my dear feminist friends who may be reading this, you can be aghast and well you might be, and in no way am I trying to defend myself. It was as if all the love, care and sensitivity I often found so difficult to give the women I would be in relationship with, would get poured into my female clients, as there it was safe and I know that I genuinely wanted to help them. Of course none of my therapy clients or the people who attended my courses knew what went on in the secret life of this externally very caring and responsible psychotherapist and transformation teacher who was quietly helping people to live happily and wholistically! This all said, in my defence, I was never abusive or a sex pest or forced myself on women or was one of those abominably pervy gropers. I couldn't stand those hideous behaviours and always wondered what men thought they could get out of it other than encouraging revulsion towards them! I was also never nasty and I never took advantage of my position of power to manipulate female clients. In my work there was always integrity. I took pride in being very professional. Enormous damage can be done by therapists abusing their positions of power and over the years I have had women come to me who had been abused by their psychotherapists and I always did my very best to support them.

As I look back at myself at this stage in my life, I find it interesting to observe how some parts of me were really becoming quite evolved, while other dimensions of me continued to exist at Neanderthal levels. I think I couldn't seem to direct the spiritual energies that I was certainly drawing into myself—or you could say, was starting to generate inside myself—into the part or parts of myself that concerned themselves with love and relationships. Those areas of myself had their defences all around. Perhaps my ego, which seemed to have taken up its residence there, was saying to me, 'Well, you are taking the juice out of my existence in so many areas of your life, so I'll be damned if I'm going to disappear from taking up my residence in, and thus being the prime motivator in your love life!'

There were, however, a few women who, during my time in California, I really tried to do my best with and give both my heart and soul to and I want to tell you briefly about two of them. I fell very much in love with a girl called Sandra Wilson. Although she was only in her early twenties, her thick hair was starting to turn grey *à la* the folk singer Emmylou Harris, which made her all the more mysterious and beautiful, and what particularly bonded us was that she had had a background that in many ways was not dissimilar to mine—she was also a bit of a trust-fund hippie and didn't need to work.

I loved Sandra for her great sweetness of being and innocence, and I felt very comfortable with her. At one level, we were both little rich kids (although I was becoming decidedly unricher by the day) and we found solace in each other's arms.

However, like all of us, she had a strong dark side, and I learned from my journals that she actually gave me a pretty rough time and that as she had never had any psychotherapy herself, a lot of her issues got projected onto me. In addition to her becoming increasingly aware of my many faults (not too hard to detect), which she found it difficult to desist from continually reminding me of, things began seriously to unravel when she became pregnant and insisted on getting an abortion, which I didn't want and which greatly upset me. In those days, 'proper girls' didn't have babies when they were unmarried and Sandra was a proper girl, and I, at this stage of my life, had no thought of getting married.

The result was that to my great sorrow, instigated by her, we gradually floated out of each other's lives. I felt very hurt. We didn't reconnect until many years later, when I found out quite by chance that she lived on a remote island and I got her phone number and rang her. She would have been in her mid-sixties. She had never married. 'I wish I had had your child,' she told me, 'I live alone on this island.' I felt sad as well. Our child would have been middle-aged today.

My other great passion at this time was an English woman called Sofia Stainton whom I had met on a trip back to London. Sofia could not have been more different. Full of spark and sexiness and chutzpah, she was so imperious that my nickname for her was 'Madam'. I adored her. Tall, dark-haired, beautiful and with fiery brown eyes, Sofia was also on a spiritual path and was also very much 'out there' in the world as she worked as an interior designer and did up the houses of the rich and famous—exactly the kind who in the past I used to hobnob with. Thus, she embraced both my old and my new worlds and satisfied a lot of my criteria. Sometimes she'd come and stay a few weeks with me in California, and other times I would fly back to London and stay in her flat, or she'd come down to Gloucestershire. I always kept my barn unrented as I liked popping back from time to time for a bit of contrast. I remember Brugh telling me that 'consciousness loves contrast' and he was absolutely right.

My relationship with Sofia was one of the most tumultuous and passionate I have ever had and it awoke powerful feelings of huge ecstasy and terrible agony. One moment she'd tell me things like—I quote from my journal—'You are my source of love energy. I love you more than I've ever loved anyone and feel I cannot do without you,' and the next moment I'd be pushed away and accused of every sin under the sun. Again: Shadow projection. She had had a distant, cold father and so, like me, had problems around intimacy. I heard on the grapevine that all the men she'd dated in the past eventually had got cast aside. But despite a lot of castings-out—and I also did my bit as on certain occasions I felt I couldn't take this anymore—I managed to hang in there because I was so besotted by her and knew that each time I would start moving away—which I often did just to protect my vulnerable heart—she would move towards me again. Continual exhausting games of push and pull. But we managed to hang in there together for four years and both of us were faithful.

Yes, dearest Sofia was for me the archetypal femme fatale. One moment I felt I loved her so much that I would die without her, the next moment I would say (again a diary quote): 'Thank God I am on my own now. Sofia drives me crazy.' I found I'd written down in my diary the quote—I don't know where it is from—that 'the pain of love is the dynamite that breaks open the heart even if it be as hard as a rock'! Well, our time together was also a kind of seminar on the heart, albeit of a very different kind, as my heart got broken many times. With Sofia I discovered the truth of the words of the Sufi teacher Pir Vilayat Khan when he told me that 'if the heart is to open, it first has to break!'

I had my first MDMA or ecstasy trip with her, and I've never forgotten that experience.

If overused or used unwisely, this psycho-chemical may certainly be unfriendly to our brain cells. But like all psychedelics, if utilised wisely, it can have an important purpose, and today a lot of research is going on with regard to MDMA's potential effectiveness for treating victims of trauma. Certainly, it temporarily opens the doors of perception into a whole new reality of unconditional love. And that was exactly what it did for Sofia and me, and those eight hours that we spent lying in the warm forest around my little home, entangled in each other's arms and only seeing the divinity in one another, are indelibly imprinted in my heart.

In Aldous Huxley's book *The Doors of Perception*, he suggests that the reason why psychedelics are important is that most of us have difficulties both attaining and sustaining higher states of awareness, as something within us operates to close off to them, and thus 'we know only what comes through the reducing valve and therefore what is consecrated as "real" by the local language'. And basically, what all psychedelics do is temporarily overrule this inner reductor, thus enabling us to have a sneak preview into higher realities or into how our lives might be if we were to live in greater harmony with our true nature.

However, we must always remember that they only offer us a peep into eternity, allowing us to realise that higher-order realities really *do* exist; they do not enable us to live at that level. There is all the difference between temporarily accessing grace and living in it all the time. Therefore, while MDMA certainly opened Sofia and me to the higher echelons of love for a certain length of time, sadly it did not heal the wounds inside both of us that made us vulnerable and fearful of that deeper love that we both so yearned for.

I basically lived in California and Sofia lived in London. Her work was in England and I was a Californian resident and gradually we found ourselves seeing less and less of each other. I think we both found that we just couldn't avoid our dramas and they were getting too exhausting and were no longer enhancing our lives but were starting to cramp them. Eventually Sofia decided to end things, and while I felt very, very upset, I also realised it was for the best, as I certainly was beginning to pay too high a price for those moments of joy and ecstasy which were now becoming few and far between. She was a wonderful human being in so many ways and I learned a lot from her, but I think in retrospect that I somehow lacked the ability to stay in my power with her. I don't think I was necessarily wimpy anymore but there was still a certain 'je ne sais quoi' that was needed to properly handle her, that I felt I did not quite possess! Or that's what she told me.

We moved out of each other's lives and I heard that Sofia married a very young Australian IT consultant. I met him briefly and he didn't seem that fantastic to me. I was reminded of the young man in Conan Doyle's book *The Lost World*. He was spurned by the lady he loved who asked him to go out and do something courageous. 'Then I can really admire you,' she told him. So he volunteered to join Professor Challenger's party and they went and discovered a lost world full of prehistoric animals, i.e., very Jurassic Park-ish and the young man has an extraordinary time, battles these monsters, saves the lives of everyone and when he returns, eager to let his sweetheart know of his heroic exploits, is bereft to find that in his absence she's gone and married a little balding ginger-haired man with a moustache.

'So what did you do?' our disconsolate hero asks him. 'Have you saved lives, battled dragons? What is your profession?' 'I am a trainee bank clerk, sir,' the little mustachioed man tells him! Or I think he said something along those lines.

Sofia's marriage lasted a few years and then they drifted apart. Many years later I heard that she was very ill with cancer and then died very suddenly. I attended her memorial service and it was a very sad occasion as many old memories came flooding back and I realised I really missed her. At that service, I met up again with Annunciata whom I had been so fond of all those years ago when I'd just left Oxford. She was there in all her loveliness but I found we no longer spoke the same language. How bizarre life can sometimes be.

Chapter 19

Returning from the Mountaintop

I was now almost forty and I had been seeing clients and teaching workshops and groups for quite a few years. I'd established myself as a Californian—had even, as I said, managed to get a green residency card by somehow proving that I could do something no other American person could do (I was always a good wangler). I had found my tribe and had a wide circle of friends. My life was working well.

However, I was gradually becoming aware of a little voice inside me that was whispering to me that my Californian adventure may be coming to an end, and that if my life was to be lived more in service to my fellow human beings, then the place where this could best happen would be back home in England, as that is where the people lived who I felt most needed what I felt I now had to offer. There were plenty of Serges in California, most much better qualified than me. Indeed, we were a dime a dozen. But not so in England. Perhaps, to use Joseph Campbell's lingo, it was now time to come down off the mountaintop and return to my roots, to bring back with me into my old world what I had learned over the last decade in my new one. And I felt I had learned a lot.

I felt I had a duty—no, actually, a calling—not just to sit atop the mountain in the sun, but to try to help those who are stuck in the darkness. I was also envisioning myself as more than just a psychotherapist. I was now seeing myself as an educator and a change agent, realising that it was not just the souls of individuals that needed healing—although that was my main focus—but also the soul of society. People back home needed educating in the art of living more wholistically. They needed to learn some of the things that I had been picking up over the last decade. As Thomas Moore put it in his book *Care of the Soul*, 'The great malady of our times and implicated in all our troubles and affecting us individually and socially, is loss of soul.' My role, I felt, was to be not only a heart man but also a soul man! I felt I had a calling to try to inject my rather soulless old world with some of the soulfulness I felt I had gradually acquired in my new one.

This also tallied with my idea that transformation needed to happen within the world, not by our escaping it. I felt my calling was, in my little way, to bring 'heaven down to earth', not the other way around. In other words, the game was not to run away from civilisation and its discontents and go and live in a monastery or complete some initiation in a temple far, far away from the madding crowd, but, on the contrary, to do one's 'spiritual training' in the middle of all the craziness of modern-day living and use the many problems it served up as catalysts to help us mature our humanity. And I wanted to help others understand this.

OK, I admit that there were still vestiges of Lord Snooty inside me. Probably always will be. Sofia had often brought him out of his closet. But perhaps this was no bad thing, as many of the people I might be working with back home could be Lord or Lady Snootys; so I was not only well informed about the kinds of problems that might come up for them, but I had a side that I could, if necessary, bring to the table so they wouldn't feel uncomfortable with me.

However, for me to say that my problems with women were now all solved and I no longer projected my issues onto them or was no longer so vulnerable would not be to tell the truth. I wish I could say that I had brought Chuang Tzu-ism into my relationships, but it would be a lie and I knew there was a great deal more work to be done in this area of my life.

But what I *could* say was that over the last eleven years, I had done a lot of growing up. That desperate sense of chaos and feeling lost that I had felt just before going to America, had completely disappeared. I put this down to the fact that I had found my purpose, and that purpose I likened to a ship that had both a tall strong mast and a solid rudder. Even if strong storms lay in front of me—and they did—I was not going to capsize. Something inside me had grown stronger. It felt like a new self that understood the meaning of sacredness was gradually being birthed inside me. No matter what hassles might assail me in my personal life, they were not going to affect my professional life. And I have to say that they didn't. In fact, often if I happened to be going through some personal crisis, my work with individuals became more sensitive.

Well, I put 'Operation Return Home' into action and within a few weeks I had sold my lovely little redwood house to a delightful family who I knew would derive as much pleasure from it as I did. I had a big farewell party, inviting all my friends and giving away bits of stuff I no longer needed, including my lovely old open-roofed VW Beetle that had done me so well over the years, together with my hi-fi equipment and television. Then, hey presto, I found myself on the plane bound once more for England and back in my old barn with its familiar high roof and old beams and the mezzanine gallery where I slept. It had always been a special friend to me and I felt that it was pleased to see me back home again!

In coming back to England, however, two problems immediately came up. Firstly, I had really worked hard to create a new life for myself in California and I never realised how nourishing this was until it was no longer around me. I also missed being part of our Institute. Yes, I was friendly with everyone in my village, but I had yet again to confront the ghastly world of class and the British stiff upper lip, where everything was always so 'nice' and where conversation was often so superficial.

On paper our village was a community. In reality, we were nothing approaching it. We were a bunch of individuals who each had their own house and preferred being in the company of those whom they felt were 'their kind'! Although I became chairman of our Hampnett council for many years and did my best to integrate the different segments of our village, in reality it was no good. As my friend Coralie pointed out to me: 'Serge, you've got to accept it. There are chiefs with a big feather headdress and braves with only one feather and they each live in their own world.' After all those years of loosening up in California, the stiffness I encountered seemed all the stiffer, and once or twice I found myself asking myself if I had perhaps been a bit impetuous in deciding to come home.

A further problem also came up: the problem of money. As you know, I had never taken much care over this area of my life. The days of trust-fund hippiedom were fast coming to an end. I had always been adroit at getting my trustees to advance me money whenever I needed it, and although I never lived extravagantly and always ate simply, the money spent on my various trainings and conferences, and travelling back to England and then to Switzerland to see my mother, which I would do every Christmas, all added up and the cupboard was getting a bit bare. I needed to do some rapid earning.

But how? All I could do was what I was trained to do, and I had been away in California for so long that nobody in England knew about me. I remember sitting in the garden and thinking, 'O my Gawd. If I don't get something positive together, I am going to have to sell my beautiful property.'

But again, the helping presence was not going to desert me. I knew lovely Brenda, the head of the College of Psychic Studies, from the old Wrekin Trust days when I lived in London, and before returning, I'd asked her if she could arrange a workshop for me on the topic of Awakening the Heart.

She did so and, arriving at the college on the Friday evening, I was amazed to find that nearly thirty people had enrolled; and after the weekend I suddenly had eight new clients who wanted to do ongoing therapy with me, plus a couple of people who volunteered to help me organise my workshops, and within the space of a few months, my work had magically taken off and I was teaching courses all over the place; I also found myself being asked to teach in Sweden, France and Switzerland. There was also a festival that had been going on for years, called the Festival for Body, Mind and Spirit, and I happened to know the guy who ran it, and so I was invited not only to lecture at it but also to introduce all the speakers. So, from a networking position, I couldn't be in a healthier place and I found I had so many clients that I needed to rent a small studio flat in London.

All was going very well when, six months later, I decided to return to California for a few weeks, as I'd been asked to give some lectures. I also wanted to see Iris, an old girlfriend who was a musician, and many of my other good friends. However, on arriving back, I experienced yet another bout of a high fever that I'd been having from time to time over the last few months. It would hit me for a couple of days and knock me out, and then go and I'd be fine.

But this time it was different. It wasn't fine. The fever hit me but it didn't go away. In fact, my temperature spiralled up to 105 and I was becoming delirious. As I lay sprawled out on Iris's sofa, all my wholistic friends clucked around congratulating me, saying, 'Have some more wheatgrass and carrot juice, you are eliminating toxins, how wonderful.'

But I was worried. I knew this was something bad. I remember my old friend Rick Carlson, who'd written a book on wholistic medicine, saying to me that if you were *really* ill, then you needed to go to one of those stethoscope-carrying, white-jacketed doctors, not a homeopath or acupuncturist. And I felt I was really ill. I remember screaming out, 'To hell with your bloody carrot juices, get me to a bloody hospital and a real doctor who drinks whisky not apple juice.'

I remember an ambulance coming for me and having to rummage for my insurance documents in my delirious state. By a stroke of luck, or very amazing grace, just before leaving for this trip I had taken out private health insurance for the first time in my life. God only knows what would have happened if I hadn't produced those papers. This was America. Probably I'd have been left on the floor to die!

Well, I was rushed to hospital and I remember all sorts of tubes being put in me to help me to breathe, and here I refer to my journal written at the time: 'I don't know what the hell is wrong with me but I know I have to be brave and find a deep core of strength inside me.' This was just as well, as the doctor in charge of me said, I quote: 'We have just done an X-ray of your lungs. You have six shadows there. They're about a quarter of an inch in size. We are not ruling out tuberculosis, AIDS or cancer.'

Fucking hell. We were learning round that time that AIDS was not just prevalent in the gay community; many heterosexual people were also getting it and in the months before I left California, I had not always been too careful.

It was eventually discovered that I had a rare disease called histoplasmosis, caused by inhaling spores created by parrot droppings. I must have caught it as a result of spending so much time with Daphne, the mother of my friend Chris Dreyfus, who lived opposite me in the country, and whose house was full of macaw parrots, which she bred. It was ironic that it was also Daphne who had suggested to me, just before I left, that I should take out health insurance! And I am very glad I did as I needed to stay in hospital for three months and be treated by intravenous doses of a drug called amphotericin B, nicknamed 'ampho-terrible' because of its dreadful side effects, which would send me into convulsions.

Well, it was back into Shadowland again. Big time. I obviously needed further purification. As I was too ill to read or watch television, my dark side—the part of ourselves we like to repress, don't want to see—came up very, very powerfully and began to parade itself in front of me, and I had no choice but to look much more deeply at aspects of myself that needed more work doing to them: my selfishness and my narcissism, my vanity and timidity, my capacity to be manipulative, my fears around intimacy and where I still resisted standing fully in my deeper sacred self.

It was horrible. For weeks it felt as if anything good about me had been well and truly sucked out of me, and that I was a terrible human being who the helping forces had totally abandoned and the Tao had moved away from me in disgust. I felt very afraid and very alone, but luckily my psychological training allowed me to be aware that I was facing what was known in the trade as a 'dark night of the soul' crisis, one of whose characteristics is that we feel completely abandoned by anything good or virtuous. I remembered a quotation by Thomas à Kempis from his small book *The Imitation of Christ:*

> *Grace is given to us to train us and is removed to test us.*

This was another goddamn test! As such, I had a perspective on what I was going through. I knew that if I could take my pain right into the flame inside my heart, and feel it deeply, that it would begin slowly to burn away. I also knew that what I was going through was all grist in the mill in my journey to become a more human, human being, and I chose to 'go with' my process and do my best to not resist it. It made me sad though that, during this time, Moonie never thought of coming out and visiting me. I guess she felt I'd grown away from her, which I suppose, having lived all those years in California and only seeing her at Xmas, I had.

Well, I made it—just, although the doctor told me that for a week, before they realised what was wrong and so knew the right drugs to treat me, I had been in a pretty precarious state. When I eventually left the hospital three months later, my insurance having paid a bill for several hundred thousand dollars, I was skin and bone and weighed exactly half my normal weight. I was also much lighter psychically. I smiled to myself. I could have put on a good show as a breatharian! I'd had a powerful spiritual initiation and I felt I'd come through.

There is one amusing little story that I can't help including.

I needed to attend the hospital as an outpatient for six weeks after I had left, and three times a week sit for a few hours and have a drug drip fed into me. It was the same powerful medication that many AIDS patients were also having, and someone told me that it could be a bit dangerous if the guys being treated for this disease found out that I didn't have it. 'I have heard stories of gay men stabbing others with their infected needles,' I was told. Wow.

So just to be on the safe side, I thought I'd better try to look gay—or rather, how I thought gay men looked. I had long floppy blond hair, well thickened by having recently had more transplants—I've always been a bit obsessed about my receding hairline—and as I anyway like gaily coloured clothes, I arrived the first day at the outpatient clinic attired in a pink shirt, light green trousers and a yellow jacket with a big, scarlet-spotted handkerchief sticking out of my top pocket. (I'm a big top-pocket-handkerchief man.)

As this apparition entered the room, I noticed all attention focussing on me, and one or two gasps. I stood out like a sore thumb as I was standing there in an ocean of men all similarly attired in black T-shirts, tight black leather trousers, bullet crew-cut haircuts and big moustaches, absolutely *à la* Freddie Mercury.

Fucking hell, I thought. I've bloody well gone and done it. I'll surely get pricked by someone for this attire. I could not have been more wrong. It was the most supportive environment, of the sweetest and gentlest guys who welcomed me into their little community, although one person did ask me why I had come thus attired and I decided to come clean. 'Well,' he said after he'd heard the story of my fears, 'you need to get your decades right. Us gay men haven't dressed like that since the days of Somerset Maugham!' I guess he was right. I became good buddies with him and another guy, and when I later returned to England, we stayed in touch. Sadly, both died within the year. AIDS had only just started and they didn't then have the drugs they have now, which enable people with the disease to live a full life. However, one of the gifts of this episode in my life was that it enabled me to get close to a community of people whom up until then I had had few dealings with, and the result was that I was able to release some rather large chunks of homophobia that I realised still lingered on from my past.

My dear old friend Yola, an acupuncturist, very generously let me stay and recuperate in her guest house. I felt so grateful that I had many wonderful friends who were always there to support me. When I left, Yola gave me a beautiful old Thai Buddha that I greatly treasure and which welcomes all visitors who come into my house today. While I was staying with her I also met a good friend of hers, Pragito, whom I slowly got to know and become very fond of.

This was a very different type of woman from the ones I'd primarily been with, so obviously I must have burned out 'something' during my illness. Pragito was not her real name—which was Liana—it was a name given her by her then spiritual Master, a man called Osho, who had been a very controversial guru in the seventies and eighties.

The wonderful thing about being with Pragito, who was from Chile, was that there was no drama. I think I'd drama'd myself out with Sofia. She was pretty *and* she was soulful. And she had a big, loving heart; she didn't play games, and she was able to see the real me. And I think I was able to start seeing the 'real her' and offer her some of my soul. I felt loved for who I was and so didn't feel a need to try so hard or always feel I was walking on eggshells as I so often had felt with dear Sofia and, to a lesser extent, with Sandra.

That was so important. And so, healing. I began to experience the healing power of love at first hand, and during the months that we were together—as with Sophia, it was a transatlantic affair as her home was in California and I was now back in England—my happy heart was increasingly coaxed out of hiding.

Over the months, however, we gradually drifted apart as it became clear that my world now was the world of being back in England, and English ways and customs were not Pragito's reality and some British rituals, around, for example, 'smart' dinner parties and how you dress for certain occasions, rather infuriated her. I had a lot of sympathy for her, but I wasn't going to return to where I'd just come from any more than she was going to go and live in England. It wouldn't have worked. But we ended well. The affection remained. There were no regrets, resentments or loose ends, and we have remained good friends.

I think that when we sense a relationship has come to an end and it is time for us to move on with our lives, that if there has been a wholesomeness in our togetherness, we need not banish our ex-partner from our hearts. Some things aren't destined to last for ever, and that was true about Pragito and me. Our relationship simply came to a natural end and I can say with all honesty that my heart is that bit bigger and stronger today because echoes of sweet Pragito-ness still reside inside it.

Chapter 20

Shamanic Journeying and Creation Spirituality

The Chinese refer to a crisis as a 'dangerous opportunity', and I felt that I had taken the opportunities for inner growth that my time in hospital had offered me; and, buoyed up by my loving connection with Pragito, I decided that another adventure beckoned to me. I decided to spend a few months in the jungles of Mexico to study shamanism.

What is it? Basically, it is a nature-based spiritual path of direct revelation going back 30,000 years. The word shaman is an Evenki word from Siberia meaning 'one who sees' or penetrates to the source. Basically, the shaman goes into altered states of consciousness and interacts with the power that Mother Nature offers, and communicates with plants and animals to produce an energy that is able to heal or help people. For the shaman, everything is infused with divinity. All of us are part of a living, breathing, interconnected web of life. Air, earth, fire and water, rocks, plants, animals and trees are all sacred. In the *Svetasvatara Upanishad* we read:

> *Glory be to that God who is in the fire, who is in the water, who is in the plants and trees, who is in all things in this divine creation.*

Shamans teach their followers to look inward to the source of consciousness as the invisible ground of the world that we see with our senses. For them, all of life is sacred and divine and the material universe represents the 'body of God'. It is said that the Buddha had a shamanic initiation on the night of his awakening under the bodhi tree, and thus sat for forty-nine days in a high state of consciousness out of which emerged the four Noble Truths and the Eightfold Path to Awakening.

We had two shamans guiding us, an American lady, Joan Halifax, whom I already knew slightly (a wild, spirited, attractive and inspirational lady—I heard that a few years later she had entered a monastery and became a Zen priestess!) and an old man from the area who spoke to us through an interpreter. We all lived in the jungle, sleeping in the caves where initiates who had undergone their initiations for thousands of years had slept, and consequently there was a great power there.

One of the tests I was put through involved me sleeping one night inside a particular cave just fifty feet down from the jungle floor, with creepers and tendrils swooping down over its entrance. The old shaman led me there and told me exactly where to put down my blanket and reminded me that I needed to be very aware.

Well, I awoke early the next morning and found my head about a foot away from a large snake that was climbing up the creepers. It stopped climbing as it saw me looking at it, and we gazed at one another.

I was terrified. What should I do? If I suddenly pulled away it might lunge forward and bite me. If I stayed put, it might also bite me. I just stared at it in confusion until I received a message that seemed to come directly from my heart telling me that 'this snake is your brother. Eliminate your projections onto it that it is your enemy and will bite and hurt you. It will only do so if you project those thoughts into it. So take them back. Take this snake into your heart. It is like you, a creature of God; you are connected to it as you are connected to all of life and it deserves your love and respect.'

I remembered how on my vision quest I had seen the mountain lion as my friend and how I'd felt that my thoughts affected it. So suddenly I found myself looking at the snake through the more awakened eyes of my heart, and as I did, it also seemed to transform. I had created a new reality for myself and this snake had now became infiltrated into it, and as a result it was no longer a fearful reptile ready to attack and bite me. It had morphed into being a fellow inhabitant of the planet who had as much right to exist as I did. The snake and I were both part of the great world soul, as were the rocks and trees all around us. I began to feel affection for it and was aware of a silent understanding that existed between us. I no longer wanted to pull away. Now I was looking at it as my friend. Yes, we both have a right to be, I felt, and I truly respect you for your divine snake-hood. I can appreciate your beauty.

As I experienced this, the snake decided to continue climbing up the vine. Later, I saw the shaman and told him what had occurred and he said that I had passed the test. I described the snake and he said it was very poisonous. If I had jerked back quickly, he said, it might well have lunged at me and I had done exactly the right thing, had shifted the reality. He gave me a shamanic name that I am afraid I have forgotten.

But my friend Peter, who was also in our group, had a much tougher initiation. He got given the name 'Jaguar man' as he had been asked to spend the night in a cave that the shaman knew was a haunt of jaguars. Peter told us all the story of how he'd woken up in the night with a huge weight on his chest and found a jaguar lying on top of him.

'The worst thing was its terrible breath, smelling of rotten meat,' he told us, 'I was so terrified that I passed out and when I woke up again, it had left me.'

One had the feeling somehow that this old shaman had a certain power over nature. How could it be that a jaguar just lay on top of him and didn't gobble him up, or that that snake didn't have me for lunch!

I was given a large flask of water and ordered to stay in that cave by myself for the next four days and fast and pray. During this time I had further encounters with snakes, this time inside the cave, and I have to say that they no longer troubled me. Something had definitely changed. Here from my journal is a long prayer I wrote down for myself over those days. I am so delighted I found it as I have printed it out and now use it as a prayer for myself today.

O great spirit of the Universe—you whose presence embraces all that is and is celebrated in the sun and moon and earth and air and water. Thank you for your loving embrace of me and being with me to help, support and inspire me.

Thank you for the gift of my life and please help me to be grateful for the many blessings that fill it. Thank you for all the tests you give me to make me stronger as a human being. Thank you for guiding me through my recent illness and giving me the strength to recover.

And thank you for enabling me to live a life where I don't have to work in some soulless job but am permitted to do what makes my heart sing. For this my heart is full of gratitude.

Help me to live more as a spiritual warrior, allowing myself to flow with the Tao.

May I be strong of heart.

And fluid of body.

And let me be kind. To myself. To other people and to the world around me.

Please deliver me from the terrible habit of judging others, which I know I still sometimes do.

Instead, help me to respect the divinity in everyone whom I meet and to hold them inside my heart, whoever they are so I never ever again feel either superior or inferior to anyone.

And help me also to no longer divide my life into separate compartments, but rather enable me to be aware of its underlying intrinsic wholeness whereby all its different parts continually flow into and out of one another.

Please help me to move ever more deeply into the sacred worlds.

And inspire me more and more to be of service to my fellow human beings.

Please also help me to continue to heal my wounded ego so that it may allow my deeper soul self to come increasingly to the fore and take more and more charge over my life.

Let my ego become my servant and not my master.

Guide me that I may be in the right place at the right time and that I act with appropriateness in the face of whatever challenges I am confronted with in the future.

Please help me always to tell the truth and act out of integrity.

O great spirit, please also give me the gift of your peace so that I can take it into my heart on those occasions when I feel stressed, lonely and unhappy.

Please help me to give up my theatrics with women
So I can be a real man with a big open heart at all times
Able to stand in my gentle power
And in my divine ordinariness.

Let me be loyal and compassionate.

Able more and more to live my life as an opening to your divine promptings.

Please help me to let go those stories of my past which I no longer need to hold on to,

And allow them to be gently washed out of my system.

O great spirit, teach me to open my heart to life, to trust life, to value myself and see the beauty and bravery and power in myself and in all people around me so that when despair, fear and timidity stalk me, I have a powerful antidote.

May I be blessed and free and may all human beings be blessed and free.

On this retreat I was encouraged to confront my fear of taking full responsibility for my life, and my tendency at times to want to play helpless and get others to rescue me. The old shaman was often quite fierce with me, also helping me look at the part in me that still somehow felt that who I was, was not enough and where I at times still blamed myself for not being more of a mover and a shaker like my father.

'Divine consciousness doesn't ask you to prove anything,' the shaman told me through the interpreter. 'Just let yourself be a space to allow it in. Let go and feel your kinship with the power and beauty and naturalness of nature, and then you can come more and more to accept the power and beauty and naturalness of your own nature. You recently did a lot of important inner work when you were very ill, but there are still many uncompleted threads inside you and you have a lot more work to do.'

I asked him about my 'stuff' with women and he told me that I had a lot of unfinished karma still to work through in this arena, and that when I was ready, I would draw the right partner to me. I had now had a lot of wise people tell me that. He kept telling me that I must continue to trust the spirit of life. His message was very similar to that of Chuang Tzu and Lao Tzu, just expressed a little differently.

What the old shaman also helped me realise—or rather, I knew it but now I had it confirmed at a deeper level—was that most of the questions that we ask others can be answered inside ourselves. In other words, there is a part of ourselves which, if we can access it, has great knowing. I had realised this at my vision quest but now I realised it at a whole new level. It reminded me of an old musician friend who had written a song with these words:

It's in every one of us to be wise
Find your heart, open up both your eyes.
We can all know everything without ever knowing why.
It's in every one of us.
By and by.

One more little interesting thing to add. We were visiting the pyramids at Chichen Itza and were asked to climb one of them. It was steep but had steps up it. Hardly had I begun my ascent than I began to feel very frightened. I felt I was going to be hurled off the top and I would die. This feeling was so strong that I just couldn't go up any further, and as on this retreat we were all helping each other, about four of the men carried me up to the top, where I curled into a little ball. It was interesting what our guide said when we all gathered around her.

'This pyramid goes right back to the matriarchal era and was a place of sacrifice. Men would be taken to the top, and then would be hurled off to their death.'

Was I tuning in to a past life where I had been one of those unfortunate men, or was I tuning into a thoughtform that still hovered around that pyramid after all those hundreds of thousands of years? I will never know the answer, and it doesn't really matter, but it was again an example of the power of thought.

I returned to England very highly invigorated and to my base in the Old School House, and after all the drama of illnesses and shamanic initiations, life suddenly felt a little empty. As I said, I really liked the people in my little village. I was very friendly with everyone, but apart from Chris and Coralie and their mother, whom I felt I had real relationships with, none of my other encounters happened at a level that I found particularly nourishing and I know they all knew I did weird things like hold 'spiritual retreats' at my home and so they considered me a bit odd. Though I never ever tried to lay any 'spiritual trip' on anyone and I never have, and despite my sometimes intentionally choosing to bring Lord Snooty more into the equation to try to show them that I was 'one of them', I am sure they picked up that in some way I wasn't and I think it slightly unnerved them. I was coming to see that what essentially separates people is the level of consciousness that we resonate at. At the higher levels, we will naturally see all people as our fellow brothers and sisters regardless of their sexual orientation, religion, class, nationality or race. At the lower levels, differences are much harder to accommodate and people often view those whom they see as 'not being one of them' with a certain discomfort, or at worst, fear or suspicion.

In my work with my clients, the whole art was—and of course still is—to try to find a space inside myself that resonates with where the person I am trying to assist is at, and this needs to be intuitively sensed. Go too high and they won't get you. Go too low and you don't help them. And here again I am not talking about intellect but about consciousness. Many people can be high in intellect—have two PhDs—but still be low in consciousness. Similarly, you can find people who are barely educated but whose self-awareness or spiritual intelligence is very highly developed.

Put simply, I realised that I lived in different worlds and had different aspirations, values and life aims to those of many of my old English friends. Again, this didn't mean that I was a 'better person' or anything like that. It just meant that I saw the world differently and that different things touched and interested me. However, I had also calmed down a lot and those old habits of mine of liking to cock a snook at the establishment had all vanished. The local hunt could now meet in the field around my house without any fear of being blasted out with raucous rock 'n' roll.

I chose to continue my psychotherapy training (I feel I've never ever stopped being a student) and I thought it would be good to continue with the English-based Psychosynthesis Trust. I did so for a year but was then asked to leave by Diana, John Whitmore's wife, for challenging some of the assumptions that I was being taught. Perhaps I was a bit arrogant but I felt that having studied all those years in California had given me a much broader perspective on the psycho-spiritual scene and that the people teaching psychosynthesis back home were a little limited.

One of the very good things that came out of this experience, however, was my meeting a very lovely Jungian analyst who was on the staff, called Dale Mathers. He started out as my therapist, then graduated to being my supervisor and is now a close buddy. Dale was, and still is, an exceptionally sensitive and brilliant man, and on many occasions has helped me out with clients when I had got a bit stuck. His liking for going around barefoot and in torn jeans, sporting a long, dyed-blond, 'beach-boy' hairstyle, hid a great sweetness, a wonderful sense of humour and a fearsome intellect, and he is the author of several immensely erudite treatises on Jungian psychology. I am so happy to have Dale as a dear friend in my life even though as I now live in Mallorca, I've not seen him for a long time.

What I found much more useful to me than more psychosynthesis training was spending six weeks at the Schumacher Foundation doing a course on Creation Spirituality, or the Christian mystical tradition as it was expressed through adepts like Hildegard of Bingen, St Teresa of Ávila and Meister Eckhart, all of whom spoke from the heart and were very much united with the source they were speaking about. Their teachings aligned beautifully with what I had learned from Joseph Campbell, Chuang Tzu and the shamans.

Matthew Fox was my teacher. A truly delightful man. Big-hearted and with a great intellect. A real spiritual renegade. He was a Catholic priest who had been excommunicated from the Church for the 'sin' of talking about the divine feminine and Goddess consciousness and for suggesting that the greatest tragedy in theology over the last three centuries has been its dryness and its divorce from poetry, dancing, music, painting and moviemaking.

His assistant was a wonderful woman in her mid-eighties, M.C. Richards, a fantastic, long-grey-haired old hippie, who danced and sang with us and was full of vital energy. M.C. was a potter, painter, essayist and poet, and she gave us classes in poetry and pot-making. All us students adored her as she had in no way fogeyfied, and there was an incredible youthfulness and joie de vie about her. It was clear that she'd never been part of 'the system'! She helped me make my first little pot and it felt so good to recognise artwork as having an important spiritual dimension to it, as I had never before been aware of the connection.

Matthew's Jesus could not have been more different from the crucifixion-obsessed and judgemental old sad-sack that I learned about in my scripture classes at Harrow. For him, Jesus was a cool dude, a poet, a healer, a storyteller, a lover of women, an awakener of the kingdom and queendom of God for us all, and his gift was to show us how we could also make our lives into a work of art and beauty.

Creation spirituality was similar to shamanism in that it told us that all is God and all is in God. Dear old Chuang Tzu might not use the word 'God' but he would not have felt out of place in this retreat! For these mystics, the whole universe is God's temple and a tree, for example, is good and valuable in itself, not because it has an economic purpose. I loved this thinking as it so tied in with my own emerging vision, which I have recently expressed in detail in my recent book *Gateways to the Soul*.

I particularly loved Matthew's definition of sin. It was 'being off the mark, not honouring who we are, denying awe and wonder and being inert as regards our refusing to start new things'. In this worldview, we are sinning when we are doing work solely because we want to grow rich but which does not make our hearts sing!

Creation Spirituality taught that life was divided into four segments, all of which needed respecting. There existed the *Via Positiva*, where we need to surrender to the joy of existence, and learn to open our hearts up to the beauty and sublimity of all of life. 'The poor not only need bread,' Matthew told us, 'they also need beauty.' Then there was the *Via Negativa,* where we are challenged to confront the dark side of life (which I think I'd by now got quite good at). The importance of *Via Creativa* was discovering our imagination and bringing our artistic or imaginative self out of the closet, thus enabling art and worship to come together. He saw this as a powerful antidote to war, and we learned how threatened all totalitarian regimes are by the free-thinking genuine artist. The last part of the equation was the *Via Transformativa,* whereby we work to bring the fruits of our creative discoveries to find our own unique way or ways to bring transformation into the world. In other words, we choose to be part of the forces of change, as opposed to being part of those forces which resist it. All issues that deeply resonated with me.

Indeed, what he was teaching me was simply to go deeper into, and have more faith in, principles that I had already been working with. Here, very briefly, are some of the best nuggets that I obtained from that month.

We need to befriend all of creation and see divine presence or soul in all things.

We need to work at developing our capacity for awe and wonder at the beauty and magnificence of life.

We need to be aware both of the holiness and also the wholeness of each moment. (The word wholeness comes from the Anglo-Saxon world 'haelen', which means to heal.)

We need to praise all of life and never forget that sacredness also lies in the dark, i.e., we need to see Shadow work as sacred work. This meant that all my 'wretched stuff' with women, turgid as it often was, had a sacred purpose!

We must remember to bring more play into our daily lives.

We need to create rituals to honour grief and anger as the patriarchal system has demonised them, as it is scared of the powerful deranging forces they can release.

The best way to get what we want is to give others what they want.

Punning on Jesus' statement about 'many being called but few being chosen', Matthew suggested that:

Many are called
But most are frozen,
In corporate or collective cold
These are the stalled who choose not to be chosen
Except to be bought and sold.

How very true. Yes, higher consciousness or amazing grace calls out to all of us in some form or other. In other words, we are all 'chosen'. The problem is that many of us refuse it; we close off to it. We don't allow in the blessings that spirit wishes to offer us; we resist aligning ourselves with our source as we are so hunkered down in our old rigid, self-centred and materialistic identities.

Matthew also stressed the importance of inner as well as outer work and that we ensure that our outer work makes a difference to the world, that is, is work that enhances, as opposed to reduces, life. In this arena, he was fierce. He stressed how important it was that we all face our greed, see how we crush and lie and cheat and don't care for those we need to, and only focus on becoming richer. In his words: 'We may glorify drama that we see on TV yet never do anything to make our world a better place, just as we like to put our Mother Teresa's "above us" on a pedestal so as to give us the excuse of not being capable of doing anything other than trying to satisfy our own pleasures.'

For him, humanity has, to a large extent, 'rejected and humiliated the divine, and the parable of the prodigal son has great meaning for us today, as that son goes off and destroys his life with his greed and addiction and then he remembers where he came from, i.e., his divine nature, and so he returns and because of the depth of his shattering, his reunion with God is more intense, illuminated and humble.'

I have a sneaking sense that these words are even more relevant today than they were then, because nearly forty years down the line, the consequences of our human-collective prodigality are much more serious, and we human beings are now in the process of destroying ourselves much more prolifically. I will explore this theme in more detail in the epilogue.

Our challenge is to give thanks for the many blessings of life and learn to savour the what-isness of each moment. We need to say no to an old world that no longer works, and invest all our energies in trying to create a new one that does, and one way we can do this is through blessing ourselves, blessing others and blessing our world as this helps us let go our old fall/redemption, patriarchal, colonial, dualistic (fear of passion) models of living, i.e., all the stuff that I'd been reared on!

For him, finding our 'right work' was all about discovering our soul out in the world *as our work loves us just as we love it* (I loved that idea) and if we don't put soul into our work—that is, love it and see it as sacred—our soul suffers and our work takes on narcissistic qualities. This I think was why, at one level, I realised I had taken some big strides. Women might not always love me but I knew my work did!

Chapter 21

Doing the Sacred Work

What I now found myself being increasingly inspired to do—and this greatly nourished the teacher archetype inside me, or what Martina, my wife, calls the 'preacher man'—was to conduct week-long spiritual retreats. They would be held at different retreat centres all over England and Europe. On top of my private practice, which continued as ever, these retreats were the most important things in my work life for the next twenty-five years.

Everything that I had been learning since the time I first arrived in California was now starting to coalesce inside me and beginning to bear fruit. Therefore the retreats came to me very organically. I had a lot of fun designing them and even more fun teaching them. I would give them names like 'Living with Joy', 'Embracing Your Shadow', 'Living Life as a Celebration', 'Journeying into Wholeness', 'Learning to Be Your Courageous and Outrageous Self', 'The Empowerment training', 'Exploring the Path of the Spiritual Activist', 'Finding the Heroic You', and of course 'Awakening the Heart'.

I now had a fantastic team working for me and their efficiency would always make up for my ADD'd vagueness, as all the administrative details that I was so bad at would get done for me. To start with I had wonderful Carla and Grant helping me, who had met each other through a workshop of mine and became a couple, and later a lovely young man called Martin (I called him Martino) took over.

They all knew me so well that they would not hold back from sometimes challenging me if they felt it was called for. At one time I remember, I was very busy and was getting a little cocky and giving myself one or two airs and graces—very un-

Chuang Tzu-ish—and they had no compunction, bless them, about reminding me about it. 'Remember what your teachings are about, Serge. Have you ever heard the word "humility"? Perhaps you ought to listen to some of the lectures you have given!' While sometimes the truth would be hard to hear, I greatly respected them for it and always asked them for it. I think we all need to have friends around us who will not hold back from telling us the truth. At the same time we also need to be open to hearing what they have to say!

My ADD, however, never interfered with my work. Indeed, the moment I had a client in front of me or was in front of a group, it would be as if a screen would come down and filter off all my symptoms. There was none of that 'vagueness and woolly-mindedness' that I was rightly accused of in my schooldays, and similarly, if I happened to be going through difficulties in my personal life, they would also never intrude into my professional life. When I was doing the work that my soul intended for me—that is, work that loved me—I always felt that it both protected and empowered me!

Essentially, what my personal work and all my courses focussed on was helping people learn to confront, understand and gradually let go their rigidities and clenches and attachments to their old stories or old conditioning, all of which served to curtail their ability to be free. In a word, all the stuff that I had also been struggling with in my own life. Many people would come on my retreats simply because they were suffering and wanted a way out. Some turned up because they were generally dissatisfied with their lives, and others because they wanted a break from their everyday routines and be given the space to look more deeply inside themselves.

Although all my retreats were on different subjects, there were certain themes which they all had in common. Basically, as I said, all of us come into the world wounded or blocked in some way, with our divine nature hidden deeply inside us.

Are we or are we not willing to try to 'out' it? I repeat once more: the more we learn to work through our personality blockages, the more we open up a space for our divinity to peek through. By the same token, the more we work at opening up the shutters leading to the more transcendent domains of who we are, the more energy we have pouring through us to assist us in working with our blockages. My approach then was, and still is, to see all a person's issues as interconnected. I regard all genuine transformational work as sacred work, regardless of what subject matter or level one happens to be addressing at any one time.

One of my specialities was helping people release traumas. The deeply traumatised person is carrying something so painful inside them, something that so scars them, that often to survive they feel compelled to numb down completely. This can potentially also lead to self-harming, depression or addictions, as they may have learned to internalise the wounding that was originally done to them and thus believe that this 'bad thing' happened to them because they were a bad person and so 'deserved' the punishment which they received. With many people, their wounds would be buried very deeply and one would need to sift through many layers until one arrived at their core. Interestingly, I started to find that the more I was able to unblock certain parts of myself, the more easily it would happen for the people I was working with.

I realised that while everyone had a different story and different dramas to contend with and thus different paths to walk, that there tended to be certain things that were important for most people. Most people needed to learn to open their hearts and be more mindful and find their own best ways to meditate. Most people also needed to connect more with nature and practise 'witness consciousness' so they could stand back and learn to observe themselves and thus be less identified with their various dramas. Most people also needed to find more joy and a sense of deeper meaning in their lives. Indeed, a lot of people came to me because they were suffering from those wounds that traditional or old-school Christianity had foisted on them, whereby one is led to believe that one should be 'God-fearing' since we were born sinful, and it is therefore right that we should carry a lot of guilt which we can only 'atone for' by working 'til we're wrinkled and grey' (as that old song goes) and denying ourselves pleasure. What balderdash!

I remember once working with a woman who was very quiet and persisted in dressing in black as she told us she was mourning a husband who had died. Something about her behaviour felt inauthentic to me. I discovered that he had died eleven years ago. Why was she still in mourning? I went to the local town and bought a clown outfit—red nose, funny hat, floppy shoes, etc—and insisted she stay thus attired until the end of the retreat. It utterly changed her life as she came to see that actually she had been delighted by her husband's death, as he had been a cruel man and very mean to her, and all her games around mourning him and remaining miserable, had been 'enacted' out of guilt because she felt she should have missed the old bugger, when in actuality she loathed him. Surprising what guilt trips we can lay on ourselves! Anyway, something big shifted inside her. She was quickly able to let go her guilt and thereby release those barriers preventing her meeting a new man, which soon after the retreat she did, and four months later got remarried.

One favourite process I would sometimes do with people who found it difficult to trust, was to have the person stand on my Cotswold stone wall (I did many of my retreats in my old barn), close their eyes, fold their arms over their chests and then let themselves fall backwards into the arms of those waiting to catch them. (You need six burley blokes for this process to happen!) I have literally seen lives change overnight. One of the problems with so many of us is that we get caught in our old 'comfort zones' and are scared of taking risks and going to the edge. What we need to realise is that it is at the edge—and it can be a physical, emotional or intellectual edge—where the biggest transformations actually take place.

I also worked a lot with music as it has very transformational characteristics. For helping people be calm I might play my friend Tim Wheater's beautiful flute music. In my retreats on joy, I would use Beethoven's *Ode to Joy* and to assist people with opening their hearts, I loved Pachelbel's *Canon in D.* Dear Brugh used that a lot. If I felt things were getting a bit sleepy, I would play African drumming music and get people to dance wildly, and if someone had a fear of what was going to happen, I might grab my guitar and get people to dance to Bob Marley's *Three Little Birds* that has the words 'Don't worry about a thing... Every little thing's gonna be all right!' I particularly loved Arvo Part and Constance Demby's sacred music and would get everyone to lie on the floor and play it very loudly in order to allow the music to enter their bodies and retune their chakras. I would also use Bach's B minor mass for that same purpose.

For the next twenty-five years over New Year, I very much enjoyed putting on a five-day course that I called 'Completing the Old Year and Creating the New One', e.g., Completing 2001, Creating 2002. In these retreats, I would always have a fire ritual, which took the following form. On New Year's Eve, everyone would go out into nature and collect symbols for things they wished to let go of. For example, a stone could represent a heavy heart, clinging ivy a co-dependent relationship, a rotten piece of wood some old rotten habit they wished to relinquish, etc. They would then make a bundle of their symbols and take it to the group for the evening session, and everyone in turn would share with the rest of the group what their bundles represented, what they wanted to let go of and how they'd like their new year to pan out for them.

Meanwhile, we would have built a big fire and people would then in turn hurl their bundles on the fire, watch them go up in flames, and while I would play the bongo drums, they would then improvise a dance to symbolise the emergence of the new life they wanted for themselves in the new year. While they were doing this, it was very important for everyone attending the retreat to focus on the person having their dreams realised. While the 'conventional' us may poo-poo things like this, I can tell you that this kind of work is very powerful. One of the many sad things about modern life is that we've completely lost the use of ritual.

I stress once more: *the great problem with so many of us is that we don't take enough responsibility for trying to lead the lives we are destined to lead, and this accounts for so much of our misery*. And no one can change this for us but ourselves. Yes, I can help a person come into a place where change can be possible, but if it is to happen, they need to really want it. Old patterns or habits, or old ways of living or looking at the world that no longer work for us, won't fall away unless we a) make the effort to recognise them for what they are, b) see what we need to do to release them, c) commit to doing the necessary work to have this come about, and d) be clear about the kind of life we really want for ourselves.

The wonderful thing about groups is that one has the power of the whole collective working for one, and as we all know, the whole is much more than the sum of its parts. Thus, a person who, for example, is attached to some old dysfunctional pattern or is afraid of being more joyful or of feeling freer, may find themselves being 'lent' a new kind of capacity to work through their resistances by receiving the empowerment of the whole group. People can also learn a great deal by observing the challenges and shifts that their fellow group members go through. Let us say that a pattern around pain over deep loss emerges. It may be that half a dozen people present have issues in this arena and find the opportunity to work through their individual issues in conjunction with each other. It also sometimes happens that if one person experiences a strong breakthrough, it can bleed through and affect the others.

In my experience, a group if appropriately focalised, becomes an entity unto itself and individual members may experience that their sense of 'I-ness' temporarily transforms into the experience of 'we-ness'. The 'help forces' or grace, I find, operates very powerfully in a group context, and this also applies to me, the group leader. I have experienced quite a few occasions where a group I have been orchestrating has got out of hand and I have felt confused as to what to do next, only to then be aware of an inner guidance or a 'helping presence' instructing me exactly as to the appropriate course of action to take.

At all times I realised that the 'me' capable of helping people in this way was a much more 'all-encompassing me'—in fact was a 'me' who was connected to the 'higher worlds' of grace and healing—and very different to the ordinary little 'me' that accompanied me when I was just 'doing' my ordinary everyday life. This is why I have come to see that helping others on their life journeys was such an important ingredient in my own personal journey. Not only did it increasingly take me out of my own narcissism and so allow that part of me gradually to dissolve, but it also enabled my own soul life to come more and more into its own.

Chapter 22

The Magus of Strovolos

Women dramas, however, continued to pursue me. A very attractive, slim, young blond tax lawyer whose profile perfectly fitted my psychopathologies bought a cottage in our village, and hardly had I met her than I became besotted with her and consumed with the idea that she was 'the one', and that if I teamed up with her, I would be happy for life. Despite our having nothing whatsoever in common—her aim was trying to enter the world of the so-called 'great and the good' that I had been doing my best over the last twenty years to exit from, and she had not an iota of interest in the things that touched me—I made the dreadful mistake of asking her to marry me. I was so infatuated with her glamour that I no longer listened to my heart. I was distancing myself more and more from the Tao and the Lord Snooty dimension of me seemed to have been invited back once more to play a major role in my life.

The result was that I grew increasingly uncomfortable with the self that I found myself reverting to and at the lack of 'feeling fed' at any deep level by her, and after six months of our being together—during which time I had taken her out several times to Switzerland to meet Moonie, and the two had got on very well—in a moment of desperation, I told her that I had made a mistake and that I now felt I could not go through with it.

While I am sure that she too must have been beginning to have her doubts about me, the net result was that I very deeply hurt a woman who had done nothing wrong except be the way that she was. She was intelligent, ambitious, sincere and basically well-meaning and I had pulled her into my web and then had spat her out, and if she felt badly betrayed and let down and angry with me and refused to speak to me for a long time, she had every right to feel that way. While in retrospect I am sure I saved us both from what would have been a disastrous marriage as we were totally incompatible, the whole episode threw me as much as it did her, and when we eventually split up, I missed her a lot. I no longer had her at my side making me feel more whole.

By this time, I was branching out a lot and was teaching regular retreats at the beautiful Spanish centre called Cortijo Romero, and was continually being invited to teach courses at Skyros, another retreat centre on a Greek island. I was also getting more and more into my writing and wrote a regular column for the magazine *Kindred Spirit*, giving people advice on how to live. In essence, I was a kind of Agony Aunt, but preferred to refer to myself as an Ecstasy Uncle! I came up with the title 'Spiritual Sergery' and people would write to me at my 'Sergery' and ask my advice. I remember in the middle of all my traumas, I received a question from a woman asking what she should do as a man whom she had just become engaged to had just called it off. Cripes!

But as I have already emphasised, whatever dramas I might be going through in my personal life never affected my work with people and I was always grateful for my work's love for me and its capacity to ground me and connect me back to myself. It felt as if the me who worked with his clients, gave his lectures and taught his workshops and retreats was quite an evolved me. In fact, you could say that in this area of my life, the Tao was with me and I would always feel both 'over-lighted' and 'empowered' by the archetype of the 'wise man'. My problem was that I couldn't seem to remain connected to this dimension of myself when I was outside the session room or the retreat space.

I had been having the feeling for some time that I needed to speak with a truly wise person again, and my friend Rob, who had just invited me to teach my 'Exploring the Path of the

Spiritual Warrior' retreat in his beautiful house on the island of Hydra, was always talking about a spiritual teacher in Cyprus called Daskalos who had meant a lot to him and whom he had just written a book about. Yes, I thought to myself, I need to meet this man.

His real name was Dr Stylianos Atteshlis, and he was also known by the enigmatic title the Magus of Strovolos! He didn't have a phone, so as I knew where he lived—Rob had given me his address—and what he looked like, I thought I'd try my luck and fly out to Cyprus.

I had no idea that I was soon to witness a small miracle.

From the airport, I took a taxi to Daskalos' address and got out and walked down a little road until at the end, I saw a very tall man whom I recognised as the sage. He'd had no idea I was coming, but I told him I was a good friend of Rob's and I badly wanted to see him and he motioned to me to follow him. I had to walk through a cluster of chickens to get into his small house.

'Please come in. You are welcome,' he said, 'I just have to do some healing first.'

I saw an old lady sitting on a sofa who was all bent over. I could tell her spine was deformed and she was in a lot of pain. As I sat down on a chair opposite her, Daskalos went and sat beside her and began touching her in different places on her back. She began to make little whimpering noises.

As I watched, she seemed to straighten up more and more, and after about three quarters of an hour, she sat up and began to weep and hug him. An hour before, she had looked as if she could hardly walk. Now, to my amazement, she got off the sofa and began to waltz around the room crying with joy. I had been sitting watching this spectacle and I was utterly amazed, and found it interesting that I should arrive in Cyprus in time to witness this little miracle. Had the force 'arranged this' further to broaden my mind? Daskalos had no idea that I was coming. Nor did the old lady. It was not dissimilar to that washbasin crashing onto the floor all those years ago when Brendan and I were chatting with Uri Geller. I felt that all these experiences were messages to me to open up more to the essential mysteriousness of life and know that extraordinary things really do happen that cannot be explained by normal means, and that the more we can be open to these experiences, the more we become a 'space' to allow them to happen.

When the old lady had gone, I spoke to the Magus about this. He was very tall and graceful and I was conscious of an enormously warm heart. He reminded me a little of dear Joseph Campbell. In perfect English he told me that if one was in tune with higher forces, they could work through one and that there is a great healing power in life and we all need to recognise it and find out how it wants to work with us. 'Yes, God's grace exists,' he told me, 'but we need to honour it and then it can not only work for us to heal us, but it can also work through us to heal others, and you have a healing gift and always have had. It comes through your voice, and the more you can allow divine consciousness to flow through you, the more good you can do in the world.' He then asked me why I had come all this way to see him, and I said that I had heard he was a great Master and I felt I was still making bad mistakes in a certain area of my life and that I needed to learn more about love and that some part of me needed more healing.

'Yes you do,' he said, 'but not in your body, but in your heart. Despite all the work that I see you have already done on your heart, it still carries big wounds and more healing is needed.'

I had a small tape recorder and asked him if I could tape his words but he asked me not to. I was a bit naughty. I pretended to turn the recorder off and put it in my pocket but I actually kept it on. He then proceeded to give me the most wonderful and poetic lecture on the need for unconditional love in the world and I realised I was in the presence of a very extraordinary human being.

Halfway through his talk, he stopped and apologised. 'Excuse me, I have to leave you for a little.' I expected him to get up and go away, but he stayed exactly where he was with his eyes closed for about half an hour. I also stayed where I was. Then just as suddenly he opened his eyes again. 'There was a small problem I needed to attend to,' he apologised, and I could sense that he didn't want to talk about what had happened. I remember Rob telling me that Daskalos was 'the spiritual master for the Middle East' (whatever exactly that meant) and that he could leave his body at will and travel wherever he wanted. I remembered reading stories about certain spiritual masters being able to be in two different places at the same time. Don Juan also talked about that in the Carlos Castaneda books. Maybe Daskalos had just paid a short visit to Palestine in another body, as a lot of problems were happening in that part of the world at that time. I questioned him about this, but he didn't seem inclined to enlighten me.

That said, he could not have been more courteous, giving me coffee and a little cake and using a friend's phone to call for a taxi to send me back to the airport. I felt so inspired by his beautiful words and decided that I needed to 'up' the way I dealt with love; I saw that though over the years I had talked a lot about unconditional love, I was still very limited in my practice of it. I began to see that this kind of love is in fact a very rare and evolved love.

Ultimately, it means loving and asking for nothing in return. No conditions. No 'I will be good to you on condition that you are good to me', which is the way most of us ordinarily operate. Unconditional love truly is a spiritual love. Thinking back on this today, I think the only person from whom I truly ask nothing, and love her however she is, is my daughter Irena. I just adore her and would willingly give my life for her, and she doesn't need to do anything in return. I think that sometimes, if I am very connected to my inner self, I also experience this with my wife Martina.

Anyway, sitting in the plane back to London, I took out my tape recorder looking forward to listening to his words once more. But nothing had been recorded. I was certain the machine had been on. I let it run to the end, but there was nothing there.

Chapter 23

Death

Moonie and George, now getting on in years, had meanwhile sold their chalet in Gstaad and were living in a flat in Geneva. I learned from my diaries that Moon and I had grown a bit distant. I think all those years that I had spent in California, when we would only meet up at Christmas, had somehow disconnected us, and as I said, I never heard from her during those three months when I was ill in hospital in San Francisco, and that had upset me.

I happened to call one evening to say hello, and spoke to George—he was then over eighty—who told me casually that my mother was not well and was in hospital. Hell! Why hadn't he thought of ringing me to let me know?

I got on the plane to Geneva that afternoon and found my old Moonie lying sleeping with her eyes closed in her hospital bed. I knew she was dying. She had had a rasping cough for so long but had done nothing about it and ignored all our warnings to go to the doctor. As I said, she never wanted to look at anything unpleasant, be it inside her or outside in the world.

I visited her again the next day with George, and she was more awake and evidently pleased to see me. George had brought some champagne, which she liked, and she took a sip. The next few moments I will never forget. I was sitting beside her on her hospital bed holding her hand, and she gave me one look that felt like the most genuine connection I had ever felt with her. It is still with me today. It was a despairing look that said, 'I don't know what to do; please help me as I know I am dying and it scares me.' But it also conveyed love. I felt in that instant connected to Moonie in a way I had never been before. I squeezed her hand and our eyes met, and in those few seconds,

Moonie let go and gently bared her sweet soul to me. I saw her inner goodness and I told her that I loved her very much. If the effects of our not-altogether-satisfying relationship still continued to reverberate, at that moment I felt fully at peace with her.

It was the last time I saw her. I remember that I returned to London that evening and looking back, I wonder why I did this and didn't stay on, as it seemed rather cold-hearted given that I felt she was near the end. I think the reason was that I didn't want to stay on in the flat alone with George, who by this time was beginning to act very strangely and aggressively towards me, which I only later realised was because he was beginning to suffer from dementia.

Anyway, three days later and back in London talking to a psychotherapist I had begun seeing, suddenly the most extraordinary sadness and heaviness came over me for no reason, and I began to cry. At the same time, I noticed something very curious start to happen. On the shelf just behind my therapist's head was a vase of flowers, and as we talked, I saw all the petals begin to drop off as if being plucked by an invisible hand.

Within half an hour, the flowers had been reduced to stalks and the floor was covered. I remarked on how curious this was. When an hour later I got home, I received a phone call from George telling me that Moonie had died a short time ago—at the exact time I watched the flowers shedding. Moonie had always loved flowers and when she was younger, she used to paint them. I saw this as her way of saying goodbye.

Both my parents had had their very different ways of letting me know that they had passed on. Interestingly, Moonie's death opened up some kind of door in that my half-siblings Anna and Geordie and myself all got married within six months of that occurring.

As Moonie didn't want a funeral, there was no way properly to mourn her. But something came to my rescue quite out of the blue: the death of Princess Diana. Princess Moonie had died just a few months before Princess Diana was killed, and when young, she had looked rather like her. Here is what I wrote in my book *Awakening the Universal Heart*:

> *The Princess's death was resulting in a collective 'field of mourning' coming into being... I found myself tuning into a grief that felt far bigger than my own personal sadness, and which also seemed to not solely be centred around Diana's death so much as around the spirit of death itself. All of us on the planet had something or somebody to mourn or grieve over and many of us had buried these feelings, and the emergence of this 'grief field' seemed to be 'giving permission' to anyone who tuned into it, to work with or go into whatever issues came up for them.*

Basically, then, Diana's death opened up a space for me properly to grieve Moonie's death. I remembered all her sweetness and kindness and I took my sorrow deeply into my heart and allowed it to do its alchemical work. I saw that for years I had blamed Moonie for all my dramas with women and my difficulties with loving and in allowing myself to be loved. What I found myself now entering into was a vast reconciliatory 'heart space' that was enabling me to let these resentments go.

What incredible grace.

Yes, my dear friend, I found myself accessing the archetype of forgiveness and experiencing that forgiveness is not so much something you *do* so much as a space of consciousness that you enter into and which resides deeply inside one's heart. Thus you don't forgive someone by saying 'I forgive you'. You forgive someone by allowing your heart to expand and enfold them, and by being able more and more to experience them through a lens of unconditional love. Perhaps my short experience with the Magus had helped awaken another dimension inside me that was now being reactivated by everything that was happening around Princess Diana. I found myself experiencing a huge amount of compassion for my old Moonie. I realised that given her difficulties, she'd always tried to do her best for me and had loved me as much as she had been able to. I realised that I also needed to forgive myself for all the blame I'd pushed on to her, and saw that I had also loved her as best I could, given my many limitations! An image came to me of a great fire and Moonie and I sitting beside each other on a bench holding hands and gazing into this fire, and me feeling that the blockages we had had with one another were beginning to melt away.

I then began to have the curious experience that 'my' grief was actually not just 'mine'; that is, it didn't belong exclusively to me, but to all grieving people; and that grief is actually a powerful unifying force, and that I wasn't only grieving my mother; I was also grieving the plight of humanity, the lovelessness of humankind. I also had the sense that humanity as a whole was doing some of its grieving through the personal me, who, as part of the whole, also *was* that whole! Our planet was in great pain. So many people were suffering all over the world. There was so much sorrow everywhere, and too many of us shut it away, and now a small crack was opening up, enabling some of us to enter more fully into its mournful embrace.

As my process deepened, I observed that it also became personal once more, and I became increasingly aware of an anguish that I still carried inside myself as a result of some of my interactions with women. It was reflected both in terms of the pain that, in their unconsciousness, I saw that they had unwittingly 'given' me—that is, had projected onto me and which I was consequently still carrying—and which I, too, had similarly projected onto them.

I was just coming out of a three-year relationship with a woman called Sima, whom I had gradually grown to love and who was qualitatively different to most of my other girlfriends. Sima, who was Iranian (her parents had had to flee their homeland in much the same way that my grandparents had), was deep and soulful and was interested in my work and in training as a psychotherapist, and had the same kind of intuitive intelligence that I had, and it felt as if we had much in common. She also came from great wealth. While she could have rented a palace, she came with her two young sons and lived in my little cottage after having come out of a loveless marriage. She worked with me, helping arrange all my courses and training programmes, and another little team built up around us and it felt as if we were not only linked romantically but also spiritually.

Darling Sima, however, had her own wounds and expected me, as an older and 'trusted therapist', to always be understanding and put up with her little shenanigans (she had always lived very conventionally and in her past had never ever had any fun with men—had never ever been a 'naughty girl'), and when I didn't and told her that her 'naughty' behaviours hurt me, things began gradually to break down between us and she decided to move out. Again, I felt very wounded. Unlike most of the women I had been with, Sima had entered deeply into my heart.

Her leaving took place at exactly the time that my darling Annanie died of exactly the same virulent lung cancer that Moonie had had.

A few months later, I suggested that my half-brother Geordie and his new wife drive down to the Old School House (I was now living there alone) and we would together plant two trees in my garden in Moonie and Anna's honour and put their ashes in their roots so that there would always be something beautiful to remember them both by. I used Peter Deunov's book of prayers, the one that David Lorimer had put together and translated, to conduct a little funeral service in my garden.

While for me this felt like an appropriate ritual to honour them, I sensed the whole thing rather confused and maybe frightened Geordie. He and I had never quite hit it off and he was certainly not on a spiritual path, though what his path was I never quite discovered.

Sadly, after that day, despite my often trying to get in touch with him, I never heard from him again and he never answered my calls. I heard he went to live in Spain. I was sad as this reflected yet another dislocation in our already dislocated family, but at least he was true to himself. I was much older than him and we hadn't grown up together and I am sure he felt he had as little in common with me as I felt I had with him, so why try to pretend things? So, Geordie, however you are and wherever you are, I wish you well. I hope your life is working out. I've not seen you for over twenty years.

Some kinds of grief seem to get resolved quite easily. We feel it, face it and don't run away from it, and it gradually melts away. With other kinds of grief, this is not so easy. The blockage is more complex. It gets bunged up in deeper areas of our psyches. While I felt I now had very little 'unfinished business' with Moonie, and had also worked through any lingering issues with my ex-fiancée, I observed that this was not the case with Sima, with whom I felt I had really 'gone deep'.

As such, despite all my therapeutic and meditational efforts, I could not seem to dislodge a big stone that felt wedged inside my heart. Indeed, nearly two years later I was still feeling constricted, and this was starting to intrude on me getting on with my life. I also realised that the sadness I was feeling was not just mine, but that a lot of it also belonged to Sima. There had always been a deep melancholic streak to her, and I realised that I had somehow 'taken it on' and I couldn't seem to dislodge it!

I happened to be giving a talk at a conference in London and a Danish woman whom I met there told me that she was going to visit a guru in Germany called Mother Meera, and would I like to come with her. I had recently read a book about her and had also heard very good things about her, so not quite knowing what to expect but welcoming a little break in my routine, I said 'yes', and a couple of days later we both flew to Germany.

About sixty other people had also decided to come and visit her, and when we arrived at the Mother's House, we were all crammed into a room and Mother Meera came in, a tiny little Indian woman in a sari. She smiled brightly at all of us and then settled herself in meditation. This lasted three hours. No talk. Nothing. We all sat quietly in her awesome presence. This was exactly how the great Indian saint Ramana Maharshi worked. In silence. So we sat in silence with the Mother for four days.

After the fourth day, I went back to my hotel with my friend and looked at her, and lo and behold, I felt that the spell had been broken. That block of sorrow inside my heart had now fully melted. The healing had happened in complete silence and—as I saw it—totally as the result of what I can best describe as the very powerful emanations that Mother Meera radiated. Again, I was aware that the help forces were looking after me and had intervened yet again to enable me to encounter two wonderful wise women, one who took me to a place of release and another who successfully effected it.

Chapter 24

Papaji and Parties

Again, I felt something more was needed. I observed that despite stones no longer being lodged in my heart and my doing regular meditation, that something had once more slowed down in my personal development. After my short encounters with Mother Meera and the Magus, I was becoming increasingly aware of the awesome transformational power that genuinely awakened men and women possessed, and I was sensing that I needed to make some kind of real quantum leap in my development. Just as when I left Oxford, the soul food I required was the experience of being at Findhorn, and when I was in California I needed my experiences with Brugh Joy, Larry, Joseph Campbell and the shamans, now I felt in need of a wholly different kind of stretching.

Yes, my friend, I realised I needed once more to 'up' my game. I needed to be more quiet and more centred and to become more adept at doing something that I was always advocating to my clients and students: namely, living more fully 'in the now'—being more present to the experience of each moment. In short, I realised I needed to expand my self-awareness and that one of the best ways I might achieve this was to sit not just for a few, but for many days at the feet of a properly awakened Spiritual Master, and allow myself to be gradually reconfigured by their grace field. As I said, I had read stories of people sitting in meditation with the great Indian saint Ramana Maharshi and, without him saying a word, they would have profound awakening experiences. I also remembered what those four days with Mother Meera had done for me.

Finding the right spiritual teacher for oneself is very important. When I was in California, I had once spent ten days with a very eminent Tibetan sage and got very little from the experience. This was not because he was not the 'real thing'. It was because he was not right for me and probably, at that time, his teachings were also too advanced. In this 'game' of spiritual development, the idea of 'levels' is very important. You need someone who can help you at the level that you need helping. For example, if you are doing O level maths, you won't benefit much by attending lectures by professors of mathematics for doctoral students. And similarly if you are doing a PhD in Mathematics, an O level schoolteacher probably won't assist you much either!

The key thing is that we find a Master whom we feel we resonate with, and for many years I had heard very good things about a man who lived in Lucknow, India, called Papaji. Interestingly, he had been a direct disciple of Ramana Maharshi. I heard, and found it rather endearing that like me, Papaji liked watching Test cricket on the television and unlike so many supposed Masters, didn't continually rabbit on about how enlightened he was. Intuitively, I knew that Papaji was the real thing.

I invited my friend Johnnie Reed and his wife, Dominique, to come out to Lucknow with me, as I felt it would be good to go on this very intimate adventure with my old soul brother, whom I hadn't seen in a while. I also brought with me an ex-girlfriend who was curious to meet him.

Unlike therapists, most Spiritual Masters tend not to be especially interested in our personal lives. They are more concerned that we *be* better—that is, that we learn to operate more out of our genuine, as opposed to our egoic, self—as opposed to that we *feel* better. Their logic—and it absolutely resonated with me—is that the more we tune in to who we *really* are, the more this will also make us feel better.

As I see it, Masters have a function analogous to a power station, in that in being themselves connected to a higher energy source, they are able to bring this source energy directly to us, only stepped down in such a way that it may hopefully expand and illuminate us without in the process electrocuting us! I see their role as not only being to remind us of who we really are by giving us a direct experience of a self that is much more expanded and exists beyond our ego identifications, but also to show us what we need to do to come closer to this self. Thus, they instruct both by the wisdom of their words, either spoken or written, and by the emanations of their presence.

Spiritual Masters come in all sorts of different shapes and sizes. Some are loud and authoritative, others are gentle and sweet, and they also teach in many different ways. For example, there is a tradition called the Crazy Wisdom tradition, whereby the adept uses trickery to help us understand how absurd are the guidelines by which we live our conventional lives; often they will do something designed to *shock* us out of our habitual complacency. Osho, who had been dear Pragito's guru, was a 'shocker'. But I felt I'd had enough shocking. I chose Papaji because there was a gentleness about him and his way was quieter.

Whereas you and I may look at a person and just see them in terms of the stories we have about them and the boxes we like to put them in, the genuine Master sees only the divinity within us and where we might need help. By focussing on who we really are, or on our true or divine self, they are able to evoke that dimension of ourselves to come 'out of hiding'.

As lovely Papaji put it:

The real Master looks into your heart and sees what state you are in, and gives out advice which is always appropriate and relevant.

I had gone to see Papaji laden with books to read so I could also spend the time 'improving myself', and on my first day of satsang—where all the students would gather together in the presence of the teacher to hear him lecture—I stood up and asked him a question about what I needed to do to bring more balance and harmony into my life. Here was his exact reply (all his satsangs were recorded):

> *Stop struggling so much to get better. Know you already are what you wish to become. Give your heart a chance to breathe and realise that real knowledge does not come through the mind. You are someone who talks a lot about peace but you are always anxious and you bring that anxiety into your quest and that always hampers you. While you are here with me, I don't want you to do anything. Just be. Let go of all your books. Allow yourself to rest into your deeper being.*

Chuang Tzu would certainly have approved! Papaji looked directly at me as he spoke and while I know it sounds corny to say what I am about to say, the truth was that his gaze utterly zapped me! I was gently propelled into a whole new world. I was given a direct experience of what it was to be awake, free, quiet, surrendered, simple, without anxiety or the need to impress others or prove myself! Wow!

After the satsang was over that day, Johnny and I walked together around the town of Lucknow for a few hours, quietly enjoying each other's company and making sure to avoid all the cows wandering about in the streets. In India, they are regarded as sacred.

What I was experiencing was nothing like a drug-induced 'high', i.e., that whooshy kind of whoomphy feeling that I had had with ecstasy. On the contrary. I had entered a state that was equally, if not more awesome, yet very, very different, where I felt completely tranquil and my world became genuinely and even, yes, absurdly simple. I realised that simplicity isn't just arrived at because you choose to downsize and only confine yourself to dealing with essentials. In other words, it's not about how much or how little you have going on in your life. It's an inner state, and you can live simply even if there are complications in your life, as you won't allow your mind to become discombobulated by them!

Yes, my friend, I think I was probably experiencing for the first time what in Zen is known as 'Beginners mind,' which I had never managed to access during my stay at Tassajara. I observed that I was becoming quietly enchanted by the moo of a cow, the smile of my friend, a person crossing the road, the wind rustling the branches of a tree—all these simple things became very pregnant with meaning and I realised that I was also probably visiting the world that my buddy Chuang Tzu probably dwelt in all the time!

What Papaji's presence had done to me was temporarily remove or certainly lessen the pull of my ego identity in that I was no longer seeing the world through its reductionistic lens that loved to put everything I experienced, including myself, into boxes, the better to understand them. This reality was now unravelling and I now observed that I no longer felt a need to define myself through absurd categories such as 'well-built Serge' or 'artsy-fartsy Serge' or 'oh-so-clever Serge' or whatever other identities I might choose to conjure up. As this unravelling took place, I also saw how much I tended to 'weaponise' what I regarded as my 'assets', that is, use them to make myself either superior to people or inferior to them, or simply see them as a kind of 'badge of credibility' both to present myself to the world as well as justify my place in it.

How utterly absurd!

Especially my height. Six foot two. So what! All that wretched macho stuff that I thought I'd left behind. It still had a hold of me. Sheer goddamn ghastly vanity. Again, I saw that why I put so much stress on my physical height was because I often felt small. In exactly the same way that my girlfriends needed to be pretty because deep down I felt ugly! As I observed myself,

I felt these patterns begin gently to melt away in all their ridiculousness.

I began to realise that I was OK anyway and always had been, and most important, my OK-ness had nothing whatsoever to do with what I deemed to be my wretched 'assets'. As these fragments of my identity began dropping away, I experienced myself being *expanded* into simply 'being'!

Being! The one thing I had avoided all my life. Yes, I talked the talk of 'being' well enough, but in truth I was really a covert 'doer', and that much my life was built around trying to justify it, almost like if I couldn't prove that I had helped a sufficient number of old ladies across the road, taught enough retreats, written enough 'clever' articles—I wasn't good enough, hadn't made the grade. But what goddamn grade? And for what? No one was judging me but me! I was doing this to me. I was inventing this drama. How crazy it all was!

I understood for the first time what a book that my stepfather George had once given me, written by a Buddhist nun, with the enigmatic title *Being Nobody, Going Nowhere,* was really about. My real somebody-ness or my true me-ness lay in accessing my nobody-ness; and the more I could be in that state, the more I could also embrace my fellow human beings and the larger world around me with integrity, the more truly 'me' I became. What a paradox! And goodness me, it felt so liberating.

To my amazement I saw that this wasn't a reduction of me. On the contrary. It was a huge expansion. Release a little of the ego clench and so many of the insecurities vanish. As I looked around me in the crowded streets, everything became impregnated with quiet meaning. All the drama had faded. Nothing hyper. Total divine ordinariness. I wasn't above or better than any of these millions of Indians in the street. I wasn't less than them either. We were all human beings together doing our best to survive.....

I think for probably the first time in my life, I felt free of stress and anxiety, and during my visit I did exactly what Papaji told me, i.e., I did nothing. Basically, Chuang Tzu's teachings. No 'I must improve myself' rituals, as the true me was already improved and it was all about my allowing this 'me' out of the closet. I slept and ate and talked a lot with Johnny and Dominique and the people I met there, with no need to impress anyone or prove anything, and it was a sheer delight.

I was, however, very disturbed by the enormous poverty all around me as I had never experienced anything like that before. I remember walking up the steps to a tailor's where I could have an Indian-styled suit made for me very cheaply, and sitting all the way up the steps were scores of beggars asking for money. Many had twisted, broken legs. I was told that their parents did this to their children soon after birth so they could earn money by begging. And there was I, by comparison, the rich foreigner going into a shop to buy clothes that he didn't really need! I confess that I did have one Indian outfit made for me, but I gave the rest of my money to the beggars. All this poverty that I had never before encountered to this extent, greatly affected me. And I let it and that felt appropriate. So often in life, we block out everything that is uncomfortable and in so doing I think we muzzle our humanity. My humanity had been well and truly muzzled, and here in Lucknow, it was slowly being unravelled.

Yes, my friend, I think more of us need to allow ourselves to be more upset at the state of the world and not distance ourselves from it as so many of us do. I think that our upset-ness, if genuinely felt, is so often what pushes us to do something about it. It became clear to me that many of us allow ourselves to feel so constricted by the conditions or sheer weight imposed upon us by our wretched somebody-ness or our ego-ness, that we already feel so burdened that we don't bother to try to help those of our fellow human beings who have genuine burdens, like: how am I going to survive? I also think one of the reasons why many of us are so resistant to really opening up, is that we fear it might move us to ask deeper questions of ourselves and of the way we live, which in turn might require us to make some radical changes! And secretly the thought terrifies us!

I thought then of the way many rich people live today, cloistered behind tall iron gates, moving from one exclusive activity to another and never having to concern themselves with world pain. And yet this suppression actually brings with it another kind of pain, the pain of being isolated. OK, rich people may not have to worry about their physical survival, but they still have to play all those games around defending their somebody-ness! Over the years, I have had many very wealthy people as my clients, and in no way have I found them happier than other people. As the Beatles put it: 'money can't buy me love!'

But now, in my new, simple inner state, I was girlfriend-less and living within this poverty zone and I was allowing it to touch me and disturb me and I was feeling very, very abundant. I felt much richer at that moment than any multimillionaire! I also saw that in comparison to many of the people around me, my own puny little emotional problems that often absorbed so much of my time and energy were simply my typhoons in teacups!

I had another important teacher here, as well as Papaji, and his name was Deepak and I found him to be one of the most remarkable people I have ever met. He literally shone with love and generosity of spirit. He was a servant, but there was nothing servile about him. He saw his looking after us—tidying the house, cooking meals, washing our clothes—as a service, not as menial tasks. You could tell that he felt neither above us nor below us. I realised it was the Deepaks of this world who were the true noble people, the true salts of the earth. I could see that he pretty well lived all the time in this new space that I was only now beginning temporarily to touch into. Yes, he lived very abundantly!

Deepak and I got on very well. I would always feel very happy in his company, as one does with very open-hearted and genuine people, and one evening he invited me to have dinner with him and his family. He got paid very little and lived with his wife and two young children in a tiny house, but there was a huge happiness there and I was greeted as if I were an old friend. His wife had prepared a veritable banquet for me, and I realised this must have cost him quite a few weeks' wages. It reminded me again that often the most hospitable people are those who have the least.

When eventually it was my time to leave the ashram and return home, I tried to leave Deepak a big tip, but when he found it, he returned it to me. 'O no, Serge,' he said, 'I am very rich. There is nothing I lack in my life. You need your money as you are going back to the West.' I had to somehow smuggle money into his little dwelling when I knew that all the family were out, just before I left, so he couldn't give it back to me!

What a guy! Here, I felt, was someone who really represented how we all needed to be and that if we were like that, there would be peace and harmony in the world. He was humble in an extremely noble way—nothing Uriah Heep-ish about him. His heart was big. He was generous and wise and a good husband and father. And he loved people and he saw the purpose of his life as being to serve Papaji and the evolution of humanity by being a good human being. Bless you, Deepak. I am writing this nearly thirty years later and I hope you and your family are still abundant. I want you to know how important you were in my life and that you have been a great inspiration to me.

I would love to say that my 'Papaji-induced' state remained for ever and that the old Serge with his old clenches and dramas never returned. Sadly, as with so many other profound experiences, that would be an untruth. As I returned to my old life, slowly my old ego clenches returned. But—and this was important—not as powerfully as before, and now I could see them much more clearly for what they were. I realised that if I were to remain in this expanded state, I really needed to do a lot of inner work and do so consistently. Staying awake is not a 'given'! The athlete who trains to run a marathon will soon lose his fitness if he stops his training.

I didn't feel moved to become Papaji's disciple or to return to Lucknow. I felt I wasn't a 'disciply' kind of bloke; I could never prostrate myself at his feet as so many of his disciples did. But I was very grateful for the experience of having met this extraordinary human being. One afternoon I quietly sat with him and a few others in silence and we all watched the Test match on his little TV. And it was such a joy. Papaji had a great sweetness of being. He has now been dead for over twenty years, but I still have a picture of him in my office and I feel a little bit of his spirit still quietly dances inside me as I go about my daily life.

When I got back I received a lovely letter from John thanking me for having invited him to come along, and affirming the depth of our relationship. At that time, I loved John like the brother I had never had, and ever since our Harrow days, he has been a very important friend for me and has played a significant role in my life on many levels and has helped me in countless ways. In fact, I could write a whole book just about our relationship.

Sadly, our closeness did not endure, and later both of us felt badly betrayed by the other. A few years later, when I got married, I received a letter from him telling me, without giving any reason, that he was 'bowing out of my life'. This hurt me a lot and I didn't see him for many years. Then he 'returned', but things were never quite the same, and then a few years ago he wrote a book about his life and I, very self-righteously, felt he had excluded certain things about his past that I thought were important and I made the big mistake of letting Dominique know about them, and he never forgave me. He was right. I should never have interfered. I'd again forgotten Chuang Tzu's teachings. Who am I to say what John shares with his wife and decides to write in a book! Sadly, all attempts on my part to have a meeting to try to iron things out (big Shadow issues can often emerge in close relationships) got nowhere. I am someone who by nature is a confronter—if something isn't right, let's look at it and put it out on the table—whereas John's strategy is always to hide away in his lair. We've had no connection for several years and I don't think we ever will again, and I miss the affection we used to have for one another. I don't think John will ever forgive me and that is sad. He is a good man and has written two important books about how to live more simply and more consciously. Bless you, my dear old friend. I wish you and your family well.

When I got back from India, my fiftieth birthday, on 29 June 1995, was looming and I decided I was going to have a fantastic party to celebrate it. I love good parties and I used to have a lot of them in my California days and I thought it was high time I had a big, elegant 'black tie' one in England in the celebratory spirit of the Via Positiva. I thought I'd hold it at my home in Gloucestershire and I'd invite all my many different friends from the many different segments of my life. I wanted to thank them all for the gift of their friendship and let them know how important they had been in my life.

I had a good friend, Sheila Reeves, who lived nearby and who, bless her, organised everything very inexpensively and beautifully; a huge marquee was set up in the garden and I invited about seventy-five guests. It was all *très chic*. But it was not artificial. It was done in a spirit of generosity to thank people for being my dear friends and to give everyone a great evening. Drinks were served by the swimming pool and I arranged the seating for an excellent four-course dinner. I gave a little speech and so did a few friends.

But the *pièce de résistance* was the cabaret after dinner. I had a lot of buddies who were musicians and I asked all of them to perform. Dearest Alice Friend, who used to help me with my New Year retreats, sang her spiritual songs, her husband Rod played the piano, and dear Marigold Dick played her harp. All my musician mates did something. And to finish the evening off was the just-formed Serge B-B Blues Band starring yours truly, my good friend Chris on the harmonica and bongos and, yes—what a privileged guy I was—none other than my friend and next-door neighbour (he lived just down the road from me) Steve Winwood, blues musician extraordinaire!

As you know, I have always been a great blues aficionado, and just to have met Steve, who for many years had been a great hero of mine, would have been great. But to actually get to play the blues with him—well, it was the very greatest of honours.

Remember what I said earlier about how, if you play tennis with someone much better than you, it lifts your game. Well, the same could be said about if you play music with a genius, and during the forty-five minutes we played together, I felt temporarily transmogrified into Ramblin' Boy Behrens! I'd written a song especially for the occasion and just to let you know how corny I really am (as if you haven't discovered by this time!) here's the first verse!

Well, I woke up this mornin' realised I was fifty
Lordy Hallelujah, that's a mighty age to be,
Suddenly realised I ain't a young guy any more
But middle aged and paunchy and a terrible old bore.
That's the price of middle age,
Givin' up being all the rage.

Shortly after this birthday, my very dear friend, Carinthia West, whom I had known since her deb party days, came and rented the Old School House for six months as she had started dating my old mate, Lawrence Blair. Carinth was tall, slim and voluptuously beautiful, with a veritable mane of honey-blond hair. She looked very much like the singer Carly Simon, who was actually a close friend of hers. She was very creative and had fingers in many different artistic pies.

It was great having my two old friends living next door to me. Carinth was one of those terrific people who knew everyone and everyone loved her. If a friend was in trouble, she would always be there to lend a hand or a shoulder to cry on. She has contributed to my life in so many ways and has been the most loyal and generous godmother to my daughter.

At this time, I also started up an affair with a Swedish woman, Kikan Massara, who for many years had worked as a model, and from the very start of our relationship, never held back from letting me know that she was angry with men as she felt they just looked at her for her prettiness and not for her brain. I had a vague sense that this probably signalled that trouble lay ahead. And I was not wrong. My ability still to draw wounded women into my orbit told me that I still had a lot more healing to undergo in this area of my life.

The story was familiar. I knew it well! As my affection for Kikan began to grow, so too did her capacity to unleash on me both barrels of the shotgun. Dear Kikan was a lovely bright, creative human being but had a side that was not only a punisher of men but also of herself. As I was writing this, I thought of her and wondered what had happened to her—I had lost touch with her for many years—so I googled her and found out she was living in Paris, and I rang her. We had a long conversation and she told me that the last fifteen years of her life had been very hard and she'd barely survived. I felt sad for her.

With Larry Spiro in Jerusalem

With 'Heart Man' Brugh Joy in Maui

Wonderful, loving Papaji

With dear friends Mike the psych, Alain Adam, Alan and Danny-boy

Sir George Trevelyan with his great friend Rhoda Cowan

Happy days with Averill and little Irena

Playing with Irena

On holiday in Mallorca with Averill and Irena

Great Honour playing with Donovan at my Spiritual Retreat

With Irena in Paris

My beautiful Martina

Martina and Leah

With Irena in Vienna

Camel riding with Martina in Marrakech

Marrying Martina

on my 70th Birthday

Celebrating my 75th birthday with Martina in Vienna

Celebrating my 77th Christmas in Mallorca with
Martina, Irena, Leah and her father Tim

Chapter 25

Marriage

I've always attended a lot of conferences, a) because they are wonderful places to keep on top of the latest thinking in one's field, and b) because they are wonderful places in which to bump into one's colleagues, and one of my favourite conferences was one entitled Mystics and Scientists that my dear friend David Lorimer had put on every year for the last twenty years, through the Scientific and Medical Network.

It was a fateful decision. At it, I met Roger Woolger, who was to become a special friend and teacher for me. He was one of the presenters and had been a contemporary of mine at Oxford, although we never met—he being scholarly inclined and utterly without dandified or jockish inclinations—and I subsequently trained with him over the next three years to qualify as a past-life psychotherapist. At the same time, I met the woman who was to become my first wife, Averill Gordon. She told me later that she had sat behind me at a lecture and, having psychic abilities, had seen that I was the man she was going to marry.

Things didn't get off to too good a start as just before meeting her I had become smitten by a woman much younger than me. But this little flingette did not last long and Averill and I came back together and started going out seriously. During my three-day stints in London, I would stay in her flat as opposed to in my studio.

Meanwhile, my cousin Alex Ranicar, whom I had not been that close to as we hadn't seen each other for many years, suddenly bounced back into my life. As he worked in the medical field, he suggested that as I was no longer a young whippersnapper—really!—it might be a good idea if I had a medical check-up, especially as I had never had one before.

I did as Alex told me and this was when I found out that I had chronic lymphocytic leukaemia.

The news initially absolutely floored me, and it occurred to me that as I was growing increasingly close to Averill and if my days were to be numbered, I perhaps should get married. Yes, that was my weird logic at that time. Besides, unlike the saga with my lawyer friend, this felt like the 'real thing'. Averill was interested in the same things that I was and I was gradually letting her into my heart. At the same time, she announced to me that she was pregnant.

I had two main fears. What if I married Averill and we found we didn't get on? And what scared me about having a child was the same thing. Yikes! Well, life is a risk, I reasoned to myself. I've loved women in the past and not married them. I'm getting on in years and the more I know Averill, the fonder I am becoming of her. So, let's go for it. There was a great sweetness and softness to Averill and I felt safe with her and I trusted her.

And suddenly marriage was upon me and I felt terrific about it. Actually, we had two ceremonies, a formal one in London at the King's Road Registry Office, and a more informal one a few days later, at the little Norman church in Hampnett, along with a reception in Chris Dreyfus' big barn just opposite. Sadly, none of Averill's friends or family came over except her best buddy Sue, who was her 'best woman'. Alan Gordon Walker was my best man, Johnny Reed by this time having 'bowed out'! Averill looked very beautiful at our Hampnett wedding and all my good friends were there. It was a very, very happy day.

Well or wow, I had now joined the ranks and become one of 'them', a married man, a 'grown-up', with a responsibility not only to look after my new wife but also our child who was on the way. Anyhow, after the reception, Averill and I flew off to a tiny island in the Bahamas for our honeymoon. The fact that Averill was carrying our baby made me feel very close and protective towards her. I began to have the sense that we were a unit and that at last I could move out of my old 'lone-wolf' identity.

Soon after our return came the most important moment of my whole life: the birth of our daughter! While secretly I had been hoping for a boy—someone to continue the lineage of Serge B-B—the moment our daughter arrived, I was so happy it was a girl. Our midwife at the Cheltenham hospital where she was born, placed her in my arms still attached to the umbilical cord. Here is what I wrote in my journal that evening:

> *Wow. I am a father and I am the happiest man in the whole world. What a wonderful wife I have. How brave Averill was. I am so proud of her. When the midwife handed Irena to me, and as I clutched this tiny little new-born creature close to my chest, tears of joy just exploded out of me. I felt my heart catapult open so powerfully and I felt so much love that I thought I would explode. And I did explode. With gratitude and joy. I loved Irena deeply the moment she was in my arms and my tears poured down onto this tiny little creature with her mass of thick dark hair. (It later all fell out as she was a blonde like her mama.) I probably experienced unconditional love properly for the first time. All those feelings about wanting a boy evaporated. I am so, so, so, so happy I have a little girl. My little girl. Our little girl... What a celebration.*

Again, I thought of Wordsworth's famous lines in 'Intimations of Immortality' about a newborn coming into the world: 'Trailing clouds of glory do we come... from God, who is our home...' This is why newborns are so precious. They have just emerged from a place where they have been experiencing a oneness with life. Remember what I said earlier about the soul wound and how it had affected me? I was damn well going to make sure that Irena was not going to suffer in the same way. I did my best to see her immediately through the eyes of soul, and over the first ten years of her life; I have endeavoured consciously to continue seeing her in that way. I also remembered what Kahlil Gibran said about children in his beautiful little book *The Prophet*, namely that 'they are the result of life's longing for itself... They come from us, but they do not belong to us.' I have done my best to bear that in mind and have tried never to be responsible for telling Irena what I think she should do.

I think that being present at Irena's birth was probably one of the great spiritual experiences of my life, as the love came up so suddenly; and now, twenty-three years later and Irena is a grown-up woman, those loving feelings are inside me as powerfully as ever. I often ponder on how marvellous nature is, endowing all creatures, animal and human, with the instinct to love, protect and nurture their young.

My life changed for ever the moment Irena came into the world. I was fifty-four and this was my first child—and as things have transpired, my only child—and I wanted to be a total 'hands-on dad'. I realised I had to be very conscious all the time, make sure that I didn't drop her, be careful that when she slept in our bed I didn't crush her. In those early years, I changed Irena's nappies just as many times as her mother and looking after her became my main priority. People talk about parents being teachers for their children. I think it is the other way around. I felt Irena was my teacher, inspiring me to surrender my tendency to be self-centred and to try to put my daughter's requirements first.

I sometimes reflected that in any one day, I have been more there for Irena than my father had ever been for me in my entire life. Averill was also a superb mother and her psychic abilities enabled her to know exactly what Irena needed at any moment, and so she grew up a happy child. It also felt so good living in the countryside where the air was fresh and green trees and fields were all around. I have wonderful memories of Irena and I playing hide-and-seek in the hay loft, sledging together when it snowed and going for long walks and examining the large rabbit holes in the forest nearby. Sometimes in the evenings, when it was my turn to give her a bath and I'd dry her and then get under her eiderdown and read her a bedtime story, I would sometimes fall asleep in the middle of reading—the giant at the top of the beanstalk or the adventures of Mr Messy didn't sufficiently interest old Mr ADD!

I would still go to London for my three days a week to see my clients, and when I returned, Irena would see her dada and run into my arms; and each time I held her, I felt I loved her more and more. All my fears of Irena and me not getting on proved groundless, and something very deep gradually grew up between us. I had the sense that perhaps I knew my little creature already, that we may even have had a past life together in some capacity, as something about her felt so familiar.

Averill and I had a lovely christening party in Hampnett and nine of my friends became godparents: Jose Fonseca, Alan and Louise, Pete Kyte, Ralph Blum, the infamous writer of the best-selling books on runes, my dear old friend Peter Adler (who had first turned me on to tribal art thirty years ago), Marigold Dick, my dear harpist friend, and Joanna and Michael Brown.

When Irena was a few years old, we went to New Zealand so she could meet Averill's parents. Here's what I wrote:

> *My darling little Irena. Every day you give me such happiness. You are a blessing from God and I could not have asked for a more wonderful child. I hug you with all my heart.*
>
> *I am having such a wonderful time with Irena, whom I love more and more every day, and I love 'us' as a little family and the affection between Averill and myself is growing and I am increasingly learning to appreciate her and see her deep sweetness. As if the trip home has somehow freed up her beautiful loving nature.*

At about this time, as I said, I also began my training in Past Life psychotherapy with Roger. He called it Deep Memory work. The underlying idea is that many of us come into the world carrying unresolved issues or chunks of 'difficult karma' that don't just relate to traumatic or painful experiences in our early childhood, but may also connect to our having had a traumatic birth or to 'unfinished business' or unresolved painful experiences 'bleeding through' either from other lifetimes or even from the collective pain pool of what humanity as a whole is struggling with. The closer a person is able to get to the core memory or to experience the deeper source of the trauma coming up for them, the more likely the charge from the negative pattern will be reduced.

To give an example, a very angry and destructive young man, who hates authority figures and may perhaps be into self-harming, may not necessarily be that way because he experienced bad parenting. It may well be because he is holding a deep memory, say, of an incarnation where he lay dying on a battlefield, his last thoughts being ones of huge rage. 'Why am I dying? This war is so purposeless and the life I could be having the opportunity to live is draining away from me.' As he dies, his last thoughts are of the absurdity of it all. Thus, in his next incarnation, he enters the world with this unresolved desperation and rage locked inside him. In my practice, I have worked with several angry young men for whom not dissimilar stories constituted the core source of their rage.

It was at this time that I unexpectedly became a *cavaliere*, which is the Italian word for knight. A good friend of mine, Julian Allison, a bit younger than me, who also had had a baby late in life, became very interested in the work I had been doing and felt that as I seemed to be helping quite a lot of people, I should receive some kind of reward.

Some years ago, he had himself been knighted in the Order of Saints Maurice and Lazarus, a Roman Catholic dynastic order founded in 1572 by the then Duke of Savoy, and felt that despite my not being Catholic, I should also be given this honour, and so he put forward my name to the committee who decide these things.

Lo and behold, a few months later I got a very formal letter signed personally by the current duke to inform me that I needed to go to Geneva to attend the ceremony where I would be knighted.

So, a few weeks later, I found myself in Geneva in a suit and tie kneeling down in front of the current Duke of Savoy who tapped my shoulder with a sword and said something along the lines of 'Arise, O Cavaliere', only in Italian! To be honest, I found it all a bit of a lark. A few years later, though, I happened to be in Rome and a group of us went out to a nice restaurant, where we were told there were no tables available. Whereupon yours truly stepped forward and introducing himself as 'Cavaliere Sergio Beddingtoni', said in his best Lord Snooty accent that, 'This is simply not good enough and we demand a good table!' Whereupon the maître d's manner changed at once. He apologised and the best table suddenly appeared for us. I thought to myself: 'Goodness, this is exactly the kind of thing that my father—Sir Edward B-B—would have done!'

Chapter 26

Mallorca Revisited

When Irena was three, she and Averill and I were invited by my good friend Peter Reichwald to spend ten days in Mallorca as he had just rented a finca there. He had married his third wife Ellen just before I married Averill, and they had had twins who were just a year older than Irena. It was very special to be on this magical island again, as I had spent many happy summer holidays there when I was much younger. Basically, my idea of paradise has always been a long swim and lying on a beach in the sun all day. A part of me is a real lazy old sod.

When I was a little boy and my parents were still together, we would either stay in the beautiful villa of my father's good friend, the Yugoslav Vane Ivanovic, or at the rather plush Formentor Hotel, just across the bay.

Vane had been my official guardian (whatever that meant exactly) and I enormously looked up to him. He was tall and immensely handsome and athletic, and had represented his country in the Berlin Olympics for the 110- and 400-metre hurdles. He taught me how to swim and many of my happiest memories of Mallorca revolve around time spent with him and his children, especially Minja, who was exactly my age and who, very sadly, has just died of cancer. Not only was Vane a great pioneer in underwater spear fishing (he had written several books on it), but he was also the British consul in Monaco and his wife June was one of my mother's best friends.

So just as I have many happy childhood memories of Zermatt, so the same thing holds true for Mallorca, and many of them are associated with Vane. He would often take my father and I out on his fishing boat early in the morning and we would swim on the surface and watch him and his friends swim many metres down and spear fish. Afterwards, we would all have a delicious breakfast on board, consisting of the catches of the day!

Vane was immensely charismatic and charming and, unlike many men at that time, he had long hair. Even when I was young, I started learning some of my dandyisms from him, and for many years, going back to the days when I used to have my jackets tailor-made, I would ask that they have turned-back cuffs like Vane's! Anyhow, all these memories of my past came flooding back on this visit, as the villa that Peter rented for us all just happened to be right next to where Vane used to live. I felt very nostalgic and wondered who owned it now, as he had been dead for many years. I particularly loved the smells of Mallorca and I found that the island had lost none of its allure for me.

I knew that my old school friend Julian Moulton, whom I used to see around and about in my Gstaad days, now lived in Mallorca, and as I drove over to see him, I suddenly thought to myself: I love this place. I'd love a little *pied-à-terre* here, and as I had just sold the flat that old Gwennie had left to me in her will, I consequently had a bit of spare cash. I always felt safe when money was in bricks and mortar, as a) it meant I couldn't touch it, and b) it felt a solid investment. By now, my thinking around money had become much saner!

Julian had a friend who was a real estate broker and the next day Sheana took me to see a half-built finca with no electricity or plumbing. It was cheap and had about an acre of land around it, and in my ADD-ish impulsive way—I didn't do anything to check its legalities—I went and bought it. It needed a lot of work doing to it and, again by chance—or can we say those good old helping forces came to my aid yet again—I also reconnected with another old friend, Chris Carter, who also lived on the island and who, interestingly, had also received help from Gwennie in the past, which had very much bonded us. And dear old Chris had now morphed from Afro-styled hippie and confused young man, to being a very respectable-looking, shrewd and successful property developer.

Indeed, he was an absolute godsend. If it had not been for him I would have been left with a wreck, unable to do anything to the house. But Chris knew the ropes, and within a year, I had a superb little holiday home with electricity, built to look like an old finca, with two bedrooms and two bathrooms and a main room with high ceilings that I loved and which reminded me of my lovely old barn in Gloucestershire. Over the years, Averill, Irena and I would go out for our holidays and we made a lot of new friends. It was especially delightful meeting Paul Gittings and Tim Dyas, who lived just round the corner from me, and who had been contemporaries of mine at Oxford (although we didn't know each other then). They both became close friends and regular tennis partners.

Later that summer, I decided to hold a major spiritual retreat in Mallorca and invited my very dear old Californian friend Martine Algier, who was one of the first people I met when I arrived in the States, to host it with me. That meant we had a balance of the masculine and the feminine. Martine had been trained in many different disciplines including as a dancer, and she brought a wonderfully delicate presence into our work.

Many of my old English friends came on this course, like Pamela whom I had been unofficially engaged to while at Oxford, and my old friend the lovely Anne Dunhill. One of my heroes from the 1960s also enrolled—Donovan, with his wife Linda, whom I'd met at a dinner with friends a few months ago. Don was very generous with his music and whenever we'd go out to restaurants, he would always play for people.

As I loved all his songs and knew most of the words, and as the chord formations were simple, he allowed me to accompany him. Just as with Steve Winwood, when you get to play with a maestro, it lifts your game. I felt as if the fairy sprinklings of

Don's delicious troubadour-hood-ness were being showered on me and I felt blessed by the experience.

Averill, sadly, did not have the same enthusiasm for Mallorca that I did. Maybe because she came from a country that was all about sun and beaches anyway. She was upset that to make up the cost of fixing up the little finca, I had had to sell some Fabergé pieces and jewellery inherited from my mother that she felt Irena ought to have had. I think she had a point. She felt—probably quite rightly—that it was *my* place with *my* vision, not *our* place. Small cracks in our relationship, which we'd both managed to paper over and ignore, were widened by the Mallorca project.

That said, having Irena, whom we both adored, greatly served to unite us and I felt proud to have this very attractive, capable, wise and effective woman at my side doing her very best to love yours truly, who, as no doubt you may have gathered by now, was not always the easiest of people!

Chapter 27

Ayahuasca

About seven years into my marriage, another adventure in consciousness began calling out strongly to me. My journey of self-discovery had not solely been about my trying to become a 'better human being' or to wake up to be more of who I truly am (and therefore less of who I was not!), I also felt a strong urge to deepen my spiritual understanding in general.

I felt I wanted to *know* 'the Friend' more fully; I felt I wanted to become more intimate with my beloved 'helping forces'. As a result of my journeying up to this point, I could unequivocally say that I not only *believed*, but *knew* that a Being or a Beingness of extraordinary love and intelligence existed, and at different times and in different ways, I had certainly experienced some close encounters with this Being. What I wanted now was to draw even closer. In Aldous Huxley's lingo, I wanted to open the doors of my perception into the higher worlds that I had begun touching into in my California days and which had accelerated during my time with Papaji. However, despite meditating regularly, I again felt myself closing down a little and there seemed to be a place beyond which I was not able or, it sometimes felt, not 'allowed' to go!

At present in my life, things also seemed to be slowing down. I was aware that this often happened just before some kind of quantum leap forward occurred and that when a 'next step' beckoned, it would often signal its approach via my encountering all sorts of resistances, and that was exactly what was happening now. I also sensed that old Mr Ego was saying, 'OK, buster, I've been your servant not your master for a long time and it's now time for me to come back and reassert myself once more.' For no reason I could point to, I was not at ease with myself. I was going through something of an inner crisis that had nothing to do with my outer life; that was flowing along comfortably enough. I was basically very happy with Irena and Averill.

I knew enough about what was going on with me to realise that I needed more purification, more 'fasting of the heart', and that I couldn't go to the new level that I sensed was beckoning to me without some additional help. Since throughout my life I have always chosen to be my own 'spiritual director'—that is, I've always been the one who has decided in what direction I needed to go or who or what to work with at any time—what I was currently feeling was that ayahuasca might well be very supportive to me. I had done a lot of research into this particular sacrament and had several friends who had reported very positive experiences. I had also been especially touched by the fact that Jonathan Goldman had written that

> *Ayahuasca offers us a chance to interact intimately with a Divine Being of unimaginable intelligence, compassion, clarity and spiritual power.*

That was exactly the interaction that I yearned for. So, what exactly is ayahuasca? It is a Quechua word meaning 'vine of the soul' and it's a natural psychedelic that had been used by shamans for the last 2500 years to expand their consciousness. The substance is prepared by soaking the bark and stems of a particular tree with various other plants, which is then made into a substance that one can drink.

Yes, my friend, from the Eleusinian mystery rites of ancient Greece to the peyote ceremonies of Native Americans, human beings have been ingesting consciousness-amplifying substances for thousands of years, and have all come to the same conclusion: namely, that these substances are sacred and that if used in the correct way, i.e., *not* hippie-dippily, they can help us connect more deeply with who we *truly* are as well as open up higher worlds of consciousness. Remember those famous words by the philosopher William James, the brother of the great novelist, in his book *The Varieties of Religious Experience*?

> *Our normal waking consciousness, or rational consciousness as we call it, is but one special type of consciousness, while all around it, parted by the flimsiest of screens, there lie potential forms of consciousness entirely different... No account of the universe in its totality can be final which leaves these other forms of consciousness disregarded...*

I wanted to experience these other realities and was also only too aware that I still carried old emotional wounds and blockages that seemed to be resisting past-life therapy. I had attended many lectures and seminars with Stan Grof, the 'father of transpersonal psychology' and a great pioneer in the field of psychedelics, and he always stressed that if we are able to stay for long periods of time in expanded states of awareness, that important healings can often take place.

The universe, as it so often has done for me, responded to my desire. Again, I happened to be attending a conference in Germany, and out of the blue, I was introduced directly to the world of ayahuasca by some good friends who were currently working with it and were full of praise. 'Come to a meeting of the Santo Daime Church,' my psychologist friends Ingo and Dietrich suggested, 'there is one happening tomorrow!' Why not? I felt very excited, and fasted until then so that I might be as empty as possible for the experience. And what an experience it was!

The Santo Daime Church had been set up in order to bring the use of ayahuasca to the West. It had branches in many European countries and included elements of several religious and spiritual traditions including folk Catholicism, South American shamanism and African animism. Over the next six months, under the watchful and protective eye of an elderly Brazilian ayahuascero (shaman), who had come over from Brazil and who would oversee everything, I participated in some twenty 'ayahuascan weekends' in London and in all probably had about eighty 'trips'.

The ceremony would last all weekend. There would be music played throughout and we would chant hymns in Spanish, and every four to five hours, as the effects wore off, we would line up and go back to the ayahuascero, who oversaw the whole ceremony and would then pour us another cup of the brew. There was a strong structure to this ceremony. We all had to wear white and the women were on one side and the men on the other. It felt analogous to taking the wafer and wine in holy communion, only for me this was the holiest communion with the sacred forces that I could ever have dreamed of.

Some people refer to ayahuasca as 'the professor' because it often talks to us from inside ourselves and gives us important information about our lives, suggesting new options for us to consider, or answers particular questions which we might have. Indeed, the very first time I drank this brew in Germany, it introduced itself quite formally to me and informed me that as a plant intelligence, it had aligned itself with humanity and its role was to assist us in our evolution and help connect human with divine intelligence. It told me that I needed to be very conscious as over the next half-century huge changes would be taking place on the planet. I remember that after my first Santo Daime weekend in London, having slept only a few hours each night, I awoke on Monday morning full of vigour and joie de vie, sensing that a healing had taken place. Feeling moved to take myself for a long run in Hyde Park, I found myself bounding along with the same energetic spirit that I used to demonstrate when I was a young man!

These weekends were extremely profound for me. Every session was completely different and I was aware of a very great intelligence at work as, in an absolutely magical way, I would find myself being taken into exactly those areas of my life that I felt needed to be examined. Sometimes I went up into the 'heavens'. On other occasions, I'd be taken down into my 'hell'! At times, interestingly, I would even find myself being taken into my daughter Irena's reality and working through some little chunk of karma for her, and I felt so happy to be doing this. As with the Princess Diana effect, in some sessions I would experience myself being taken into some dark area of the human collective psyche, and on one particular horrendous occasion, I felt myself entering into the heart of the mindset of fascism and totalitarianism. While this was extremely painful, I found that this brew seemed to endow me with the strength and courage to experience and work with this energy pattern, which is why I suspect I was being taken into it so deeply.

Ayahuasca also served further to open the doorways into those dimensions of my psyche where my deeper love and wisdom and my capacity for feeling ecstatic resided, and some sessions were journeys into pure joy from beginning to end and very much confirmed the validity of everything that I had learned from my work with Matthew Fox, namely that all of us come into the world full of blessings and are not full of sin. I needed to be crystal clear, however, that there was a huge difference between my *temporarily* accessing a high state of consciousness, which was no indication of my level of evolution, and my being able to live in that state *all the time,* which would be. In other words, the difference between most of us and the great Masters—the Papajis and the Ramana Maharshis—is that they reside in these high states *all the time* and are able to arrive there naturally! Ayahuasca takes us into the higher worlds but only temporarily. It points the way but that is all. If we want to take up residence there, we have to work for it.

Essentially ayahuasca was reminding me what I knew already, namely, that the purpose of being human was to learn increasingly to be an open space for divine consciousness to dance inside us, but I felt I was now 'getting' this message at a deeper level. Here's how I put it in a journal entry:

> *I believe that the reason why we were created—why we have all come into incarnation—is because as we choose to embark on the journey of becoming more who we truly are, we increasingly become a space for a higher or a more divine consciousness to know itself and to celebrate itself through us. In a word, we become a space for grace.*
>
> *So, when you and I are feeling joy, when we love someone or something—say our work or a beautiful piece of art or music—or when we are acting courageously or experiencing a deep connection with nature, we become a space for this consciousness which ordinarily is hidden inside each of us, to come more and more out of hiding and manifest itself.*

A few months into my journeying, I felt adventurous and asked the old ayahuascero if I could venture a little deeper and have three cups of the brew, not just one. He looked into my eyes for a long time to see if I was ready, and then nodded and gave me this extra dose. What followed then is in an extract from a letter I wrote twelve years later to Chris Bache, a professor of philosophy and religious studies in America, a consciousness explorer for many years, and author of best-selling book, *LSD and the Mind of the Universe*:

> *Chris, after this triple dose, I felt myself being precipitated right into the mind and heart of the Cosmos. The Great Symphony of God's love for his Creation was singing a glorious hymn of Hallelujah to me and I was aware of the sacred music also emerging from within me. I was both the singer and the song. The experience felt so dear and so real now as I recall it, and I realise that I miss it, even though it happened twelve years ago. There was so much*

illumination and so much love and light as I experienced the enormous beneficence of the universe. Yes, there was definitely a plan for the evolution of humanity and it felt as if I, a little tiddler, had temporarily been offered an invitation to feast at the high table of those great spiritual intelligences working 'the plan' out, and being informed that in my infinitesimally tiny way, I was also part of it.

Yet I observed that as the light grew brighter, I couldn't fully open to it. I saw in me a resistance and a fear and yes, a definite pain. It felt as if my channels into these deeply sacred realms, were not open enough and now the light was pressing against this block, trying to push it away but not quite succeeding. I saw in me a strong resistance; I saw that I was afraid to experience that degree of love and abundance. It occurred to me that this was perhaps because at this level, these channels of mine had not been exercised enough; they were too narrow or too stiff or too weak in the same way that if one was to lie in bed for a month without moving a muscle, they would gently atrophy and one was going to find it difficult when at last one tried to get up and walk!

It wasn't that I felt that the cosmic symphony didn't want to dance inside me, as I knew it did. And it wasn't as if I didn't also desire this awesome experience, as I also deeply did. It was just that I couldn't surrender to it as fully as I wanted. I was experiencing what in transpersonal psychology is called the 'repression of the sublime' where we become afraid of becoming that sublime being that we all truly are. Perhaps, at another level, I hadn't yet undergone enough purification, i.e., my sensibilities were still too coarse fully to allow those higher vibrational frequencies to run through me. Maybe it was a little like asking an O level student in maths to understand post graduate mathematics! What do you think, Chris?

Here is an extract from Chris's reply:

> *Serge, I understand completely the dilemma you shared with me and described so well. The infinite Bliss wants to dance with us but is blocked by the coarseness of our being, and we invite it into our being at great risk, knowing it will burn before it takes us into ecstasy. But where did this coarseness come from? We see that it comes from our commitment to incarnate in this dense world in the first place. So this struggle comes ultimately from our love and our love comes from our true nature. But now once embodied, the challenge of admitting the bliss of our true nature into our physical being is formidable. As you say, you have to train for it. A passage from my book reinforces your observations...*
>
> *I saw that in the afterlife, 'hell' is actually a state of deep purification entered into only by those who are deeply committed to their spiritual development, for there are slower paths available for the less spiritually ambitious. The experience of hell is created when our flawed and imperfect personal history is brought into contact with our luminous Divine Nature and held there, allowing the power of our Divine Nature to purify and heal our historical limitations... Only when hell's work is finished can we possibly begin to appreciate its mercy. As in hell, so in our sessions, all suffering serves bliss.*

A very profound reply suggesting that the experience of suffering has a purifying element to it; it burns up karma, and it is so important that we understand this. I will therefore end this chapter by saying a few words about how I work with suffering, as it is something that, by virtue of our being human beings, all of us at some time or other in our lives will be called to confront. The only difference is that some of us are visited by it more often than others, some of us have to put up with it more intensely than others, and some of us are better equipped at dealing with it than others. When, for whatever reasons, suffering pays me a visit, I try to relate to it as follows:

1) I don't run away but understand it has come to visit me for a purpose, even if I don't always get that purpose. In other words, I see my suffering as part of my initiatory challenges, which, as Chris so poignantly pointed out, we need to go through if our intention is to become more fully human.
2) I do my best to experience my suffering or my inner burning as fully or as consciously as possible, and to do this I try to take it into the alchemical fire that I know resides inside my heart, and thus is able to transmute my 'base metal' into gold! The more I open my heart to my suffering in this way, as opposed to try to close off to it or escape it, the better. From this place, I also ask it to enlighten me and burn away all my impurities.
3) I realise that I need to pray for help and guidance to do this work effectively and trust that if I stay with my suffering and don't try to avoid it or become numb to it, a resolution will come in its own time and in its own way. I also need to remember that when night is at its blackest is when the first slivers of dawn begin to appear.

I had no idea that very shortly I was about to confront a big dose of suffering and to hit one of the lowest points in my entire life...

Chapter 28

Uncoupling

Underneath the surface, small cracks were beginning to open up in my marriage that Averill and I were both finding it increasingly hard to ignore. Initially our involvement with and love for Irena had made both of us not want to look at certain challenging issues that were coming up between us, but now that Irena was going to kindergarten and we had more time together, these could no longer be brushed aside. In my diaries of the time, I noted that those days where the waters between us were choppy were becoming more frequent.

However, it is so easy, when relationships begin to run into difficulties, to wish to ascribe blame, whether to ourselves or our partner—to say that if only we or the other did this or didn't do that, that all would be fine. I don't think this approach applied to us, and that either Averill or I were at fault for these ever-widening fissures. We both wanted our marriage to work and we both did our best to make it work. And there was a lot of love there. But the Beatles didn't quite get it right—love is not quite all one needs. If it was, perhaps we'd still be together today. Unfortunately, one also requires a few other ingredients that often can't be manufactured.

I wish they could. I wished I could have been more sensitive to her world, which I was starting to see was very different to mine. I also wished I could have shared with her a bit more about my inner world or some of the challenges I had in my work with people. Our problem was that apart from Irena, we were beginning to find that we didn't have enough things in common to bring us close. To start with, this didn't seem to matter, but as we both began to evolve, we were sadly not doing so side by side.

The truth was that dear Averill and I were discovering that we were very different people and we lived in very different universes—with neither being 'better' than the other, just different. We wanted different things from life and began to realise that we could not offer each other what we wanted. And so, gradually, and with a great deal of pain on my side, and I am sure also on Averill's, we began to draw apart. We were both increasingly losing the ability to communicate with each other what was really going on.

For me the sad thing was that, as I just said, I loved Averill. In addition, she had so many of the qualities that I, with my ADD, lacked: great practicality, the capacity to sort the wood from the trees. Also, unlike me, she was very academic. During our marriage, in addition to being a mother and still working in her job for a PR firm, she did a master's degree and got a teacher training degree; and later, when we eventually went our own separate ways, and she returned to New Zealand and began teaching at the University of Auckland, she also obtained a doctorate and wrote the key textbook on global public relations. An enormously capable and brilliant woman and, in this arena, light years ahead of me.

Some differences complement each other. To begin with I think ours did, but then they gradually seemed not to anymore. And I cannot pretend that I was an easy husband, my ADD hindering me in so many practical areas of life, as I have already explained. One therapist I had worked with in California many years ago called me an 'emotional terrorist', meaning that in my relationships I could be very pushy. I would often want to go too deep too quickly without thinking whether my partner necessarily desired this, and it was often felt to be invasive; and I think Averill definitely felt this. I didn't respect boundaries sufficiently. She, rather like Sima before her, was much more private than I was and hadn't done all the many courses designed to 'open one up' that I had, and quite understandably grew to resent my always wanting to know what was 'going on' inside her. Though things had greatly improved over the years, it also couldn't have been very secure making for her to have been married to someone as impractical around money as I was. I think our core problem was probably that we both found it difficult to talk about what was really going on beneath the surface.

Given that I always manage to put on a good show with women to start with—I was always quite good in the romantic phase of a relationship—I am sure that poor Averill married me expecting me to be the wonderful prince she dreamed of who would heal all her vulnerabilities and make her feel whole, whereas I think that as a result of my being a psychotherapist, often what my presence seemed to do was highlight her vulnerabilities. I am sure in her eyes, I often must have appeared more frog than prince! Averill once said to me that she was glad I was not a plastic surgeon as I would no doubt have been continually insisting she have surgery done—a little tuck here, a few fillers in there, etc. Oh dear!

Well, things got worse between us and we found ourselves connecting together less and less, and we began to live apart, with Irena staying with Averill but me seeing a lot of her. This coincided with me going into a serious financial crisis for the first time in my life, where I was forced to put the Old School House on the market.

This was the final straw for Averill. I never realised how important the property was for her symbolically. Why was I wanting to sell the family home and not that useless (in her eyes) second home in Mallorca that I'd spent so much money on? If I hadn't bought that and done it up, I wouldn't be in a crisis. And again, she had a valid point. She asked me if she could take Irena to New Zealand for a short time so she could see her grandparents before they died, and not suspecting anything I said of course. I remember kissing Irena goodbye at the airport, expecting to see her back in six weeks.

After a few weeks, I realised that Averill's intention was not to take Irena back to New Zealand for a short time but for good. And I panicked and became utterly distraught. I rang Averill and insisted she return with Irena, but Averill said that she had the power to stop me selling the house, and unless I let Irena stay in New Zealand, she would prevent any sale.

And here I made the worst mistake of my life, based, I realised in retrospect, on bad legal advice. I agreed. I was in a state of fear based on having very little money and various debts to settle. So instead of telling Averill that among other things it would be traumatic for our daughter to suddenly be snatched away from her father and from her roots in England—which of course it was—I meekly backed down and let her take Irena away. No wonder darling Irena for a long time felt betrayed by me. A few months later, I sold the house, interestingly, to Peter Reichwald, who had invited us all to Mallorca, and whose marriage to Ellen had by this time also broken down.

But I lost Irena. Until the sale, I don't know how I would have survived if it hadn't been for a loan to tide me over from my dear old friend Michael Cowdray. I first knew Michael quite superficially in my deb party days, when he, like Julian, had firmly established himself as a playboy of the Western world, and travelled the world on a yacht aptly named *The Hedonist*.

But rather like me, Michael saw the light in time and completely changed his life. He chose the path of Tibetan Buddhism, married a truly wonderful woman, Marina, a sculptress (she made a beautiful bronze of baby Irena's feet), and they had five children. Michael, with his long beard, not only looks like an old sage but has become an old sage, and I am honoured to have him as a friend in my life. He's stuck by me even though I've driven him up the wall a few times.

Well, back to the drama. Irena had now gone and I felt utterly devastated. I missed her so much and she must have missed me. For me this was a terrible tragedy and I couldn't believe that I had allowed it to happen. I was now living alone in my rambling Old School House chock-full of memories of my darling daughter, who was now at the other end of the world. It felt like a death. I had seen none of this coming and I came to see how essentially naïve and trusting I was, and how I tended to believe everything I was told. I found out later that Averill had very carefully planned the idea of moving back to New Zealand for a long time.

My little girl, that person whom I loved most in the world, had been taken away from me—right to the other end of the world, not to somewhere where I could just pop over and see her. I felt traumatised. However, I also realised that Averill must have felt that with our marriage souring, England was also smelling less sweet, and so she no doubt felt that her survival was at stake and she had to get back to her roots. And of course, she knew that if she had asked me, I would never have consented.

What also upset me at this time was that many of my friends in the village, who were only too happy to hang out with me in the good times and come to my poolside barbecue parties, started to shrink away when they saw me in my hangdog misery and down-and-outness. But as my dear friend Chris Dreyfus said: 'That's English people for you; they don't know how to deal with the darker side of life. It embarrasses them.'

And it's true. I had to accept that while I had many real, supportive and loving friends, like the Cowdrays, Alice and Rod, Carinthia, Peter Kyte, Mikey McIntyre and dearest Alan and Louise Gordon Walker and wonderful Joanna and Michael Brown and Tristan and Michelle Hillgarth and Peter Adler and John Drew and David Lorimer among others, I also had a lot of fair-weather ones. I remembered that at my fiftieth birthday party I'd sung *Nobody Loves You When You're Down and Out* with Steve Winwood. I thought there had been something prophetic about it! I felt down and out both emotionally and financially.

And just because I was that much closer to living out of my real self (as opposed to my false self), it did not muffle my outrage and grief. It just meant that I could deal with it more effectively and consciously, understand more clearly that suffering had come to visit me for a reason, that there was obviously a strong karma involved. But I felt that in somehow allowing this to happen, that I had betrayed Irena, and I knew that Irena must feel abandoned by me as well.

As I now had nowhere to live in England anymore, I packed up two thousand books from my library, stored them in a friend's barn and arranged to ship out my remaining pieces of furniture to my little finca in Mallorca and decided to base myself there until I decided where I was going next in my life. I had already furnished it in the style that I have liked all my life, and now I brought out the rest of my kilim carpets, my favourite kilim-covered sofa, my Russian icons, my Tibetan thangkas, and, most important, my beloved African tribal sculptures.

Of course, in all Irena's school holidays I'd fly out and see her. In fact, for a few years I would go out and collect her and bring her back with me to Mallorca and then fly back with her to take her back. These flights were pretty exhausting. I would also sometimes stay with Averill in New Zealand for Irena's holidays, but it always felt very uncomfortable because I would often feel that I was being seen through her mama's disapproving eyes, and I would feel very persona non grata! Children in divorces can't help taking sides as it is about their survival. Interestingly, my parents divorced when I was Irena's age; and the fact that I spent more time with Moonie meant that I invariably took her side.

But I no longer see Averill as the 'baddie', which I confess I did at first. Nor do I want to frame our relationship as a 'failed relationship' just because it ended after ten years. We got on very well for a long time and our differences didn't seem to intrude. We produced a fantastic daughter together and I got a lot out of being with Averill and I enjoyed being married to her. It was just that as we both began to grow, we did so in different directions and instead of becoming closer, we grew more distant.

The point of life is that some things don't last for ever. And maybe they're not intended to. Just like a business. If it ends after a certain length of time, it probably suggests that new directions and policies are probably needed and maybe the business is not equipped for them. Well, this analogy applied to our marriage. My Israeli friend Elan Neev, who'd been married four times, used to tell everyone that he had had four successful marriages. I liked that approach. Well, I had had one successful marriage, which included, as I said, our creating the most wonderful child together. And then it came to an end.

Averill and I had got on well and enjoyed being together for a long time and then somehow the climate changed. OK, I'll be honest. I didn't at all like Irena being taken away to the other end of the world. But perhaps in the greater scheme of things, Averill felt that there was no future for her any more in England and that she needed to go home and, as a mother of a young child, she had to take her little girl with her.

Perhaps, who knows, from a long-term perspective it may well have been all to the good. If Irena had stayed in England, we'd have probably sent her to a girls' school equivalent to Harrow and she might well have emerged as entitled as I had been. I don't know. Certainly, there is nothing Lady Snooty-ish about Irena today and she couldn't have turned out better and I am immensely proud of her, and Averill has been a superb mother.

In truth, Irena is a strong character like her mama, and I think dealt very well with the separation. Probably better than I did! She has a natural imperiousness to her and a capacity to inspire love and devotion on the part of all her many friends, and there's no doubt that New Zealand has been good for her. Averill always had a genius in choosing the right schools. First of all, Irena went to a mixed school and experienced kids of all races and nationalities, and then she went to a school where many of the All-Blacks rugby team boys went to, and that too, was healthy. Today, my darling daughter is a very balanced 23-year-old and is living a very balanced life. New Zealand seems to work for her and she has many friends.

Today, twelve years on from our divorce, I am happy to say that Averill and I are good friends again and I am very fond of her and wish her the best. She is now Dr Averill, having done her PhD in public relations. We have both forgiven each other and moved on, and now we chat a lot on the phone and there is a good spirit of camaraderie. And that is so valuable. In my therapy, I have so often dealt with couples who remain angry and resentful for ever, making everyone's life a misery. And that feels such a shame. In life, we need to be able to move on, and to our credit, I think we've both managed to. Averill has just got married again and I am delighted for her. Over the years, darling Irena and I have also grown very close again and things have turned out very well for her. So all's well that ends well.

Every year, except for the pandemic years when borders have been shut, Irena has come out to Mallorca for a month in the summer and in six weeks in the winter and our time has been so precious that we'd do nothing else but hang out together. We'd have our meals that we both enjoyed—and still enjoy—like duck and roast lamb and tiramisu, and she'd put up with my same old ghastly jokes and has now given up trying to teach me how computers work as I am so dumb and she is so quick. We would sometimes go on little adventures together; we'd go skiing or visit Paris or the Canary Islands. Often, we'd fly to London and stay there together for a week, with one or other of her many godparents. Every Christmas, I would hold a ritual godparents lunch and all of them would bring their friends and we would have very jolly gatherings.

Irena and I call each other by all sorts of nicknames but one that stuck was Ghastly Large Creature (me) and Ghastly Little

Creature (Irena); to celebrate our bonding, a few years ago we decided to have a small tattoo done (designed by Irena), she on her ankle very discreetly and me on my forearm, with the letters GLC with a little crown above them!

Those few weeks we'd spend together every year were, and still are, terribly precious for me. We would play tennis together and Tim and Paul, who also had a little Mallorca fishing boat, would often take us out for the day. As a bit of a fashionista, Irena particularly loved going shopping with me in Palma and I confess I rather enjoyed it as well; I saw in her the very fashion-conscious me when I was exactly her age. I confess, though, that I am a pretty soppy fellah and at the end of our holidays, when I would fly with her to Barcelona to put her on her 27-or-so-hour flight back to Auckland, after having our favourite 'goodbye' suckling pig ritual lunch at the best restaurant in the airport, I would stand at the gates and watch my GLC disappear through baggage control and I would always have a lump in my throat. We'd wave to each other until she was out of sight. I love her so much and miss her terribly when I don't see her for long periods. On the other hand, I know she is happy, could not be looked after by anyone as caring and devoted as her mama, and is returning to a country that is warm and safe.

As I write now, New Zealand's borders have just opened up and Irena flew over and is with me in Mallorca for two months before she flies back home. Indeed, I see grace shining through this whole saga. Bless you, dearest Averill. I am so, so happy for you and I hope your new man will be able to make you happy in those areas where I failed to.

Chapter 29

The Challenges of Being on a Spiritual Path

I have thus far talked only about my own personal evolutionary journey and I now feel moved to share a few of my perceptions of the spiritual journey as a whole and what I see as some of the main challenges confronting those of you who may also feel inclined to try to grow your soul life. If this is your aim, I applaud your courage and hope what I say here may be of some small assistance to you.

I'll begin by saying that I think one of the big problems the seeker faces is that while the atmosphere is certainly more tolerant towards experiencing spiritual realities—if you do yoga and practise meditation, you're no longer seen as a weirdo as you were when I started out—nonetheless, the process of actually allowing a person time and space to focus on deepening their inner life, is still in our ultra-materialistic and action-oriented society, not considered particularly important.

The problem is that we all live in a world where it is primarily outer realities that count, not inner ones, and where nothing is permitted to exist if you can't see, touch, taste, smell or hear it. As such, everything that exists outside the domain of what we consider normal—which includes many spiritual experiences—still gets labelled with the negative epithet of 'abnormal'. This means that truly holy and saintly people like Ramana Maharshi, Mother Meera or my beloved Papaji can get put in the same bracket as someone who is psychotic. I therefore like the Tibetan Master Chögyam Trungpa Rinpoche's somewhat impish suggestion that being on a spiritual path is analogous to 'licking honey off a razor's edge'!

Perhaps this analogy doesn't apply so much at the start of our journey, where, as you saw with me, the aim is not yet to move beyond our ego identifications but more to use spirituality to make our ego selves feel more secure, i.e., if we do yoga and learn to meditate, we'll experience less stress and anxiety and thus feel more confident, etc. This is important, for we don't evolve into higher states by trying to diss our egos or pretend we can transcend them, but rather by working to help our personality self to become healthier. Indeed, to reach a place where our egos are willing to step aside and stop trying to run the show and thus allow space for a 'higher' or 'more evolved' part of ourselves to enter and take greater charge of our lives, they first need to feel secure and healthy. As my lovely Ram Dass put it: 'We first have to become a somebody before we can become a nobody!'

This is why the process of working to heal our emotional wounds is so integral a part of the sacred journey and why psychotherapy is so important. I do not go along with many Eastern teachers who tell us that ego is bad and the aim is to become totally egoless. I believe that a healthy ego has much to offer us and we need to find a place where we can befriend this part of ourselves so it becomes content in the role of being subservient and is happy to not stand in our way. When I stayed in Papaji's ashram, for example, I realise that I was not wholly egoless. It was more that it had stepped to the side, so I was no longer seeing the world primarily through its limited and separative lens, which has the habit of robbing life of so much of its aliveness.

So, my dear friend, as you start out on a spiritual path, I think a few things are important. The first is that you need to choose to commit to your evolutionary development. The second is that you don't try to avoid working through your inner blockages, wherever and however they manifest; thirdly, you need to address the issue of healing and integrating the many different parts of your personalities, some of which may be at odds with each other. And lastly, you need to acknowledge and work at gradually releasing all those anachronistic beliefs, values and worldviews which you are still attached to and which conspire to keep you hunkered down in your old-world mindsets.

Some people believe the main aim of the spiritual quest is to get high. I don't agree. Given the condition of our planet at this moment, I think the name of the game is for us to become more genuine and self-aware and to aspire to live in greater harmony with ourselves, other people and our environment so we increasingly become a good friend to all of life on earth. The more we are able to live this way, the more our lives can be about making a positive difference to everyone and everything around us.

We need not only to ask ourselves how we can free ourselves from our old fears and attachments to such things as power or vanity or greed or envy or hatred, but also how we can live more simply and from that place find a work that resonates with our soul's aspirations.

It is also important to honour the evolution of our minds—enabling us to be more open to receive knowledge coming from higher levels of consciousness—and also to ensure that we have a healthy body. If we do not have a good relationship with our body, it may well hinder our progression in many other areas. Sometimes, in our spiritual journeying, we may go through periods where we become physically ill. The great mystical poet Rumi understood this and told us that 'the spiritual path sometimes wrecks the body and then restores it to health and builds it better than before'! This is also true of our hearts and minds. For a new and better us to be born, our old us has to crumble away and die and this can only happen if we allow it. Yes, my friend, as you've seen in my life, we face challenges at every corner and at every level.

However, we need to realise that we all face very *different* challenges. This is because we are all different and have different karmas and different kinds of paths to tread. For example, not everyone is on a 'path of Heart' like me, and so ways that might be right for me may not be for someone who is, say, more on a path of Knowledge or of Action in the World where their role is to be more of a mover and shaker. (In my book *Awakening the Universal Heart,* I talk about these different paths in some detail.) Also, for some of us the journey can be extremely volcanic. We evolve by erupting all the time. Others of us may take big quantum leaps that then take a long time to integrate, while others move more quietly and slowly, always making little advances, and much less drama is involved. Here is what Roberto Assagioli had to say:

> *Spiritual development in a person is a long and arduous adventure, a journey through strange lands, full of wonders but also beset with difficulties and dangers. It involves deep purification and transformation, the awakening of a number of formerly inactive powers, the raising of consciousness to levels it has never existed at before and its expansion in a new internal dimension. We should not be surprised, therefore, that such major changes pass through various critical stages and these are often accompanied by neuropsychological and even physical and psychosomatic symptoms.*

For example, if we will have had a traumatic birth when we came into the world and if this trauma is not properly worked through, it may tend to replicate itself in our spiritual journeying, making it that much harder for us to 'give birth' to our deeper self. Also, if our spiritual journey goes awry at the later stages, we may encounter further pathologies. This can happen for example, if we encounter an unprincipled spiritual teacher. (Over the years, I have worked helping many people traumatised by having been part of cults run by very manipulative individuals.) As you've seen with me, grace is not all love and light and there may be occasions where we find ourselves having close encounters with powerful archetypal forces and we may sometimes experience images of death and destruction, and if we don't have sources at hand to remind us that it is not our actual death we are experiencing but the shrinking away of our old self, the experiences can be terrifying.

Crises due to spiritual awakening are very different from the kinds of crises we experience in our ordinary everyday lives. A lot of the time they are due to our system trying to adjust itself to very different vibrational frequencies. As we gradually evolve, we start entering into more rarefied realities, and as Chris Bache just said, if we are insufficiently purified or energetically are too coarse, we may not be permitted entry! This was my experience with my high dose ayahuasca session. I experienced those elevated worlds beckoning to me and felt their love, but I could not fully make the grade! I have hanging in my office an old Tibetan *thangka* that shows wrathful deities guarding the entrance to the holy of holies and woe betide anyone daring to enter who has not yet earned the necessary requirements for doing so!

I repeat: the 'higher' we journey up into the light or into the embrace of a 'higher-order' us, the more those closets in our lower unconscious containing all the skeletons we've not yet chosen to look at begin being illuminated. But by the same token, the more we confront those skeletons—descend into our Shadow side—the more we will also evoke the light, for (as we see in the Yin/Yang symbol) both polarities exist within the other.

If, for example, we happen to be going through an existential crisis, it is often characterised by our feeling marooned and lost in a kind of no-man's-land, existing between our old world that we have not fully transitioned out of, and a new one that as yet we only have our fingertips in. Thus, we may feel scared and lonely and have the sense that we belong nowhere. As you've seen, I encountered this crisis quite a lot.

Similarly, if we are someone who has been used to a particularly emotionally and spiritually barren inner life and we suddenly start to open up and experience great joy and abundance, because we are not used to this, it may create great fear and evoke strong resistance, and we may find ourselves turning away from that very grace and sublimity that we are looking for! And then of course there is the well-known 'dark night of the soul' experience that I have a strong hunch that all of humanity is gradually slipping deeper and deeper into at this moment. I experienced this when I was in my hospital bed in America. Here again, if we are not given the right perspective with which to view it, we may feel that God is 'punishing' us for our imperfections, when in fact the very opposite is occurring. Martin Luther sheds light on what is actually going on.

> *God works by contraries so that a man feels himself to be lost in the very moment when he is on the point of being saved. When God is about to justify a man, he damns him... When a man believes himself utterly lost, light breaks.*

Perhaps we can substitute the word God for the word 'grace'! It is important, then, that we know that the deeper we allow ourselves to go into our transformational processes, the more fiercely the fire will burn inside us. However, these are the flames of our inner alchemical transmuting machine resident within our hearts and they don't behave like ordinary flames which consume everything in their path. What characterises these flames is that their aim is solely to burn away our old beliefs, patterns and worldviews that have become anachronistic and encrusted inside us, and which stand in the way of our further development.

Nonetheless, the burning can be painful. So I say this: if you truly wish to evolve, you need to be willing to accept that there will be times when you will go through periods of feeling lost, abandoned, confused, dispirited and rejected, and you must realise that this is part of your journey and thus try not to push the suffering away but rather take it into your heart and experience its fire fully, for as my friend Chris Bache put it, this is how the process of purification operates.

I like to use the analogy of mountain climbing to describe the spiritual path. At the foot of the mountain or as we first embark on our journey, the terrain is easy. If we deviate a little, it doesn't make too much difference. However, the higher up we go, the thinner the air, the steeper the incline and the more challenging it becomes. We start to realise that the game has radically changed and the rules we adhered to at the start no longer apply; we can't now get away with what previously we could. What once were small deviations now seem much bigger and we realise that less and less can we afford to take wrong turns. More mindfulness and self-discipline are required. Karlfried Graf von Dürckheim, a diplomat and spiritual teacher, spoke some very salient truths when, in his book *The Way of Transformation*, he wrote that:

> *The Man (or woman) who, being really on the Way, falls upon hard times in the world, will not, as a consequence, turn to that friend who offers him comfort and refuge and so encourages his old self to survive. Rather, he will seek out someone who will faithfully and inexorably help him to risk himself, so that he may endure the suffering and pass courageously through it, thus making of it 'a raft that leads to the far shore'. Only to the extent that man exposes himself over and over again to annihilation, can that which is indestructible (i.e., his true, deeper selfhood) arise within him… Only if we venture repeatedly through zones of annihilation can our contact with Divine Being which is beyond annihilation, become firm and stable. The more we learn wholeheartedly to confront the world that threatens us with annihilation, the more are the depths of the ground of being revealed and the possibilities of new life and new becoming opened up.*

The Sufi poet Kabir said much the same thing. He told us to be grateful to those who challenge us by making life difficult for us and to 'worry about the others who give you delicious comfort that keeps you from prayer', that is, who distract us from our path by creating situations that lull us to sleep once more. As that's exactly what we *don't* want; we must remind ourselves that *the reason why we are on a spiritual path in the first place is that in our normal (not our natural) state, we are too asleep to who we truly are*. Indeed, the whole aim of our seeking is for us to wake up from our 'slumber' and realise who we *really* are, that is, come to see that that divinity which previously we may have recognised as only existing outside of us or beyond us, also exists within us, and *that in actuality we ourselves are the One that we are looking for!* In this context, often our seeming worst enemies may actually turn out to be our best friends, because in confronting us with difficulties or obstacles, we are somehow being challenged to stretch ourselves—to begin to develop qualities such as resilience, forgiveness, tolerance, compassion, kindness and courage, all of which help take us more deeply into the heart of ourselves. I continue this theme in my Epilogue, only I apply it to political and social realities.

It is also important that we are not naïve and that we recognise that there is evil out in the world and that this evil also lives inside each of us and that we don't push this realisation aside. I recently came across this little poem by the great saintly Buddhist monk and peace activist Thich Nhat Hanh. In his words:

I am the child in Uganda, all skin and bones,
My legs as thin as bamboo sticks.
And I am the arms merchant, selling deadly weapons to Uganda,
I am the twelve-year old girl, a refugee...
Who throws herself into the ocean
After being raped by a sea pirate,

And I am the pirate, my heart not yet capable
Of seeing and loving.

Yes, my friend. All of us carry patterns both of what is best and of what is worst about the human condition, and each of us carries different facets of these patterns. When we do deep Shadow work—when we work, say, at transmuting our anger or our capacity to manipulate or to hate or act dishonestly—we are not only purifying ourselves, but as we are all connected to the larger whole of humanity, we are also doing our tiny, weeny bit to help the purification of all of humanity.

I think one thing that is definitely very different about the spiritual path today, compared to when I first embarked on my journey in the late sixties, is that in the past we were primarily looking for freedom for ourselves. Now the name of the game has shifted to liberation for humanity as a whole, and consequently our undertaking is much more of a collective one. As a species, we journey together. Humanity as a whole is looking for its soul and is doing so through each of us increasingly coming to experience our interconnectedness.

One of the main ways, then, that we learn or that we evolve, is through our continually being confronted with different kinds of initiations. In much the same way that at school if we pass our tests, we move up a grade into a higher form, so the same analogy holds true for the spiritual path.

As I just said, at the start our tests tend to be gentle, but as we gradually evolve, they become increasingly more difficult. How well are we able to forgive someone who has deeply hurt us or cheated us? How kind are we to those less fortunate than ourselves, or how loving can we be to those who feel particularly unlovable? Similarly, how willing are we to take a stand for truth knowing that everyone around us has chosen a path of dishonesty and we won't be thanked for it! Conversely, how courageous can we be when violence is all around us?

In this context, I think of Nelson Mandela. After all those years in prison, not only did he unconditionally forgive his jailors when he came out, but as president he averted a civil war in South Africa because his heart became so big that it was able to hold his entire nation inside it. Mandela for me was an example of a truly evolved human being, a rare example of a politician who operated at a very spiritual level and was in the game not because he wanted wealth and power, but because he deeply wanted to heal the conflicts in his country.

Whereas in centuries past, the initiate would forsake the world and go to caves in the Himalayas or temples far from civilisations and its discontents to face their tests, today this is no longer the case. As I've said, each of us is not only embarked on a collective journey, but we are now having to face our initiations out in the big, bad world, out in the highways and byways of London, New York, Moscow and Rome and Moscow!

What I am suggesting, then, is that all the problems we face today—including social and economic unrest, inequality, war, Covid, rogue politicians, difficult relationships, poverty, genocide, homophobia, Islamophobia, xenophobia, etc—all the complexities and problems of life itself—constitute the 'stuff' of our tests. All our emotional, relational and financial difficulties, all our psychological wounds—exist not to thwart us but rather to teach us to grow our humanity. We need *to see all our challenges as Dürckheim's 'raft' asking us to stretch ourselves so we might reach the further shore.* I will develop this thesis in more detail in my Epilogue.

I think our really big challenge is to regard all of our daily activities—from brushing our teeth in the morning to cooking our dinner in the evening—as being incorporated into our spiritual practice. How can we bring heart and soul into our work, our relationships, indeed, into everything about our daily lives, so that the way we live plays a role in helping a transformed and healthier society come into expression? This requires a lot of discipline and mindfulness. Today, I see us all being challenged in our own ways to be 'change agents' in a deeply discombobulated world, and this starts to happen as we begin to tune into the sacred activist archetype inside us which Andrew Harvey defines as being '*the fusion of the mystic's passion for God with the activist's passion for justice, creating a third fire, which is the burning sacred heart that longs to help, preserve and nurture every living thing.*'

Here are a few guidelines to help us as we start out on our journey:

1) It is good to have help, particularly at the start, so always gravitate towards a teacher/guide/psychotherapist or a teaching that you feel drawn to and feel good about. Best if you can find someone whom you sense is a bit further along the path than you are—but not too far; if they are too evolved, their teachings may be too advanced for you to benefit. Also, do not work with someone of the old school who denies the validity of altered states of consciousness. And don't worry if you hit a few brick walls. Often, we learn what we need by first discovering what we don't need.

2) Beware of shysters or false prophets; there are plenty around. Because the starting-off seeker is vulnerable, we can be potentially open to being conned. There are three main areas I want to warn you about:

- Beware being sucked in by a fundamentalist cult. Many intelligent and well-meaning people have fallen for the very successful conversion tactics that cults use.
- Beware cowboy/cowgirl therapists or so-called 'life coaches' who are untrained and can unwittingly lead you into deep water and not save you from drowning.
- Beware manipulative so-called 'gurus', who may talk a good talk but don't walk it.

3) Know that the more you pray for grace and ask grace to be increasingly present in your life, the more it will be. So, talk to it. Connect to it in as many ways as you can. Imagine yourself reaching up to higher states of consciousness and make it your daily practice to treat your fellow human beings with kindness, graciousness and respect at all times. Know that the more you share grace, the more you will draw it to live inside you. Here, discipline is needed. We need to do the work even when we don't feel like it.

4) Don't worry about mixing things up. All genuine paths to God come from the same ground of being. For example, there is much we can learn from the Buddha's 'middle way' about how we might live more harmoniously and peacefully, while Shamanism teaches us to open up more and more to the spirit of the Earth. I see no conflict.

5) Know that there is appropriate suffering, which we often don't do enough of, and neurotic suffering, which we tend to engage in too freely. Appropriate suffering has a spiritual aim. As I just said, we experience it when undergoing a purification or a burning through of old patterns inside ourselves. It is very different from neurotic suffering, much of which is avoidable and comes from our having an insecure ego and not living in the right way.

6) Don't worry if you think you are not making significant enough progress and find yourself slipping backwards a lot (which as you've seen, has very often happened to me). Lao Tzu told us that 'Going on is going back', and it is true. Each new step forward requires us to 'return' and revisit our past so we don't leave it behind or reflect it, but rather discover how to 'bring it up along' with us.

7) I recommend that from time to time you go on a spiritual retreat whereby you remove yourself for at least a week from your everyday existence. What this does is give you time and space to focus only on your inner life. I've gone on many

spiritual retreats and I continue to teach them and I regard them as invaluable.

8) Don't forget that being spiritual is all about our capacity to become more fully human, so try as much as possible to seek out and spend time with people who already *are* more fully human so you can move in their slipstream. I quote again from Ramakrishna: *Seek spiritual advancement from one who is advanced... take trouble to live in the society of the good.*

9) It is also important that you find work that both feels appropriate and enables your creativity to flow, and in some way makes a positive difference in the world. We can serve the evolution of life on Earth in so many different ways, and the more effectively we manage to do so, the more our inner life will expand and flourish.

Chapter 30

Mallorca and Martina

In the last chapter I've just had my little outing as 'preacher man', so let me now return to my personal life which was starting to change very rapidly. My Hampnett days were over. My beautiful old barn which had looked after me so well and had been the sturdiest of companions for almost forty-five years, was now full of memories of my little girl and it had a terrible emptiness to it that I just couldn't bear, and I was delighted to move on from it. I never once looked back. That phase of my life was well and truly over. I was only too delighted that my friend Peter, who was responsible for having brought me to Mallorca again, was now taking it over.

Thank God then, that I had my little *pied-à-terre* in Mallorca. I felt happy being based there. The great thing about it was that it had no sad memories. I would sit out in my little garden under my favourite carob tree and do a lot of prayer and meditation, and gradually my sorrow and hangdog look began to evaporate, my mojo started to return and a spring came back to my step. While I had no clue which direction my life was going to go in—half my work was online and half, as I said, was returning every ten days to London to see my clients—it certainly felt good being in Mallorca. I threw a lot of energy into writing a book *Awakening the Universal Heart: A Guide for Spiritual Activists*. I had a sense that possibly my future lay in Mallorca.

When I was in London, however, I would do a little bit of online dating, particularly with a site in the *Guardian* newspaper called *Guardian Soulmates*, and while everyone I knew had terrible stories to tell about it, I only had positive experiences. I met some extremely nice women, whom I would arrange to meet for lunch in my favourite little Vietnamese restaurant, and if I felt we got on well, we'd meet once or twice again and I might invite them out to stay with me in Mallorca. For six months, I had a good relationship with a woman I met on a train called Monica Godwin and we have stayed very close friends and been very supportive of each other as she had also been going through a divorce.

Then an event happened that totally turned my life upside down in the best possible way. Thank you again, dear 'help forces'! My old friend Chris Carter, who, as I said, had rescued my finca in Mallorca, decided that he simply had to take me to a birthday party that was being given by some close German friends of his wife's.

His wife Julia was opposed. 'You can't take Serge. This is last-minute and you can't ask them now.' Well, Chris didn't ask them but took me along all the same. It was a very chic party given by Karin and Axel von Poelnitz, in the grounds of their beautiful finca. The only people I knew there were Chris and Julia.

There was a delicious buffet. Having helped myself to food, I looked around, wondering where I was going to sit, and saw a table that had six women on it and decided to join them. 'Wow,' I thought, 'there are some fantastic ladies here. How can I get to know them, I wonder!' A plan came to me. It was going to be full moon in three days' time. I addressed the table. 'Hey, you guys, I am doing a full moon meditation workshop at my little finca. I invite you all to come. Could I please have your phone numbers and email addresses, so then I can either ring you or write you to give you directions.'

It was a saucy strategy but it worked. In three days' time, all of them came to my workshop. And of course, I had their phone numbers. I decided I would go through my list and invite them one by one to lunch and see if any sparks would fly with anyone.

The third person on my list was Martina, and after I had had lunch with her, I never contacted any of the others. I fell in love with Martina almost at once. I had never met anyone so beautiful, inwardly and outwardly, and so genuinely kind and good and honest. I had just started doing what I called 'personalised spiritual retreats', that is, week-long retreats, not for large groups as I'd done in the past, but for individuals or couples—father and son, husband and wife, etc—and a few days after our lunch, a couple arrived, Rupert and Veronica, to work with me.

Every afternoon, Martina would come and visit me for ten minutes and Rupert, who has since become a close friend, said very prophetically to me at the end of the week, 'Serge, I think you are going to marry Martina.' Martina's then eleven-year-old daughter, Leah, eight months older than Irena, said the same thing to her mother after I had taken them both out to dinner a week or so later. 'Mama,' she said, 'the way this man is looking at you, I think he wants to marry you.'

How right they all were. I was then sixty-six and Martina was eighteen years younger, but when Cupid shoots his little arrow, all the norms get blown away. When, a few months later, after having had lunch at our friend Claudio's restaurant—perhaps not the most romantic of environments, but I'm an impetuous old so 'n' so—I popped down on one knee and posed the big question and yippee, yippee, I got a 'yes', I was suddenly the happiest person in the world. It felt so good after all those dark months of being the unhappiest!

Martina was like me a free spirit, and things like marrying had never been part of her itinerary and when later I asked her, 'But how could you fall for an ageing old scallywag like me?' her answer was, 'Because I feel you see me and I have never felt that any man has seen me before.' If she had asked me *why I* wanted to marry *her*, along with fifty other reasons, that one was also high on the list. The point is that when people see us—*really* see us, as I felt Martina *really* saw me—we are somehow 'allowed', or subtly 'given permission', to be ourselves. Soul is invited out of the closet. There's no need to explain certain things or try to be someone or something that we are not. With so many women in my past, I've always felt I've needed to adorn myself with various bells and whistles to be loved. So exhausting. Not so with my beloved Martina.

It was therefore easy being with her. There was a natural harmony. Our values and beliefs tallied. We saw the world through a similar lens. With all my other relationships, there was always so much stuff to work through; I was always finding myself either needing to walk on eggshells or somehow apologise for being me. With Martina, no apologies were ever required, and I think that because she 'got where I was at', it was probably much easier to accept my many faults. Or perhaps she didn't see them that way but just as different aspects of this funny, rather eccentric, elderly Englishman she was choosing to team up with! The lovely thing was that I also grew to love her daughter Leah, and all her close friends, and vice versa.

Where I was ADD impractical and impetuous, Martina was eminently hands-on and always thought things through carefully before she made any decision. Whereas I was (and still am!) capable of sitting at a desk and focussing for hours on end on a project that interested me, Martina always liked to be on the move. As Leah was only a few months older than Irena, I got extra coaching as to how to relate to teenage girls! To start with, she was understandably somewhat suspicious of this old buffer who had suddenly stormed into her mama's life taking away the attention that up until now had always all gone directly to her. But over time, she came to accept me and today, Leah and I are great buddies and she has a very tender place inside my heart.

Martina was incredibly sensitive and was always right in her intuitions and impressions about people. She had an extraordinary sixth sense about everything. I always tell people that we get on so well together because we never had—and still don't have—conflicts or power struggles. The reason is that Martina is invariably right and I am nearly always wrong. You may laugh but that is the absolute truth. She also managed something that only someone with her consummate intuitive skills could have done. She has not only remained great friends with Tim, who is Leah's father and who had abandoned her before Leah was born, but she has also worked together to co-parent Leah with him. In addition, they both worked together to build up a wonderfully successful yoga retreat centre called La Serranía. Over the years Tim and I have become good mates.

Martina was one of those people whom everyone loved, and it was not surprising. She was the most loyal and generous of human beings and had an integrity and generosity of spirit that was awesome. I trusted her 1000 per cent. I realised that if Martina was to be my wife, I had a lot of catching up to do. While it would be untrue to say that Martina did not sometimes (quite rightly) reprimand me—especially on those occasions when Lord Snooty would suddenly emerge out of the closet with his somewhat bizarre, outdated, naughty-boy, public-school humour, or when old Mr Sad Sack would have one of his rare outings—so big was her heart and so much love went into everything she did, that I never ever felt made wrong. I think this was because I was given a huge space to be myself; and in these last ten years with Martina, I feel that I have not only become a better human being but also a more creative one. She is the greatest teacher I have ever had.

Martina always had both Leah and me pulling at her for her attention, and it is to her huge credit that neither of us ever felt excluded; and when Irena would come and stay for the holidays, Martina's big heart would also extend to her and make her feel welcome, which was so important for me. While I have had to do so much therapy, attend so many workshops, visit so many gurus and partake of so many sacraments just to open my heart a teensy-weensy bit, Martina's heart was already open. And it was vast. It went into everything she did, whether it was her cooking, her intimate friendships or her work. She is one of those rare human beings who carries an atmosphere of goodness about her wherever she goes, so that everyone whom she touches feels that little bit blessed by her radiance. And I was the lucky man now who had it all the time. After all those years of searching—and I stress again, I don't think I am an easy person and I definitely think I've been the wrong kind of man for many of the women I've been with in the past—I at last found someone willing—or should I say 'big enough'—to tolerate me and put up with my many irregularities and eccentricities.

Another of the joys of being with Martina was that I got to spend a lot of time in Vienna (Martina is Austrian) and especially in Baden, where her delightful parents lived and who, bless them, despite being only a few years older than me, were incredibly generous in accepting me as their son-in-law. In all the years I have known them, they have shown me nothing but kindness and support. As have Martina's brother and sister. What I also loved about being in Austria was the food. Venison, goose and red cabbage and those gorgeous apfel-strudels and sacher-torten and linzer-torten. Yum. Martina could dump me in one of those fantastic cafés that Vienna is well known for, and I'd be as happy as a sandboy pigging away and pushing my cholesterol levels into overdrive.

We had intended to get married quietly in Jamaica, where I had been invited by dear David Lorimer to teach a ten-day spiritual retreat with him, and Irena very much wanted to be part of the process. However, for reasons I can't remember, at the last-minute Irena couldn't fly over, so in order to placate her, I put off the wedding. Understandably, this greatly upset Martina and for three weeks—the only three weeks ever—I experienced being persona non grata in her eyes.

But we eventually married, on 29 June, on my seventieth birthday. We had two celebrations: first, a formal wedding in Vienna, which Martina's parents and Viennese friends attended, and where dear David Lorimer flew over to be best man; and another more hippiefied celebration a week later in the field outside my little finca, where I invited thirty of my closest friends, who came over from abroad. Here, Johnnie Reed was my best man as he'd now returned into my life. My good friend Teckla conducted a beautiful ceremony where Martina and I created our own vows, and we had a wonderful dinner for about sixty people. Irena, who is a true master of the art of public speaking, gave very moving speeches at both weddings and I was so grateful for her incredible support for me. I felt so happy I thought I would burst! I had the two ladies I loved most in the world right beside me. I was so lucky that Irena liked and felt comfortable with Martina, and, while our two girls are very different characters, they also get on well and are fond of each other.

I felt with Martina that I could fully put into practice what I had learned about marriage from my time with dear Joseph Campbell. For him, it is the reunion of the separated dyad. Originally you were one. But now you are two in the world and as such, you recognise the spiritual identity that emerges. In a love affair, there is no real responsibility. Not so in a marriage. For Joseph, true marriage occurs on another mythological plane of existence. If we live a right life, if our mind is on the right qualities regarding our partner, we'll find our proper male or female counterpart. In his words:

> *By marrying the right person, we reconstruct the image of the incarnate God and that's what marriage is. When you make the sacrifice in marriage, you are not sacrificing to each other but to the unity in a relationship. Thus, it is an ordeal and the ordeal is the sacrifice of ego to a relationship in which the two have become one and that is not compatible with the idea of 'doing one's own thing'.*

Marriage, therefore, is a spiritual exercise and a context to assist us to be more capable of being of service to society. This corresponds with my dear friend Susan Campbell's final stage of a relationship, which in her book, *The Couple's Journey*, she calls the 'co-creation stage'. This is reached when the surplus energy created by the couple's synergy impels them to feel moved to give something back to the world. A truly sacred space begins opening up. I felt that after so many years of my life being immature, I was at last, at seventy, starting to grow up and was ready for this.

And now, seven years down the road, this is exactly what is happening. Martina has single-handedly started an organisation called *Pollensa Cares* to raise money to help local people who've been financially badly hit by the pandemic. It began by just producing food for those who were starving and now it has expanded to buying computers for children living in poverty and organising mindfulness courses for people who have become depressed. A tiny seed has now turned into a huge plant and Martina and her gaggle of terrific girlfriends who joined her, have raised many thousands of euros. All this has happened because Martina watered her little seed in the right way and gave it love, and I am so, so proud of her. *Pollensa Cares* now offers an awesome service and helps many people in many different ways. Martina has been so modest about it. I think that at the deepest level, what unites us is the desire, each in our very different ways, to make a difference in the world.

Sadly, my little finca was not big enough for Martina and me to live in and so we have been renting it out or using it ourselves, and living in the lovely townhouse in Pollensa that Martina lived in before with Leah, which is big enough to house both of us and gives me a little room as my office and plenty of space if Leah and Irena both happen to be staying at the same time. I liked being in town as one of my great pleasures was strolling down to the café in the main square, buying a newspaper and meeting up over a cappuccino and croissant with my new friends Donald Trelford, who used to be the head honcho of the *Observer*, Ian Smith, or my old schoolmate Julian Moulton. I'll say a few quick words about Julian as he's been in and out of my life for many years.

Dear old Jules had had a background in some ways not dissimilar to mine, only when he was twenty-one he received many, many millions and, again, with no guidance as to how to deal with it, and being handsome and charismatic, it was the simplest thing to turn himself into a full-blown playboy, jet-setting around the world in pursuit of beautiful women, with all the snazzy cars that such a lifestyle required. Unlike Michael Cowdray, however, Jules never saw the light until nearly the end, and eventually his trust-fund money began to run out. As he had never thought to buy himself anything like a house, he had no solid investments to his name and, never having properly worked, had no qualifications to enable him to do anything to supplement his dwindling income. For twenty years he'd rented a small house near where we lived, but then got kicked out for not paying the rent!

Jules gradually became a kind of hobo figure around town, by now somewhat ravaged by a lifetime of heavy smoking, drugs and alcohol, and wholly dependent upon handouts from his mates. He ended up in a care home, plagued by a most horrible cancer that had eaten up most of his face. I was with him the last few hours before he died, and he was puffing on his beloved ciggies to the very end.

For the last month he knew he was dying and he faced it with incredible bravery, and, as his life slowly dribbled away, he became increasingly more human. In the old days, when he had been riding high, he never had a moment for anyone. Now he was becoming gentle and tender and humble and interested in other people and genuinely grateful for the help he received. We'd have long talks and he told me—and I believed him—that he had no regrets. I very much enjoyed our chats at this time, and felt very close to him. I gave a small speech at his funeral service and found a trickle of a tear in my eye.

What Jules and I had had in common were fathers who didn't have the time to teach their sons true values and instil in us an idea of what it truly meant to be a man, probably because they didn't know themselves. In the last months of his life, Jules's ego grew increasingly less prominent and his true sweetness shone out of him. Once more, I think there's so much truth to be found in the parable of the prodigal son: we need to lose if we are to find ourselves. Certainly I count Jules as another important teacher.

As you may have gathered, my friends are very important to me and, soon after meeting Martina, a new wonderful one came into our lives, Charles Montagu, a hypnotherapist, whom Martina and I have both grown to love.

We met in curious circumstances. I hadn't smoked for many, many years but suddenly, out of the blue, the habit returned. I had known Charles very slightly from the past and when I was on one of my trips to London, I decided to have a hypnosis session with him. Afterwards, we went out for dinner together and found we had so much in common that we didn't stop talking until one in the morning, and over the years our friendship has blossomed. Charles is a generous, humorous and wise man and joined the ranks of wonderful and special friends whose home was always open to Martina and I whenever we'd come to London.

Being married to her not only gave me a new sense of freedom, but also helped to further the simplification of my life that I'd been working on ever since Papaji, and which has particularly enabled my creative life to blossom. In these last five years I could not have been busier, and in addition to my private practice and writing my books, I have held many more 'individualised retreats' and also branched out and worked at a drug rehabilitation centre near Marbella, which I found fascinating. I had been asked to join by another friend of mine, Mark Collins, who over the years has also become close. Mark is now retired but had been a very eminent psychiatrist. He is the younger brother of Richard, who had been a great mate of mine in my teenage years and who went up to Oxford the same time as I did and when he left, went on to become a dancer with the Bolshoi Ballet.

While I still often feel like a student, at another level I realise that now in my late seventies, I have become an elder in the movement for the transformation of society, which, in my fumbling ways, I have always tried to champion. It is extraordinary to think that I am now the same age as—often older than—many of my heroes who all those years ago, when I first arrived in California, I had looked up to so much.

But life was not just work. Martina and I found time to travel and one of our most memorable excursions was ten days in St Petersburg, where I was giving a lecture at a conference. I had two old Russian friends, Dimitri and Irina Spivak, and they took great care of us, taking us to see my ancestor Peter the Great's summer palace, and guiding us through the vast labyrinth of the Hermitage. I also learned that a whole square in the central part of the town had been named after a particular Obolensky relative who had been a revolutionary. (Have I, I wondered, perhaps inherited some of those rogue genes!) My intention had been to take Irena and Martina on a long tour through Russia as soon as all lockdowns are ended and we are all free to travel once more. In view of what has just happened, though, with the horrific invasion of Ukraine, I suspect that this will not be on the agenda, or certainly not unless there is regime change in that country. How tragic that this beautiful country whose soul finds expression in its great art, music and literature, has once again been led down a dark path of conquest and destruction by a psychopathic neo-Nazi leader.

Chapter 31

Reflections

It is now time to come to an end and I will try and gently sum up my life. I am now seventy-seven, living in Mallorca, and I feel very at home and very blessed to live on this beautiful island. While over seventy years have gone by since I first set foot here, despite the uglification that rapacious developers seem to have inflicted upon certain areas, Pollensa, the town where we live is essentially unchanged. It is only ten minutes' drive to the sea and, as a Cancer water sign, I need and love my seawater and I go for long swims most days in the summer. What a delight. Some people need grounding. I need watering.

The fact that Martina has lived here for over twenty-two years and knows how the 'Mallorca world' works gives me a strong foothold. In addition, my life is enormously helped by the fact that she speaks fluent Spanish (she actually speaks five languages fluently) as I confess that despite all those years spent first in Ibiza and now here, I have never bothered to learn Spanish. I can speak French because of my mother having lived in Gstaad for so long, but I'm afraid that languages have never much interested me, and this has certainly limited my ability to connect more deeply with many of the local people, and it's a shame and it's a mark of my laziness.

That said, places, just like people, have always found a way of letting me know when it is appropriate to stay or if it is time to move on, and I feel that Pollensa is not punishing me for my negligence but, on the contrary, strongly welcomes me and it feels very right to be living here. I love the little townhouse where we live and I am happy in my little office surrounded by my sacred art and of course, my beloved African sculptures. An art dealer told me recently that my tribal art is about to become the 'next big thing', and I confess that this thought didn't especially excite me. I've always collected my tribal figures because I love them and I don't care whether they are fashionable or not and I dislike the habit people have of putting a price on everything. I think it was Gandhi who said that 'we know the price of everything and the value of nothing'.

I have called this book *Amazing Grace* because, as I said earlier, I have always felt very graced. Even amidst my self-absorption and narcissism, even before I had any knowledge about higher power or sensed that a very profound intelligence existed in the cosmos, I was all too aware of a certain good fortune seeming to stalk me! And so many important synchronicities have taken place throughout my life. Over the years I grew increasingly to understand that it was definitely grace that encouraged me to question the kind of life I was living, and grace that moved me to work at trying to open up deeper dimensions of my Serge-hood, en route propelling me to encounter all the many teachers and teachings who played such important roles in my life.

As you've seen, grace has taken many different forms. At times it has shown its fierce face—Irena being taken from me, being ill with histoplasmosis, my depression around my father—while on other occasions it has been gentle and loving. I especially feel grace with me when I work with people and experience a healing energy flowing through me.

I repeat once more: I am very blessed in never having had to face a truly terrible tragedy where someone very, very dear to me has been killed or where I have lost everything or been traumatised by war or a severe mental disorder or some very debilitating disease. For this I really count my blessings. I am sure that if I lived in Afghanistan or Yemen or currently in Ukraine, and I had written a memoir, it would not have been given this title! There is evil and great tragedy in the world and I have written and lectured about it quite extensively and feel extremely lucky that I have managed to live in countries not ravaged by war, excessive corruption or rabid authoritarianism.

One way I measure my development is that I observe an increased capacity to live with an appreciation of my life and of life in general. Today, I feel my heart is both my best friend and my guide, and it teams up well with my mind. If I can also say that I have more self-worth than I had in my past, I think it is not only because I have addressed many of my emotional wounds, but also because over the years I have gradually grown more accepting of myself despite my many limitations. More dimensions of me are now out of the closet and can therefore be brought to the table. I still watch myself and sometimes see less savoury sides of myself pop out, but I no longer condemn myself for them or have my life ruled by them.

And this makes me naturally feel much more abundant. (I ask myself: how can any of us have true self-worth if the main way we see ourselves is in terms of our ego identifications!) There is a lot of difference between what I see as bogus self-worth, where we use things and possessions and power and status to bolster and define ourselves—which as you've seen, I certainly used to try to do—and genuine self-worth, which comes out of our increasingly being aware of our own and everyone else's value as human beings.

If anyone were to ask me what the best thing I've ever done in my life is, I'd answer: definitely having my daughter Irena. I wonder what she will do in this crazy, swiftly changing world we are all living in today. I am sure it will be something noble as my daughter has some very special qualities. (I know all parents would say this about their children, but I really mean it.) Mindful of how my father always wanted to try and control my life, I've always sought to stand back and give Irena space in the knowledge that she will know much better than me what direction she wants to take. As I've learned from my days of therapy, you don't tell people what they ought to do. Rather, you try to help them find a place inside themselves where they can alight on the answer. So if Irena asks for my advice, I'll willingly give it. But not otherwise.

I reflect again how very fortunate I have been in that I have always been able to do 'my thing' in life and have never needed to be manacled to a job I disliked simply in order to put bread on the table, which is so many people's lot. Though I have complained about the spiritual aridity of my privileged and entitled background, there is much that I can also be very grateful for about it, not least that it educated me to think for myself. I think it also gave me the courage to stand up for myself and thus break free from it. That said, I've never rejected my origins. I've never pretended not to have come from a background of privilege or, for example, tried intentionally to tone down my 'posh' way of speaking, as this would entail becoming something I am not. What I have done, though, is endeavoured to not wear my background on my sleeve. I hope that that arrogance I once used to have has melted away a bit, and that more than a smidgen of humility is discernible so that the way I present myself allows me to be approachable by anyone.

I am also grateful that I have a deep mythology to hang onto, which means that I do not equate happiness in my old age with needing to have acquired status and power and a lot of money to let me and the world know that I've 'made it'. I no longer live in a world where things like that are important. I have quite enough, as Gandhi would say, to satisfy my simple needs.

Yes, my friend, I think I have had a rich life, particularly in terms of many of the many interesting experiences I have had, and some of the remarkable people I have been privileged to have encountered along the way, who in so many different ways, have taught me so much. This also includes the wonderful human beings who have been my clients and who have attended my courses. Many have been terrific examples to me of what it means to be fully human and have become real friends. Here I particularly think of Sandra and Pete Salmi, and Andy, Ramzi and Joanna, Rupert and Lady V, to mention just a few. For me today, wealth is primarily an inner quality. I feel, as I said, graced and abundant, and Martina's presence and our love for one another enormously adds to this.

Rummaging through my belongings stuffed in the attic, I have just recovered a file of old letters to me from girlfriends going right back to the sixties and seventies, and I have been very deeply touched to discover that this very flawed and wounded human being of those days seemed not only to have inspired women to leave him but also, for some strange reason, to love him. It still makes me a little sad to reflect how closed my heart used to be, and how hard it was for me to receive the many beautiful gifts that so many of them had to offer me. Looking back, I can see that 'macho man' who for far too many years of my life I identified with, was basically a man operating with a fearful, closed and unfeeling heart.

I also discovered a bulky file I had forgotten about for forty years which I had labelled 'Fan mail'. This deluge of 'thank you' letters deeply touched me as I realised the transforming effect I seemed to have had on many people's lives, even when I was just starting out and often felt personally unhappy and confused. This has led me to believe that although of course it follows that the more whole we are, the more we can offer this quality to others, one doesn't always need to have solved a problem in one's own personal life to be able to help other people. I might not have been too conscious of my own soul in those early days, but it seems as if from the very start, it has been aware of me, and that the helping forces have always been with me to support and guide me in my work, and for this I feel terribly grateful. Yes, my work *has* always loved me and it still continues to do so.

Right now, in no way can I claim to have reached that place which certain Eastern sages say one needs to aspire to, namely, a place where you are always blissful and nothing ever perturbs you anymore. But to tell the truth, I am glad I *haven't* reached it and hope I never will, and that certain things *continue* to perturb me, especially man's inhumanity and the corruption and injustices and evils in our world today, as this empowers me to take stands for those causes which I believe in. I also grieve over the death of friends who once upon a time were so dear to me. Here I think particularly of dear John Whitmore, John Rendall, who died very suddenly a few months ago, Sima, Roger Woolger, my beloved Marcus who shared my house in California with me, and la belle Sophia who passed away far too early.

I regard the process of allowing ourselves to grieve as being very important and we need to honour and respect it and far too many of us try to shut it down and in so doing also shut down our ability to feel joy. Actually, I see grieving as an integral part of my abundance and I think it has helped make me all the keener to try to extend and flex my difference-making muscles! As I've said many times: I am not an island unto myself; I am part of the whole of humanity, and if that whole is wounded, then some of that woundedness has to be—and indeed is—reflected in me. And I respect this and I feel it both my duty and my privilege to serve my fellow human beings in the small ways that I do. I think it has been my anger at the injustices and pain in the world that has basically propelled me to have written my books.

I am only too aware that there's still a lot about my past and my ancestral heritage that needs working through, and I hope to do it in the years ahead, but I realise I have done just enough to no longer be *as* troubled by it, and so my personal history no longer holds me back. It's taken a long time but I think I can honestly say that I've outgrown that immature boy who continued running the show way beyond his sell-by date! I mean, if I hadn't achieved this by my age and with all the effort I've put in, it'd be a pretty poor show!

Yes, my dear friend, today my ego has lost much of its rebelliousness and its always wanting to dominate and is now much more content to be my servant. But it's a slippery old so 'n' so, and I never want to take anything for granted. I know only too well that it is all about how much prayer and meditation I continue to do every day and how well I face and work with shadow issues if and when they surface. I know that were I to stop my inner work, I could easily fall back. I think that any new state we enter into, we can easily topple out of unless we make the conscious effort to build upon it.

I admit, though, that at times getting older needs a bit of adjusting to, as the rules of the game change somewhat. Certain habits and inclinations tell you that they need to be surrendered and I see this particularly in my relationship to sport, and though I exercise briskly for at least an hour most days, I feel that my old self-image as a 'sporty, athletic guy' is one that, in my vanity, I've probably held on to for a bit too long! Perhaps this is because I felt I never lived up to my true potential and so there is always the thought that 'maybe one day I will *really* shine': perhaps I could enlist in the over-75 Geriatric Olympic games and manage to do the mile in just under an hour! I've recently had to give up my beloved tennis because I am going blind in one eye; but my goodness, even if I've never been a particularly outstanding player, it has given me a huge amount of joy throughout my life.

I am currently watching the Olympics, and yes, I admit, I feel a bit nostalgic and would love to get out there and put on my racing skis once more. I also confess that a few months ago, I happened to be driving past an athletics track and saw some hurdles up, happened to have trainers on and thought 'what the hell'. I confess, though, that I couldn't even jump over one of the buggers! But I had a good chuckle at myself.

There were a few young people training on the track and I realised I was probably quite invisible to them. I had this same experience a couple of years ago when I was travelling by tube in London. I'd just been to Moorfields Eye Hospital to receive an injection in my eye and I was feeling a trifle vulnerable. As there were no seats, I was standing up and noticed a very pretty young woman sitting just opposite me, and just for a moment I felt a pang of sadness as I realised how totally invisible this old geezer must be to her. I suddenly wished I was twenty-five once more. But I was very wrong. I *had* been noticed. She suddenly stood up and came over to me and said in a loud voice (presuming I was probably hard of hearing): 'Sir, I wonder if you'd like my seat!'

I have just had the task of going through some twenty-odd photo albums so I can dig out a few piccies for this memoir, and my oh my, has this taken me down memory lane. As I looked at all those reminders of the many different phases of my life and the many people who once upon a time were important to me, I confess I felt a little sad. All those chapters in my life; all those people I shared it with. All passed away into the mists of time. I often wonder what some of my old buddies are up to today and if we'd still recognise one another and have anything to say to one another. I know it is preferable to let go the past and to honour what has been and so move on and not try to hang on, but I own that I have a certain sentimentality to me—perhaps it's the Russian part of me. Though let me be clear. I don't hanker after the old me. I am glad I've left most of *that* Serge behind and I much prefer being the 'me' I am today. I think what at times troubles me a bit is the sense that I perhaps didn't give as much to certain situations as I might have done. I think: if only I could re-enter some of my old stories with the 'me' that I am now, I could extract so much more meaning out of them; perhaps I could also contribute so much more as well!

I wish I could be like an eagle soaring in the sky, and as I look down, I can see the totality of my life and all its many stages or phases all spread out and existing in present time—

and I am able to swoop down and re-enter any story that I want to. Sadly, I can't. The truth is that I am more like a tiny ant crawling along, and once I've moved past that blade of grass, it now exists in my past, relegated to the domain of memory. However, if I think about this a bit more deeply, I realise that not all of my past exists in my past. If its actualities are no more, many of its ramifications or its repercussions, be they for better or worse, still live on in some way inside me!

I feel terribly grateful to all those people in my life who have befriended me and given me so much and who have accepted me for who I am and for who I am not, and who over the years have satisfied those criteria I mentioned earlier concerning what I would wish of a friend. It is interesting that those friends whom I am especially close to and love very much, like David Lorimer, Peter Adler, Alan and Louise Gordon Walker, Carinthia, Charles Montagu, Chris Carter, Joanna and Michael Brown, Mike McIntyre, Coralie and Chris Dreyfus, Monica Godwin, Alain Adam, Pete Kyte and Dale Mathers I have known for a long, long time. All of them in their different ways have been so gracious towards me and I feel so blessed.

I mention again that I am sorry Johnnie Reed and I are no longer close, and as I said earlier, I hold myself responsible. I had no right to interfere and tell his wife things about his past that he had intentionally concealed from her. I have a small hope that maybe he'll wake up one morning and realise why I did what I did and that it might be time to forgive me! But I don't blame him if he doesn't!

I think two things are important about the process of ageing. The first is to *not* give in to the stereotypes of old-fogey-hood—not to say ridiculous things designed to elicit pity, like 'Ooh, I'm not as young as I was' as you grimly pull yourself out of an armchair that you've let yourself sink helplessly into, with a pained look on your face. I think that's pretty manipulative.

Why should you be pitied just because you're getting on! People who operate like that age much more quickly.

The second thing is that it is equally important that you don't try to deny your age and pretend to be young in order to fit in with our Western culture, which, unlike tribal cultures which respect their elders, primarily only reveres youth and beauty. You are now an 'elder' and it needs accepting even as we are also challenged to avoid tuning in to current myths about how people ought to be and behave at our age. I am absolutely speaking the truth when I say I feel young, even though my outwardly saggy-chinned, wrinkled and tired-looking, baggy-eyed old face may belie it.

Yup, my body has certainly changed a bit over the last few years, but interestingly my inner child or inner spirit still feels very awake and alive. And I am still a busy old bee and do a lot of mentoring of young people and, unlike my old dad who was envious of my youth, I rather celebrate theirs. In fact, I feel quite privileged to have a few buddies who are forty or fifty years younger than me. I think two of the old stories we are all called to surrender are the ones around ageism and same-ism; i.e., that say, 'I can only hang out with people around my age or who see the world the way I do.' I feel that old and young can learn so much from each other and we can also learn so much from those who see the world very differently to ourselves.

I've observed that while I think I have more *awareness* than I had when I was younger, I obviously don't have the same kind of *freshness*. Though I think that I've basically looked after myself quite well all my life, done sport, meditated, not ate too much crappy food or smoked or drunk, the old machine has undoubtedly become a bit rusty in one or two places and today needs more looking after and oiling more regularly. Occasionally, I miss a particular kind of physical intensity that I used to have. However, I always need to remind myself that the fact of certain doorways closing creates space for others to open. Today, for example, I think my *élan vital* has not so much disappeared as grown a bit subtler, as I can now sit at my desk and think more clearly and write intensively for much longer than I used to. And this gives me great pleasure.

I do still have a little confession to make. Despite my protesting that 'je ne regrette rien', I occasionally go through moments where I feel sorry that I made such bad use of my father's financial legacy, never at the time fully appreciated what I had or made any efforts to 'grow' my inheritance. I could have done so much good with it. That said, I always need to remind myself that that was the way things panned out and that if, when I was twenty-three, I had known what I know now, my life would have been very different. But I didn't and I have to accept that I have been a very, very slow developer. However, I also need to remind myself that things could have been so much worse. Imagine if my father hadn't decided to die when he did......

Many spiritual purists like to tut-tut blokes like me who have been very eclectic in our approach to transformation. They tell me that if I had only focussed in one area—had had one spiritual master, chosen Shamanism, Buddhism or Sufism—instead of rushing about like a headless chicken all over the place, my path would have been easier.

Certainly they have a point, and no doubt this is true for many people; but my path thus far has been intentionally eclectic. I've always decided what teacher I needed or what teachings I felt were relevant for me at any time and I don't think I've done too bad a job of it. In fact, I see the many different things I've done and the many different experiences I've had as all linking up and complementing each other. OK, I may have gone wildly off focus on occasions, but at least I can say that I've done my damndest to be true to myself. But just as in mountain-climbing, where you at last get to the top of your mountain only to realise that far from it being the end of the road, a whole new range now lies before you, I realise that in terms of my potential spiritual development, I have a very, very long way to go and still feel very much a beginner.

But I am glad I am my age and I am glad I have had the life I've had, and again I say that I am so blessed that I am not all alone in this last phase of it and am with a woman whom I love and who for some extraordinary reason, seems to love and wish to support me. I would never dream of retiring, for that would mean exiting from my involvement in trying to play my tiny part in helping create a healthier world. My work is what connects me with the world.

I had a heart attack three years ago after a tough game of tennis and a hefty workout in the gym, and this gave me an important shock; it woke me up sharply to the realisation that I will one day no longer be in this body, and that in exactly the same way that if you want to have a good life you need to work at it, so exactly the same thing holds true regarding death. In my last book on the soul, I wrote at considerable length about death and dying and refer you to that book as much of its contents will complement what I write here.

What my heart attack also showed up, interestingly, was that all my life I have suffered from heart disease, and have lived with an enlarged heart, which I think I inherited from my father, and which has meant that the poor old thing has always had to work doubly hard to pump the blood around. So given that I also have my leukaemia (despite the healing I had, my blood count is still not normal), I'm jolly lucky to be in the good shape I'm in! Who knows: perhaps all the work I did over the years with my inner heart has helped my outer one. But I absolutely speak the truth when I say that I now have little fear of dying and so continuing my journey in other dimensions, other than I know it will deeply upset my darling Irena and Martina. This is why I'd like to hang around on this mortal coil for a good while longer.

For me, what is most important is that I continue in my odyssey of seeking to evolve my humanity and to continue to die to my old identifications and beliefs. I know that the more I do this, and the more I focus on trying to make a little difference in the world, the more the quality of my life increases and the more the environment around me benefits. I must never forget that the journey never ends!

Epilogue

Looking to the Future

OK, it is time now to look forward and say a few words about what I think might possibly lie ahead for humanity in the future as I regard this issue as a very integral part of my personal memoir. I say this as I am increasingly observing that the more I come to experience myself as part of humanity, the more fully me I feel!

I say once more how sad and angry I am about what is happening on our planet today and the many injustices that exist. I think the biggest problems our world faces are selfishness (extreme ego-centredness), huge greed, huge corruption, huge inequality, huge apathy, and an obsession with materiality and power, all of which are symptomatic of a very immature humanity.

Hypnotised by the comforts of status, pleasure, wealth and power, too few world leaders think of what the planet really needs, as they are primarily concerned with what benefits themselves and their clan and how they can cling on to power. This process has increased during the pandemic, and world inequality has worsened, with the rich having grown considerably richer and the poor very much poorer. Today, 1 per cent of the world's population have more wealth than the rest of the world put together. And this is utterly insane.

I find it horrendous that many wealthy people are able to hide their millions in offshore tax havens and pay little to no tax. This, my friend, is not a perversion of capitalism. It is capitalism's true ugly face that has always existed, just as there has always existed a marriage between so called 'respectable bankers' and the oligarchs and kleptocrats who drain their nations' wealth and channel it into these havens. We need to understand that we live in a world where huge injustice reigns and also where many millions of us turn our backs to it as well as disassociate ourselves from those who are 'not like us', who have different skin colours, sexual preferences, financial levels, beliefs, nationalities, opinions, attitudes and worldviews, all too often seeing them as 'the enemy'. And this is tragic.

Indeed, it is clear to me that our planet is in a precarious place and is becoming more so by the day. As I write, many countries are collapsing socially, economically and politically and every day America grows increasingly divided and may well descend into civil war either if the ultra-right-wing Republicans get into power once more, or conversely, if, despite their corruption and criminality, they fail to. Many believe that within a very few years, this country may well become a failed state.

Just as I was about to give up this manuscript to my publisher, Vladimir Putin, the Russian president, whose monstrousness has been steadily marinating over the twenty-plus years he has been in power, decided to invade Ukraine to the horror of the rest of the world. In this illegal, unprovoked and brutal attack upon a democratic country, we see the same kind of viciousness that was once displayed by Ivan the Terrible and later by Stalin. In his insane vision to rebuild the empire that Russia lost half a century ago (totally indicative of an overinflated and very diseased ego), Putin shows that he cares not a jot for the sanctity of human life. It is clear that the Nazi-istic behaviour that he refuses to own in himself is being projected onto the Ukrainian people whom he portrays as less than human and therefore eminently deserving of their fate. This is evil of the highest degree.

There is no doubt that Democracy is certainly under great threat today. The general fear and uncertainty that is everywhere has been opening up a space that is very conducive to allow fear-stoking, fascistic/populist forces to come into their own, replete with their paranoid signature tunes and lies. These especially focus on how all social ills are caused by 'evil immigrants', and that as there are 'huge dangers everywhere', there is an urgent need for greater law and order, thus 'legitimising' the use of force to suppress resistance.

Yes, my friend, essentially what totalitarian dictatorships do is continually spew out a diet of conspiracy theories which conjure up an oversimplistic and duplicitous world that is more acceptable than reality itself, so that those who feel uprooted don't have to face the real shocks that real life and real experience can give them. China today is increasing her surveillance capabilities, and soon the state will know the opinions, beliefs and habits of all its subjects and I find this kind of oppression horrifying. I am particularly outraged by the vicious ways that these fascistic regimes deal with those who dare to challenge them. So many brave whistle-blowers suddenly mysteriously 'vanish', get tortured, find themselves imprisoned under trumped-up charges, get accused of being terrorists, get 'novochoked' as was the fate of Alexei Navalny, or as was the case with the unfortunate Khashoggi, get cut into little pieces for daring to 'out' the sins of the leader of Saudi Arabia.

The Coronavirus has not only claimed many lives but has also served as a catalyst in bringing up very deep Shadow issues for humanity. Whether this virus will continue as a disequilibrating force to mutate and shake up the world and render ever-greater suffering for the world's not-haves, who always suffer the most in times of crisis, at present no one knows. James Lovelock, who coined the idea of the Gaia Hypothesis, suggesting that our planet is an intelligent self-regulating mechanism, had recently been putting forward the theory that it has grown increasingly sick of us human beings continually abusing it and is now fighting back to eliminate the threat which we present, and regards the Covid virus as one of the various weapons it is using!

Few can deny that humanity en masse is currently journeying ever deeper into a collective Dark Night of the Soul crisis. As the American philosopher William Ophuls put it in his book *Immoderate Greatness: Why Civilizations Fail*:

> *What the impending crises force us to confront is that we have sacrificed meaning, morality and almost all higher values for the 'sordid boon' of material wealth and worldly power. To keep drinking from this poisoned chalice will only bring sickness and death.*

The tragic thing is that too many people in positions of power in government and in our institutions are continuing to drink from it, indeed, are addicted to its liquids and are enormously resistant to change. We see this reflected in the refusal of so many nations to cut down on their use of fossil fuels despite being aware of the consequences. I find it interesting that so many world leaders today are elderly men who won't be alive to experience the ecological effects of their rigidities. As the historian Niall Ferguson put it:

> *Civilisations behave like all complex adaptive systems. They function in apparent equilibrium for some unknowable period. And then, quite abruptly they collapse—the shift from consummation to destruction and then to desolation is not cyclical. It is sudden...*

As I see it, it is highly probable that over the next fifty years our world situation will continue to worsen. This will not only be the case for the very poor and for those living in countries continually being ravaged by droughts, storms, famines, poverty and wars and where there also tend to be a lot of crime and corruption, but it will also be true for the wealthier countries. Yes, my friend, the haves of this world are by no means coming out unscathed. Here, the crises tend often to be more internal. I see huge unhappiness, insecurity and depression fuelled by our living in a system that primarily addresses only our egoic selves and where, as I said, we are not especially encouraged to work at deepening ourselves or be kind to our neighbours!

In fact, I would go so far as to say that today we are witnessing a vast tsunami of grief in the world. OK, a few things are getting better—for example the health of people with AIDS, and gay rights are in many places improving—but many things are getting worse and worse and breaking down faster and faster. Certainly, to continue to move forward by looking in the rear-view mirror, or to persevere with a 'business as usual' mindset, which still seems to be the approach that many governments, corporations and institutions are taking—largely, I think, because they are not structured to be able to change gears—is only hastening the breakdown.

We return to the thesis implicit in my introduction about how important working on our personal evolution is. I remember in the eighties reading a book written by George Land entitled *Grow or Die*. And what he said is even truer today:

> *Unless as a species we start evolving; unless we work to come into our deeper selfhood and realise our interconnectedness and start living our true story and begin helping each other and cooperating together and being kind to one another and stop trashing our planet and instead start living more sustainably, we haven't a chance in hell of 'making it'.*

I stress once more: the main reason why we have so much evil, greed, trauma, violence, corruption, selfishness, hatred, war, cruelty, nationalism, terrorism, fascism, racism, xenophobia, homophobia, antisemitism, nationalism and inequality is because not enough of us are encouraged to confront very dark aspects of ourselves! The result is that we are utterly controlled by our Shadow sides and remain closed off to our deeper humanity and consequently never move beyond espousing worldviews that are rigid, self-serving and backward looking. The result is that we have little or no connection with those locations inside our psyche where our altruism, our courage, our kindness, our wisdom, truth, compassion, creativity and love lie, all of which are the necessary antidotes enabling and empowering us to live our lives much more wholistically and creatively.

What we need is a new vision. One with heart and compassion. One with wisdom. Old visions such as the 'American Dream', which made materiality into its God, have proved to be utterly hollow. *Our great challenge is to choose a new path for living on Earth that is regenerative not destructive, wholistic not reductive, supportive of life as opposed to detrimental to it. As I argued in my last book, we need a path of soul. With soul, we can truly begin envisioning ourselves as caretakers of our planet as opposed to abusers of it.*

In this context, we also need to remind ourselves that *we human beings hold our future in our hands*. No one else. And our future is not set in stone. And no one and nothing 'out there' is going to save us. Certainly not our governments and our institutions, not least because they are all very much part of the problem. We are the only ones who can save ourselves!

Having presented this dismal picture of a society breaking down in many areas (and I've not yet touched on the nuclear bomb dangers we potentially face), I am now going to say something that may surprise you. *In the long run I am very positive about the future of humankind.* I will repeat this. *In the long run I am very positive about the future of humankind.* In fact, I believe that despite all the horror, breakdown, evil and danger currently enveloping us, that humanity is poised for a quantum leap in consciousness. I believe that not only are we going to 'make it', but we are going to do so very powerfully. In his book *Cosmic Consciousness*, Richard Bucke, looking to the future, tells us that:

> *Cosmic consciousness will become more and more universal earlier in an individual's life, until the race at large will possess this faculty... This new race is in the act of being born from us and in the near future, it will occupy and possess the Earth.*

But how can this be given that everything is collapsing around us as I write? Am I being absurdly naïve? Is this all silly 'new age Serge psychobabble'? My reply is that I am very serious and I think it is important that we start trying to view our world from a very different perspective. This particularly concerns how we relate to the issue of death and destruction. Do you remember how earlier I talked about how it often is that our bodies need to break down in order to be put together at a new level? Well I maintain that the same criteria applies to the body of our planet. If something new is to be born or come into being, it is necessary that 'oldness' has to die in order to create the space for it. Just as in my own life, for a deeper me to emerge, I needed to work through and try to 'die to' many of the more backward-looking patterns from my past, so I view much of what is happening in the world today in a similar vein. I regard much of the confusion and chaos currently being experienced, as a necessary purification or cleansing that is serving to clear the way for a very different kind of society to come into expression. And newness, my friend, always carries its Shadow in front of it. *The road to breaking through lies through the valley of break down!*

So for example, if many countries' social, economic and political realities are teetering on the edge, it is because they do not work, and so these realities may need to disintegrate in order to make way for something new and hopefully preferable to emerge out of the ruins. It is no longer a question of just addressing the symptoms. We've been trying this for the last fifty years and we've found that in no way does it solve the great problems that we have in the world today. On the contrary, it merely pushes them aside. If a new, improved society is to emerge, it can only do so by humanity going to the very roots of all that is disharmonious and disfigured about itself. And this is precisely what is happening right now and where, species-wise, we are currently finding ourselves journeying. Nothing is hidden any more. The world's closets are opening wide and nobody can remain ignorant about the many things amiss with our planet. The evils of the regimes of many countries are plain to see despite their rulers' best attempts to try to conceal the truth.

So despite everything I have said about what is 'wrong' with our world, with all my *heart I believe that humanity will pull through and that the grace forces are not going to desert us.* I resonate very much with what the late Bede Griffiths, a Christian monk and Hindu scholar, said when questioned on this issue:

> *We will make it but it will cost everything. Just as Jesus had to go through death into the new world of the resurrection, so millions of us will have to go through a death to the past and to all old ways of being if we are to be brought by the grace of God into the truth of a new age… God, I believe, wants a new world and a new humanity to be born.*

And what I see currently happening is that grace is showing us more and more of its fierce face! Duane Elgin in his excellent book *Choosing Earth* suggests that three paths lie ahead for us.

1) In the first path, chaos reigns, and our civilisation crashes and collapses.

2) The second path indicates that we turn more and more to authoritarian rulers who promise safety.

3) In the third path, we don't hit rock bottom. We descend, as a species, into huge chaos, and the flames burn and many institutions crumble, but we don't have a full-on crash. Here, the destructive unravelling of the old dysfunctional society meets the constructive forces weaving a new world order based on planetary thinking.

Elgin believes that the third path is what lies ahead for us in the next half-century, and I fully agree. Certainly, breakdown leading to breakthrough was the thesis that I also put forward in 2013 in my book on the awakening of the universal heart. I have little doubt, therefore, that from now on, things will continue to 'heat up' and our human suffering will probably increase. There may well be a few years where initially it will seem as if everything has gone kaput. But this won't be the case. In all probability, those nations that are failing may well collapse completely. For the rest of society, there could well be food and water shortages and people may fight each other to get to them. Probably social services won't be able to cope and there could possibly be a full-blown global financial collapse. I also have little doubt that more demagogues will come into positions of power in certain countries, although it will not be a full-blown authoritarian takeover in all countries.

I think that everything in our global Shadow that, species-wise, we have thus far managed to dodge confronting, we will no longer be able to. This includes our coming increasingly face to face with all the many vicious and hostile ways in which wealthy nations have exploited the less wealthy ones over the last four hundred years. Humanity will also come to see the full barrenness and horrendousness inherent in all authoritarian regimes. Xi Jinping's China and Putin's Russia will undoubtedly be called to confront their spiritual bankruptcy.

Put simply, I think that the next half-century is going to be very tumultuous, as many of those structures, organisations and institutions that we believed in and felt made us safe, are probably going to slowly—and in some instances maybe quite rapidly—disintegrate, so that it may well be that the world we are currently sliding into will be unrecognisable to the one we have today. Elgin feels that organisations like NATO, the IMF and the UN could well cease to exist and large entities like Amazon, Microsoft and Google may experience a similar demise. In all possibility, the world's wealthy, who currently feel that they have the wherewithal to avoid these crises, will find themselves in the same boat as everyone else and discover that their money and possessions are not going to be able to save them. Yes, my friend, all the king's horses and all the king's men are not going to be able to put Humpty Dumpty together again! But in the long run, this will be for the best. It's not about fixing the old order. It is about creating a new order, a new world, a post-Humpty one! I really like the perspective of the philosopher David Spangler, whom I had the good fortune to meet up at Findhorn.

> *Underneath the patterns of instability in the world, a profound spirit of love and goodwill is at work and is using the instability and the individuals that emerge from it as the farmer uses a plough, to turn the soil and prepare it for new seeds and new harvest.*

I have certainly experienced the truth of these words in my own life as I hope I have made clear. That said, I admit it can be very, very hard to feel the love if we are suffering from the effects of climate change and have just had our whole livelihood washed away in one big tidal wave, have an empty belly or have just had several members of our family blown up in a war. It is very, very hard when in enormous personal anguish, to start thinking in perspectives that are less personal and more global.

To make things even more challenging, we also need to know that *to bring about enduring, radical, concrete change, the pain has to be great enough.* To give one small example, the problem with the 2008 financial crisis was that it wasn't severe enough to bring about a radical transformation in the financial system. The result was that after the crisis was over, everything went back to pretty much the way it used to be before and so the old regime got reinstated. *The reason why I cannot see how there will not be more suffering and more collapses in the years ahead, is because it seems that only terrible crises get us to make the necessary quantum shifts. Terrible shocks—like losing most of what we hold precious—if they don't destroy us (and they certainly have that potential) can also transform us.* Elgin puts it very clearly.

> *It is the immense suffering of millions—even billions—of precious human beings coupled with the destruction of many other life forms, that will burn through our complacency and isolation. Suffering is the psychological and psychic fire that can awaken our compassion and fuse individuals, communities and nations into a cohesive and consciously organised global civilisation.*

However, suffering on its own won't lead to this breakthrough. There is another very key ingredient that also needs to be factored in. *Indeed, the reason why I am very positive in the long run and believe that change will definitely be a change for the better and not for the worse, is because there are some extraordinarily evolved souls on the planet today.* In fact, there are many millions of them. And they exist in every country and they work in every profession. Many of these visionaries are very young people and many aren't tainted as I was with the past and so don't need to do all the discarding and releasing that was so necessary for me. Many have come into the world already pretty awake and pure of heart and they know exactly what is wrong with our world and what, in their respective fields, needs to happen to bring about transformation and thus are fully committed to creating a new and healthy planet. Indeed, many of these young people no longer see work from a perspective of 'how can I advance myself and earn more money'—the old approach to a career—but more from 'how can I best find my way to making as big a difference in the world as I can!' In both my books I have written about these new-world order activists in great detail. The media, with its tendency to reveal only the negative things occurring, has never sufficiently stressed how powerful this infusion of goodness is. Dear Sir George Trevelyan understood it perfectly and very prophetically wrote these words over forty years ago:

> *Out of the confusion of a crumbling society will emerge individuals who are touched by higher guidance. They will inevitably flow together with others of like inspiration, and a new quality of society will begin to form. This is the true adventure of our time.*

I've been privileged in my life to have met and been inspired by many of these global activists, and as I said, they exist in every profession. Their commitment is to healing the environment and building a society that works for everyone and I have learned two very interesting things from my discussions with them. The first is that all the structures for a new, more workable world exist right now, the second is that the solutions to all the many problems on our planet also exist. What we don't yet have is the willingness to implement them, as to do so would require many more people being willing to relinquish their old privileges, addictions and lifestyles, and things as yet aren't quite 'hot enough'—the suffering isn't as yet sufficient—to enable this to happen.

Duane Elgin's words also tie in with what philosopher Chris Bache believes. Chris suggests that we see the species-mind as a unified psychic field and that this field will be driven into a very tumultuous state by the extreme suffering generated by a monumental global ecological crisis; and that in this hyper-aroused state, the species-mind will exhibit the capacity for rapidly accelerated change, heightened creativity and higher self-organisation.

Under the pressure of the extreme conditions of the future, the human psyche will come alive at new levels, and the interconnections between people previously too subtle to be detected will become obvious. *And all of this will take place much more quickly than anyone could have predicted.*

Ilya Prigogine, in his well-known study of dissipative structures, also talked about the same thing. He has shown us that one of the properties of systems when they are driven into difficulties is that they don't just break down; they evolve a capacity for higher self-organisation. They generate new structures that pull higher forms of order out of the resultant chaos. Put simply, huge suffering will serve as a purifying fire leading to the awakening of the soul of humanity and the gradual diminishing of importance of all those people who still insist on hanging on to outmoded and negative trains of thought.

As the old centres of power gradually fall away to the edges of society, I see a new, higher-order centre begin to emerge on the planet, peopled by a whole new cadre of world leaders who will be conscious human beings full of heart and soul. I see many of these new leaders being women, as we will also be witnessing a powerful emergence of feminine energy being born out of the embers of a rapidly disintegrating patriarchy.

Certain countries will need to apologise for the damage they have done to other countries and to certain segments of people in their own countries, and a lot of forgiveness rituals will need to be created. Many different kinds of reconciliation will also be called for, as people start to realise the futility and huge cost of not having respected and often having demonised those who do not see the world the same way as they do, and who belong to different races and religions, have different sexual ethics or different skin colours.

In this emerging new world order, I see the haves being increasingly moved to support the not-haves. All thinking about needing to make more and more money and own more and more possessions will have fallen away, and the utter absurdity of some people being billionaires while others starve will be appreciated. All will see the necessity and the value of making their lives simpler at every level. I see this as also being a time of great mourning for all the lives lost and the huge suffering that will have taken place, as well as the devastation done to the planet in the name of greed. Elgin thinks it may take many years for the wounds we have inflicted on ourselves and on our world to heal.

It may even be that if those forces conspiring to detonate positive changes reach a critical threshold and the infrastructure required to deploy them becomes dominant, that a 'counter-flip' may occur, driving fossil fuels to extinction. I know this is maybe stretching things but, as I mentioned earlier, I have personally had experience of sudden 'quantum healings' occurring, and I ask myself if what may be possible for the individual may not also be possible for the planet! The important thing to understand is that the human race will less and less be operating out of its old egoic centre and more and more out of higher-order soul perspectives. And this will radically change the way in which reality gets viewed, enabling all problems and challenges to be seen from a broader and more compassionate context, which in turn will enable solutions to be much easier to come by.

I feel sad that my daughter and stepdaughter will have big challenges to face during the course of their lives and won't have it nearly as easy as us 'baby boomers' did. However, I also have the sense that there is something innately empowering about living in these challenging times, and that the grace forces will draw ever closer to a struggling humanity and I have no doubt that both girls will rise to the challenges and that their personal development will be much speedier than mine.

Here are twenty-four key changes that I see gradually coming about. Most of these observations are my own. Some have been taken from my general readings, and a few from Charles Eisenstein's writings.

1) With the gradual emergence of a more wholistic vision, a new consciousness of fullness of being or of abundance begins to permeate the thinking of millions of people, with the result that the mindset of separation and scarcity begins gradually to melt away.

2) Visionaries or activists working for a transformed world will be honoured and encouraged. They will come more and more into their own and will become the 'new centre' of power in the world, while those who are currently at the 'centre of things' will find themselves increasingly slipping away to the peripheries. In this new context, farmers who transform deserts to grow food or mediators who work to heal war-torn societies or journalists who work reporting in war zones, or climate change activists, will be all honoured for the immensely important work which they do and will be seen as the real 'great and the good'.

3) Personal achievement will no longer be measured in money or power, and being wealthy will no longer be defined by what we own, but by the quality of our lives—how much we are able to love and be loved, how creative we are, how holistically healthy we are, and how much we are able to live with kindness and heart.

4) We will start creating a participatory society, one where all people will have a voice in the decisions that affect their life and future. More and more people will start demanding freedom and having their rights respected, and by the end of this century, I predict the demise of many right-wing populists. Democracy, which at one stage was rapidly failing, will come bouncing back only now manifesting as an even truer voice of the people.

5) The self-centred nation state, utterly disconnected from its soul and thus from its true *raison d'être* in the world, gives way to a transnational system, where individual nations

connect to their higher purposes and see their deeper role in supporting the emerging world community.

6) There will be more peace and less war. Where war still exists, instead of brute force, new technologies around conflict resolution will begin to be used.

7) A new model of what it means to be human begins to emerge whereby we no longer deify the rich, the notorious and the celebrity. Instead, we come to see that our real heroes or the real 'great and the good' on the planet are those who live unselfishly, humbly, wisely, simply and unpretentiously. A new 'aristocracy of soul' composed of men and women who will have worked on their own evolution will start coming into being.

8) Those who have managed to hold on to some of their wealth, will be happy to share their good fortune with those who are poor and marginalised, so that the latter feel empowered and more able to lift themselves up by their own bootstraps.

9) Nations that have huge debts as a result of exploitation that goes back many centuries are released from their obligations, at the same time that those nations which have done the exploiting open their eyes to the huge damage done in the name of 'advancement'.

10) All corporations embrace a mindset of 'giving to' as opposed to 'taking from', and put the well-being of people and planet before profit.

11) Those who are most resistant and hostile to change are given opportunities to learn to see the world in a new light and the damage they do by opposing the natural flow of evolutionary advancement.

12) Understanding the Shadow and how to work with it becomes a core part of what is taught in schools and universities, so that instead of our projecting our dark sides

onto other people, races and nations, we learn to work creatively with it inside ourselves.

13) More people start moving away from their involvement in fundamentalisms, pseudo-religions and cults, and begin learning to embrace a spirituality that has depth to it, leading them to realise that we are all united, all equal in the mind of God, and that there exists a divinity that is both within us and that is greater than us. Religions are therefore stripped more and more of their institutionalisms and dogmas that have been such a source of violence in the past, so that a space can emerge for a more genuine spirituality to come to the fore, whereby people may feel invigorated and inspired by a connection with a soulfulness or a grace that feels real and alive. (This beautiful perspective comes from Charles Eisenstein.)

14) People come increasingly to realise that they are stewards not despoilers of our planet, and that their role is to help Earth's delicate ecosystems recover.

15) Politicians learn to be more authentic and honest and refuse to be 'bought', and gradually all forms of government based on repression vanish from the face of the Earth.

16) All forms of violence and oppression to minority groups also come to an end. A new value system is gradually born whereby honesty triumphs over corruption, kindness over indifference and generosity over greed.

17) Money will be used in new ways, largely spent on things that support the emergence of a new world. The economic system is therefore gradually reformed of its corruption, and bankers attend courses where they are taught to operate with integrity and honesty. The new, emerging world will be one where the wealthy don't just get richer but where money is distributed equally so that no one is marginalised and the less well-developed economies can be assisted by the more developed ones.

18) Education will no longer be about trying to help people adjust better to a deviant society, but instead to prepare and encourage them to work to create a new society, and children in school will learn life skills relative to this new emerging culture.
19) The old desacralized and de-animated view of nature that has become the foundation of modern science, and the whole mechanistic worldview, leading to a belief that one can exploit it for profit as much as one wishes, begins to fall away. Instead, people learn to recognise nature's aliveness and sacredness and realise it needs to be celebrated and honoured and related to in a wise way.
20) As a balance against the 'cyberfication' of life, we focus on what is real, purifying everything about the way we eat and think and work and generally live our lives.
21) The media, which so strongly affects how we see the world and which at present mainly deals with money, houses, celebrities and disasters and continually finds fault, undergoes a profound level-shift, gradually becoming an important ally in the game of transformation. Among other things, it shows us examples of soulful human beings who have undergone transformation.
22) Support is increasingly withdrawn from the entity we call 'the system', thus enabling it to evolve and transform into something that supports the emergence of a sustainable and harmonious world.
23) Society is happier and more balanced and people learn to think more in terms of what will serve the larger community and not just enhance their own personal lives. Because the level of corruption will radically decrease, there will be less hatred, less crime, less addiction and more people policing their own local communities.
24) More and more people allow themselves to be 'fed' from higher sources of inspiration or more unified states of

> consciousness, with the result that there is far less depression and anxiety and much more enthusiasm for life based on the realisation that true happiness comes from how full we are inside ourselves and has very little to do with how outwardly wealthy we are.

I will end by saying that one of the big challenges we all face in the years ahead is not to 'ostrich' it and hide our heads in the sand and close our eyes to some of the very terrible things happening around us. Just because we don't see things doesn't mean they don't affect us. Rather, I think we are all called to have a go at 'giraffing' it—that is, to stick our necks out and up and make our hearts strong, and in so doing, choose to have the way we live be a stand for a new world order wishing to come into expression. The more we choose to see the turbulence around us as a powerful gate of initiation asking us to develop the qualities necessary to enable us to go through it and so move beyond it, the more the forces of grace will be able to guide us and the more effective a role we will be able to play in the great unfolding of personal and planetary transformation.

Note to the Reader

Hello, my Dear Reader! Thank you for purchasing this little memoir of my life as seen through a transformational lens. I do hope you enjoyed my often-stumbling attempts to 'grow my soul' and heal the many less healthy parts of my nature.

I have written two other books dealing with transformational themes. If you would like to know more about them, if you would like to contact me, read my blog, receive occasional newsletters, or if you'd like to know more about my lectures, webinars, bespoke spiritual retreats, or you'd like to do some personal work with me, please visit my website (https://sergebeddingtonbehrens.com).

Biography

Serge Obolensky Beddington-Behrens, MA (Oxon.), PhD, K.O.M.L., is an Oxford-educated transpersonal psychotherapist, spiritual educator, teacher of transformation and a change agent. In his mid-twenties he moved to live in California and trained to become a transpersonal psychotherapist, during which time he co-founded the Institute for the Study of Conscious Evolution in San Francisco. Over the next ten years, he helped put on many global conferences, the most well-known being the Florence Congress of the New Age which took place in Florence in 1975. (It felt right to celebrate the new renaissance taking place in a city where the first renaissance was born.) For over forty years he has had a private psychotherapy practice and has trained psychotherapists as well as having lectured, taught workshops, and run spiritual retreats all over England, Europe, America and Russia.

He has contributed over forty articles to journals dealing with transpersonal issues and has written two books, *Awakening the Universal Heart: A Guide for Spiritual Activists,* and most recently *Gateways to the Soul: Inner Work for the Outer World,* published in 2020. His memoirs entitled *Amazing Grace* will be published early in 2023. In 2000 he was awarded an Italian knighthood for services to humanity. He now lives in Mallorca and is married and has one young daughter.

Other Books by Serge Beddington-Behrens

Awakening the Universal Heart: A Guide for Spiritual Activists
published in 2013
ISBN: 978-0-9541275-8-9

I invite you to come on a journey with me into one of the most important, yet often most neglected, dimensions of ourselves. Our inner heart. I want to help you discover, as I have gradually been discovering over the course of my life, that this part of ourselves not only holds the key to our being able to live a fuller, happier and more authentic existence, but if properly activated, will enable us to play a major role in helping create a happier and healthier world.
Most of all, please know this book has been written from a place of great hope and joy. It is based on the knowledge that our world is changing, that the universal heart awareness is awakening among increasing numbers of people and that the forces of resistance or of heartlessness are being powerfully confronted.

Gateways to the Soul: Inner Work for the Outer World
published in 2020
ISBN (print): 978-1-64411-045-4
ISBN (ebook): 978-1-64411-046-1

Humanity is in a great crisis of soul today. As a species, we are challenged to start embracing a new story, one that enables us to be less greedy and materialistic and to espouse peace not war, kindness not cruelty, and heart as opposed to indifference. What we need is to bring more soul into the world.

Engaging in inner work offers various gateways to reconnect with our soul. Renowned transpersonal psychotherapist Serge Beddington-Behrens, PhD, reveals how the healing of our personal wounds combined with the growing of our soul life leads us directly to the addressing of world problems.

Sharing inspirational stories from his own personal journey of becoming a therapist, shaman, and activist, he skilfully shows how, by transforming our inner world, we begin creating important positive ripples that reverberate around all areas of our outer experience.

Gateways to the Soul offers exercises and meditations that will not only help us heal and become more fully human, but also enable us to bring a very different kind of awareness––a sacred awareness––into all areas of our everyday life.

Not only will we experience more joy and meaning as we increasingly disconnect from the clutches of the current system, but we will also find ourselves opening our heart, reclaiming our personal power, bringing in new myths for humanity to live by, and gradually shifting away from being part of the problems in the world to becoming a core part of their solution.

O-BOOKS

SPIRITUALITY

O is a symbol of the world, of oneness and unity; this eye represents knowledge and insight. We publish titles on general spirituality and living a spiritual life. We aim to inform and help you on your own journey in this life.
If you have enjoyed this book, why not tell other readers by posting a review on your preferred book site?

Recent bestsellers from O-Books are:

Heart of Tantric Sex

Diana Richardson
Revealing Eastern secrets of deep love and intimacy to Western couples.
Paperback: 978-1-90381-637-0 ebook: 978-1-84694-637-0

Crystal Prescriptions

The A-Z guide to over 1,200 symptoms and their healing crystals
Judy Hall
The first in the popular series of eight books, this handy little guide is packed as tight as a pill-bottle with crystal remedies for ailments.
Paperback: 978-1-90504-740-6 ebook: 978-1-84694-629-5

Take Me To Truth
Undoing the Ego
Nouk Sanchez, Tomas Vieira
The best-selling step-by-step book on shedding the Ego, using the teachings of *A Course In Miracles*.
Paperback: 978-1-84694-050-7 ebook: 978-1-84694-654-7

The 7 Myths about Love...Actually!
The Journey from your HEAD to the HEART of your SOUL
Mike George
Smashes all the myths about LOVE.
Paperback: 978-1-84694-288-4 ebook: 978-1-84694-682-0

The Holy Spirit's Interpretation of the New Testament
A Course in Understanding and Acceptance
Regina Dawn Akers
Following on from the strength of *A Course In Miracles*, NTI teaches us how to experience the love and oneness of God.
Paperback: 978-1-84694-085-9 ebook: 978-1-78099-083-5

The Message of A Course In Miracles
A translation of the Text in plain language
Elizabeth A. Cronkhite
A translation of *A Course In Miracles* into plain, everyday language for anyone seeking inner peace. The companion volume, *Practicing A Course In Miracles*, offers practical lessons and mentoring.
Paperback: 978-1-84694-319-5 ebook: 978-1-84694-642-4

Your Simple Path

Find Happiness in every step

Ian Tucker

A guide to helping us reconnect with what is really important in our lives.

Paperback: 978-1-78279-349-6 ebook: 978-1-78279-348-9

365 Days of Wisdom

Daily Messages To Inspire You Through The Year

Dadi Janki

Daily messages which cool the mind, warm the heart and guide you along your journey.

Paperback: 978-1-84694-863-3 ebook: 978-1-84694-864-0

Body of Wisdom

Women's Spiritual Power and How it Serves

Hilary Hart

Bringing together the dreams and experiences of women across the world with today's most visionary spiritual teachers.

Paperback: 978-1-78099-696-7 ebook: 978-1-78099-695-0

Dying to Be Free

From Enforced Secrecy to Near Death to True Transformation

Hannah Robinson

After an unexpected accident and near-death experience, Hannah Robinson found herself radically transforming her life, while a remarkable new insight altered her relationship with her father, a practising Catholic priest.

Paperback: 978-1-78535-254-6 ebook: 978-1-78535-255-3

The Ecology of the Soul

A Manual of Peace, Power and Personal Growth for Real People in the Real World

Aidan Walker

Balance your own inner Ecology of the Soul to regain your natural state of peace, power and wellbeing.

Paperback: 978-1-78279-850-7 ebook: 978-1-78279-849-1

Not I, Not other than I

The Life and Teachings of Russel Williams

Steve Taylor, Russel Williams

The miraculous life and inspiring teachings of one of the World's greatest living Sages.

Paperback: 978-1-78279-729-6 ebook: 978-1-78279-728-9

On the Other Side of Love

A woman's unconventional journey towards wisdom

Muriel Maufroy

When life has lost all meaning, what do you do?

Paperback: 978-1-78535-281-2 ebook: 978-1-78535-282-9

Practicing A Course In Miracles

A translation of the Workbook in plain language, with mentor's notes

Elizabeth A. Cronkhite

The practical second and third volumes of The Plain-Language *A Course In Miracles*.

Paperback: 978-1-84694-403-1 ebook: 978-1-78099-072-9

Quantum Bliss

The Quantum Mechanics of Happiness, Abundance, and Health

George S. Mentz

Quantum Bliss is the breakthrough summary of success and spirituality secrets that customers have been waiting for.

Paperback: 978-1-78535-203-4 ebook: 978-1-78535-204-1

The Upside Down Mountain

Mags MacKean

A must-read for anyone weary of chasing success and happiness – one woman's inspirational journey swapping the uphill slog for the downhill slope.

Paperback: 978-1-78535-171-6 ebook: 978-1-78535-172-3

Your Personal Tuning Fork

The Endocrine System

Deborah Bates

Discover your body's health secret, the endocrine system, and 'twang' your way to sustainable health!

Paperback: 978-1-84694-503-8 ebook: 978-1-78099-697-4